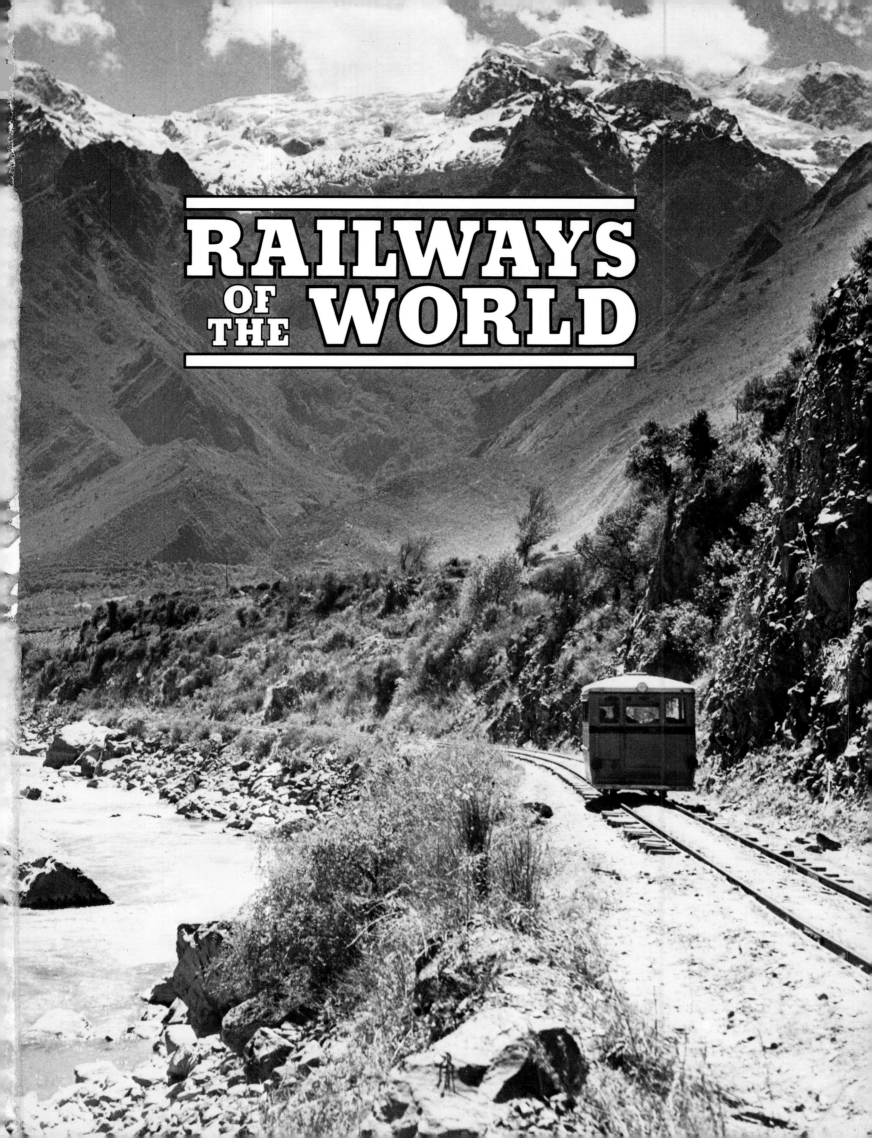

RAILWAYS
OF THE WORLD

RAILWAYS OF THE WORLD

BRIAN HOLLINGSWORTH

GALLERY BOOKS
An Imprint of W. H. Smith Publishers Inc.
112 Madison Avenue
New York City 10016
A Bison Book

Published by Gallery Books
A Division of W H Smith Publishers Inc.
112 Madison Avenue
New York, New York 10016

Produced by
Bison Books Corp.
17 Sherwood Place
Greenwich, CT 06830
USA

Printed in Hong Kong

4   5   6   7   8   9   10

ISBN 0-8317-0492-6

Contents

Below: Operating relic: Serra do Mar inclines in
Brazil. A steam brake van in action.

PREFACE

It is the intention of this book to present to the reader, country by country, an account of the world's railways. In addition to covering historical and technical aspects, an attempt has been made to bring serious instruction into relief by considering aesthetic, pleasurable and even idiosyncratic attributes – almost raising railways to an art form, without forgetting their folklore.

Except when they are the principal line of one particular country or are of exceptional international interest, railways of less than 100 miles or with less than 25 locomotives have had to be omitted. 'Exceptional interest' in this context means those which have earned the title 'first' or 'only' in some particular way. 'Public' or 'Common Carrier' railways receive a more generous interpretation of this rule than do private or industrial ones.

The geographical sections are preceded by a general description of the development and historical effect of railways in the world. In the same way the account of each country's railways begins with a short history. There follows an account of what the system is like today, emphasizing differences from the rest of the world rather than stating similarities. Special mention is made of features which were developed in a particular country which have

become standard practice worldwide. Where a country contains a number of railway systems, the account begins with a general description of its railways and their effect on its history.

Two points remain: first, traditional Imperial weights and measures are used; second, where a railway system spans two countries or continents, its entry is placed according to the location of its headquarters.

One characteristic common to railways the world over is a love of statistics, both meaningful and meaningless. Railway reference books and annual reports are full of them. Great care is needed in interpretation – there is, for example, a noticeable correlation between the decrease of steam traction on British Railways and the decline in its profitability – but, alas for steam lovers, it does not mean that modernization was a great mistake. The few statistics which appear in this book are given more with the idea of showing the kind of railway being described rather than making a contribution to the store of absolute truth.

For example, a railway will, with utter confidence, declare on an Atlas of World Railways' questionaire, that it has, say, 138,624 wagons; but on Judgement Day it would have to admit it does not really know exactly how many. Some are being built, others are being scrapped, some

have been reported scrapped but are still around, others have been scrapped or destroyed but not reported. There is usually an interesting group which has one number on one side and another number on the other side, even on the best regulated lines! It might in fact be more sensible to give the figure as 139,000 – meaning, between 138,500 and 139,499 – and this is what has been done in this book. The same applies to other statistics; even the length of route or track is uncertain. Does a railway line cease to be included in statistics when it goes out of use or when – possibly years later – the rails are pulled up?

Anyone wishing to play around with figures and obtain a mass of fascinating information regarding railways, is referred to two excellent annually published works of reference:

The Railway Directory and Year Book, published by IPC Transport Press, Dorset House, Stamford St, London SE1 9LU.

Jane's World Railways and Rapid Transit Systems, published by Jane's Yearbooks, Paulton House, 8 Shepherdess Walk, London N1 7LW.

Above: Early railroading in America: The Santa Fe express halts at Virginia City in 1885, headed by Virginia & Truckee 4-4-0 No 11 Rene.

Editor's Note

The maps were supplied by George Philip Printers Limited from their *Modern School Atlas.* The railways drawn on them are as up to date as possible but in the areas which are covered densely with railways, the main lines only are shown.

INTRODUCTION

Above: The first public railway to use regular steam traction was the line from Stockton to Darlington.

There is a plaque on the wall of the original railway station at Stockton, County Durham, England, which reads modestly as follows: 'Here in 1825 the Stockton and Darlington Railway Company booked the first passenger thus marking an epoch in the history of mankind.' While the claim as stated is not pedantically correct – regular steam passenger trains did not come for another five years – the truth remains that the coming of steam railways did have an immense effect on the way people lived.

This is not surprising when one considers that both the cost and the speed of transport were improved at one stroke by a factor of at least four. On the credit side, no longer would most inland people stay all their lives in the place where they were born; no longer need they live within horse-and-cart range of the land on which their food was grown. On the

debit side, governments found a fatal ability to move armies from place to place in days rather than weeks, detraining the troops reasonably fresh and ready for battle, rather than footsore and weary from continuous forced marches. But would William of Normandy have got ashore at Hastings in 1066 if King Harold's army had moved by train from his victory over the Scandanavians in Yorkshire a few days earlier?

The political and economic power generated by the new railways meant that they were used for the unification and development of nations. In this way the world found itself the richer, but many green and pleasant lands were spoiled by dark satanic mills in the process.

The Origins and Development of Railways

Sometime in the dawn of civilization some unsung hero must have, for the first time, laid strips of wood – still called rails when used in fences – on the ground to allow his horse to pull a heavier load. And if the wheels of his cart were fixed outside the shafts, whose spacing was in turn determined by the width of the animal's buttocks, then the distance between these wooden strips would approximate to the width between the rails of most of the world's railways today.

After a diversion into 'plateways' using cast-iron flanged plates, there came wrought-iron rails and finally steel rails. At the same time the living horse had to give way to the iron one.

By the early 1800s railways and plateways were quite common in mining areas, while steam power was also commonly in use for driving pumping machinery. The marriage of the two and hence the first steam locomotive is attributed to Richard Trevithick, a mine captain from Cornwall, England. Trevithick's locomotive, built in 1804 at Pen-v-darran in South Wales as a wager, was tried out on a local mine tramway. While it seems to have worked quite well, the cast-iron plates which formed the track were not strong enough.

William Hedley's *Puffing Billy* of 1813 which ran on a tramway at Wylam near Newcastle-on-Tyne was one of the earliest successful uses of steam traction. *Puffing Billy* was good enough to continue in use until 1859, well into the photographic age.

The first use of steam on a public railway was George Stephenson's *Locomotion* on the Stockton and Darlington in 1825, but the term 'public' then had a literal meaning; it meant that anyone could run his train on the railway by paying the appropriate toll. A high proportion of S&D traffic, including all regular passenger workings, was hauled by horses supplied and operated by independent contractors, just as if the railway was a canal. So we come to the first public railway – in the modern and more restricted sense – the Liverpool and Manchester of 1829.

The Liverpool and Manchester Railway had every element of a modern railway. Its trains were propelled by mechanical means and ran on metal wheels guided by flanges running inside pairs of rails set 4ft 8½in apart. All trains ran to a timetable, were operated by the company, stopping only at its own stations, manned by its own staff. Perhaps the most significant way in which this railway fell short of a modern one was its speed. The 38 miles between the two cities were booked to be covered in two hours and six minutes, an average of eighteen mph.

Only fourteen years later, however, we find Daniel Gooch, locomotive superintendent of the Great Western Railway, personally driving Queen Victoria's husband, Prince Albert, home from Bristol to London after launching Brunel's new steamship, the *Great Britain*. The 118 miles were covered in two hours and four minutes, an average speed which would still be out of reach on many railways even today.

By 1850 many hundreds of miles of railway had been opened in most of the countries of the civilized world and, indeed, the speed of extension during the next thirty years took the form of railway mania. In 1869 the continent of America had been spanned, in 1902 – with the opening of the Trans-Siberian railway – came Asia's turn. Australia had to wait until 1917, while Cecil Rhodes' dream of an African Cape-to-Cairo line has yet to be fulfilled. By World War I in most parts of the world the network was complete.

We may note, however, that a young man, Henry Ford, in the early 1900s had the idea of making motorcars not as playthings for the wealthy, but as cheap transport for such as you and I. By the time Ford Model 'T' production ended in 1927, after fifteen million vehicles had been made (plus untold numbers of other

makes), railways were finding their customers coming to them by choice rather than necessity. The same applied to traders and shippers as well as those without cars; they had the alternative of trucks and motor buses.

The effect on the main lines was very marked, but that on branch and local railways was catastrophic. A few small countries abandoned railways completely, while in others, great reductions in mileage were made. In France, for example, 15,000 miles of local interest railways were abandoned and in the USA the slaughter of inter-urban local lines amounted to a similar figure over this period.

The shortage of oil during World War II signalled a reprieve; the development of aircraft during that conflict led (by the 1960s) to the jet airliner. The speed of the big jets more than compensated for the superior comfort and roominess of long-distance trains.

Thus, between road and air competition the railways suffered greatly; indeed, after just over a century of existence their very survival as providers of general transportation was in doubt. The situation was compounded in many countries by continuing and inflexible systems of regulation dating from monopoly days.

However, today it has become clear that, for a whole series of reasons, the world is entering a new railway age. Ten years ago, this would have been speculation, but it is now firmly rooted in certainty.

Firstly, the exhaustion of the world's oil supplies is an event which is likely to be of concern to people living now; therefore any means of transport which does not depend on oil – or uses less oil than others – is one which should be fostered.

Secondly, it is recognized that the economics of hauling things in long trains, which flanged steel wheels guided by steel rails permit, make a railway by far the cheapest form of land transport, provided that the trains are long enough and/or frequent enough to pay for the fixed costs of what is, after all, a very specialized form of highway.

Thirdly, technology is once again on the side of the railway, with such notions as crewless freight trains or aircraft-speed passenger trains becoming practical possibilities.

Fourthly, growing concern for the environment is encouraging for railways, bearing in mind that one extra freight train on the railway means fifty juggernaut trucks off the roads.

Thus, 150 years after the first inter-city line, the future of railways can be viewed with considerable optimism. Only a tiny fraction of the world's countries are without railways; and several of these have indicated their intention of becoming members of the railway club.

The Development of Motive Power and Rolling Stock

Steam

Steam power dominated traction on the world's railways for the first 120 years of their existence, that is until the 1950s. In some places of course, it still does. Indeed serious new construction continued at least until 1978, when this was written. The final product, the *March Forward*

or 'QJ' class 2-10-2, built by and for the Chinese National Railways, was typical of the tradition of steam construction in the world. Accordingly, it is illuminating to compare the *March Forward* with the *Rocket* of the Liverpool and Manchester Railway, which took to the road 147 years earlier. It is no surprise that what impresses one is the similarities not the differences, at any rate in fundamentals. The path of evolution from *Rocket* to *March Forward* is remarkable as much for the small number of forward steps as for the large number taken sideways or on branch lines.

Rocket already had a fire-tube boiler with multiple tubes, water space round a firebox and a fire which was drawn up by exhaust steam blasted up the chimney. The more steam was used, the more the fire was drawn. There were two cylinders linked to driving wheels by connecting rods, all outside the frames in full view.

Major progress came straight away with some of *Rocket*'s immediate successors of 1830. *Phoenix* had a smokebox and with *Northumbrian* the previously separate water space round the firebox was integrated with that of the rest of the boiler, exactly as in *March Forward*.

The *Invicta*, built the same year for the Canterbury and Whitstable Railway in England, had the cylinders which, although still inclined, were placed at the front end and, in addition, her four wheels were coupled.

With the *Planet*, built later in 1830 for the L&M, Stephenson (and most British locomotives) left the main line of evolution for a branch. The cylinders were placed inaccessibly under the smokebox, the drive being provided by an expensive double crank in the driving axle. This branch line was a long one, locomotives of this layout being supplied – some by Robert Stephenson and Company – 120 years later to an order placed by the Western Region of British Railways. It will be appreciated that not only had the cranks and connecting rods to be accommodated between the frames but also two sets of gear to actuate the valves.

The cylinders temporarily reached their final horizontal outside forward position with the 2-2-0 locomotive *Vauxhall* built for the Irish Dublin & Kingstown Railway in 1834 by a Liverpool engineer called Forrester. They remained in Ireland permanently and were adopted in the USA from 1835 on. Bogies first appeared under William Hedley's *Puffing Billy* of 1813; during the time (1815-1831) it was altered from a four-wheeler to an eight-wheeler. This double-power-bogie arrangement is today – with diesel or electric drive – by far the commonest in the world.

The idea of pivoted wheels for guidance originated in the USA. The great Mathias Baldwin of Philadelphia produced a bogie 4-2-0 design as early as 1834, but bogies and pony trucks with side movement did not develop until the 1860s. On the other hand the bogie tender of our Chinese 2-10-2 is an arrangement which appeared in the USA early in the 1830s, as being suitable for America's lightly laid tracks.

Top: This contemporary print shows the opening of another very early railway, the Canterbury and Whitstable, 3 May 1830. The locomotive Invicta *has been preserved.*

Above: The causeway connecting the line from Hamburg, Germany to the island of Sylt crosses the open sea. This composite picture (in the form of a popular postcard) is rather more dramatic than the actual case.

Eugène Walschearts of Belgium in 1854 devised the valve gear that bears his name, but it saw little use for many years. Early in this century, however, it came suddenly into fashion and in the end became virtually universal for the last forty years of steam construction. The gear that bears Stephenson's honoured name can be arranged to give excellent steam distribution, but it is awkward to place it in an accessible position outside the wheels, whereas Walschearts' fits in very conveniently and remains in full view.

Brilliant engineers unfortunately can conceive complicated designs but a Frenchman called Henri Giffard in 1851 produced his injector – a simple and static arrangement of cones – whereby steam is used to squirt water directly into the boiler. In this way the expense of troublesome feed pumps became a thing of the past. Actually in making his invention, Giffard had steam aircraft in mind but this early spin-off from the space age has been of great benefit to the cause of steam.

Flat or 'slide' valves were normal in the 1800s, but around the turn of the century they began to give way to the less friction-bound piston type.

Complexity and the steam locomotive never agreed. For example, the compound principle was tried over a period – short in Britain, long

An American train runs alongside the Mississippi River in Minnesota.

in France – whereby a second set of cylinders was provided which would take in the steam exhausted from the first ones and extract additional work from it. The process had achieved big savings when applied to steam engines in factories and ships. But, for two reasons, compounding never (not even in France) became universal practice: firstly, the gain in efficiency was reduced when, as in a railroad, the demand for power constantly varied; secondly, the extra machinery needed extra maintenance and the savings were not enough to justify this. Similar remarks applied to other multiple-cylindered locomotives which did not use the compound principle.

Wilhelm Schmidt of Germany in 1891 fitted a locomotive with what was called a super-heater. By the laws of physics water boils at a temperature precisely dependent on the pressure; hence, since efficiency is improved by working at a higher temperature and increasing the pressure leads to problems in making the boiler strong enough, Schmidt thought that further heating the steam after it had left the boiler might do the trick. His simple arrangement of tubular elements inside enlarged fire-tubes worked well and superheating became a universal feature from the early years of the century onwards.

Early in the new century, therefore, the

steam locomotive reached its final form. It remained to improve the materials and the details. As an example of what could be done, one could cite an improved axlebox bearing introduced in the 1930s on a British Railway – the London, Midland & Scottish – by a locomotive engineer from rival Great Western. Failures due to overheated axleboxes on the seventy principal 'Royal Scot' express locomotives fell from eighty per year to seven in consequence. Such an instance illustrates the kind of improvements in repair and maintenance costs that could be and were achieved by careful study of every detail. In this way enormous reductions were constantly being

made in the cost of running the conventional Stephenson steam locomotive. In stark contrast was the failure, in spite of many attempts by the most skilful designers and engineers, to improve the basic Stephensonian principles.

One thing does remain to be said about steam and that is to refer to the passionate and almost unbelievable love that it evokes in men beyond any bounds of logic or reason. In all the countries which have dispensed with steam, iron horses have been preserved for pleasure purposes, to the tune of several thousand in total, many of them in working order. The effort put into this is some measure of the strength of feeling for one of mankind's most beneficial and attractive creations.

Diesel

As a competitor of steam, the diesel engine was a late-comer; the principle dates back to a type of heat engine devised by a certain *Herr Doktor* Diesel of Berlin, Germany in 1893. Like other internal combustion engines, it is capped by a fundamental weakness and it is this: unless the engine is turning, no force is produced. In traction of course, a big force is needed when stationary; this basic unsuitability has not, however, prevented diesel-driven locomotives from dominating the railway scene today.

Four solutions of gradually increasing complexity have been considered and experimented with; it is strange that while in steam-locomotive engineering the simplest of alternative solutions has usually prevailed, with diesel the most complex has been the winner. The first answer to this problem of coupling a spinning shaft to a stationary wheel is the familiar motorcar clutch and gearbox – a mechanical solution in fact. This works very well for low powers, up to say 200 horsepower, but in spite of some brave attempts, no higher.

One idea which seemed promising was to use a diesel engine to compress air. The compressed air in its turn could be used to drive the locomotive – in one 1932 German experiment an actual steam locomotive was used. However, the excess heat produced in the process proved in the end to be both troublesome and wasteful.

The coupling of the engine to the wheels hydraulically has had modest success and many diesel-hydraulic locomotives run on the world's railways. Most originate either directly or indirectly from Germany.

Nevertheless, today the standard locomotive of the world is the diesel-electric which is, in fact, an electric locomotive which carries its own power station. We note an early successful application of the principle to some low-power Swedish railcars in 1913 and experiments, some of which became successes, in many countries during the 1920s, but most of the credit of turning a dubious and complex box of tricks into a world-beater must go to General Motors of the United States of America during the 1930s. The complication of the solution may be gauged from the fact that diesels cost three times as much and some had (as a measure of their complexities) sixteen times as many cylinders as steam locomotives of equivalent performance, but the advantages prevailed.

The advantages of diesel locomotives over steam sprung much less from direct savings – when modern diesels were compared with modern steam power, these were often negligible – than from indirect ones. Diesels are push-button power – no lighting up, hours before they are needed. They are also building-block power, capable of being made up to any power required by adding units, without needing extra crews. The servicing time is also much less and there is a small bonus in smoke abatement. All these things added up to a good case and furthermore, even railway magnates are vulnerable to the 'keeping-up-with-the-Jones' syndrome.

Electric

For most railway traffic, however, dieselization is not a long-term solution. Electrification, which goes back further in time, is likely to be applied to all railways in the future where the density of movement is sufficient to justify the high fixed costs. Put another way, when there are enough trains, it is better to take power stations off the locomotives and build instead bigger and fewer ones on the ground. The inventor of electric traction was a Scotsman called Davidson from Edinburgh, who demonstrated an electrically propelled vehicle as early as 1834. On the other hand the first practical electric railway was one demonstrated at the Berlin exhibition of 1879 by the firm of Siemens and Halske. This led in 1881 to a line 1.5 miles long near Berlin and very quickly thereafter to a proliferation of electric inter-urban and local railways. The only survivor from these days is Volk's Electric Railway at Brighton, England. The gestation period for practical electric traction was therefore much longer than for steam or diesel, but its childhood much shorter.

The first major main-line, big-time, electric railway was the Swiss Bernese Alps line (now called the Bern–Lötschberg–Simplon), which opened in 1913. After the 1914 war, railways in numerous countries electrified quite long sections of main line. By 1930 it was, for example, possible to travel the 500 miles from Geneva, Switzerland to Salzburg, Austria by electric train.

Where is the longest such journey now? It goes from near the Finnish-Russian frontier at Vyborg via Leningrad, and the Trans-Siberian Railway as far as Karymskay 1993 miles from Vladivostok on the Pacific Ocean. The overall distance is just short of 4500 miles. Alas, while Czarist *laissez-faire* provided one uniform track gauge throughout this journey, Communist planning has led to two incompatible electrification systems, direct current and alternating current, over different parts of the route.

This highlights a conflict between high-voltage alternating current systems (cheap fixed equipment, costly locomotives) and medium voltage direct current (more costly fixed equipment, cheaper locomotives) which has gone on since electrification began. If compatibility with older systems is no problem, the solution of using newly developed solid-state conversion equipment on DC locomotives,

enabling them to use AC transmission, has recently resolved the matter. It has also become very much easier to build multi-current locomotives, capable of running under both DC and AC systems.

Passenger Carriages

The Liverpool and Manchester Railway commenced operations with what were effectively stage-coach 'inside' bodies in threes on four-wheeled rail chassis. This compartmented layout (with eight or more 'bodies' forming each coach, and in due time modernized with a side corridor), remained the norm in Britain until the 1960s. Early American railroads favoured the open coach – which most of the world's railways have now adopted – in which the passengers sit either side of a central aisle, entering and exiting by doors at the ends. Rougher tracks across the Atlantic led to the mounting of carriage bodies on the now-familiar four-wheel trucks or bogies as early as 1840. The present-day layout of railway carriages, therefore, evolved very early and development has taken the form of improvements and refinements rather than change. Stronger construction and automatic brakes have improved safety; air-conditioning, heating and better bogies have improved comfort out of all recognition. One major improvement involved communication between adjacent

vehicles. Access to and between open carriages was originally via open and draughty platforms at each end. By the early 1900s these were beginning to be made into closed vestibules and the vehicles joined to one another by flexible corridor connections. This feature is now virtually universal.

In the first years of railways, passengers generally either brought their own food or snatched what they could in dining rooms during stops. Similarly, they slept as best they could in carriage seats when overnight journeys were involved. In due time, dining, buffet and sleeping cars evolved to meet these needs.

The extra comforts of sleeping berths as well as meals on the move, were (and to some extent are still) catered for by two famous companies, both household words in their own sphere of influence. They were Pullman, mainly in the USA, and Wagons-Lits, mainly in Europe. Other lines, particularly those under British influence, used their own cars.

The first recorded regular provision of sleeping accommodation in a train was well ahead of its general provision. There was a 'bed carriage' on the London and Birmingham Railway in 1838, while the first regular public dining car operated by the Great Western Railway of Canada (now part of Canadian National) in 1867. Such facilities (as appropriate) are now normal on most overnight

and long-distance trains the world over. There were facilities on the Liverpool and Manchester Railway to bring one's own road carriage with one on the train; it is a pleasure to record that in recent years (after a long absence) these have now returned, on a small scale in the USA under the name Autotrain, but quite extensively – as Motorail – in Europe.

Many special types of passenger carriage have existed, such as dance cars, observation cars, gymnasiums, fresh and salt-water bath cars, and so on, but they give pleasure to the student of curiosities rather than play a serious role in the evolution of modern passenger transport. An exception is the class of vehicles built for the heads of state and other VIPs; in some countries and in the early years what was right for Kings and Queens in one decade became available for their subjects in the next. Sometimes it worked the other way; before her recent Jubilee Queen Elizabeth II of Britain used a train which included vehicles dating back to her grandfather's time and, in consequence, she could sometimes be seen travelling on the 'slow' lines at their maximum speed of 70 mph while her subjects roared by on the fast ones at 100 mph.

Left: A five-unit diesel crosses the Olifants River Bridge with an iron-ore train on the new Sishen-Saldanha line in South Africa.

Left: A steam-hauled goods train crosses the arches of a masonry viaduct.

Extreme left: A narrow-gauge 4-8-4 climbs the Raurimu spiral in New Zealand.

The Development of Operations and Services

With this development of passenger accommodation came improvements in two main areas. First, overall speeds steadily increased. In steam days, 70 mph average speeds and 100 mph maximum speeds were reached, but with diesel and electric power a thirty percent improvement on that has so far been the best that can be achieved. There seems reason to suppose that, above 150 mph, the flanged steel wheel on a steel rail begins to run into difficulties. The idea of tilting the carriages to maintain a comfortable ride at high speeds round sharp curves is being developed in several countries.

The second main area of improvement has been the development of passenger trains which run without change, over the metals of several administrations. That a traveller should be able to remain in his seat or berth while moving from one country's or one company's line to another, instead of facing all the tedium and hazards of changing trains, is one of the greatest possible benefits. Awkward problems have had to be solved, compatibility of equipment being the least of them.

Having said all this, it must be added that, regarding railroads in general, passenger services take very much second place to freight movement. Most types of goods wagon or

freight car now in use have been around since the early days of railways, (including containers and 'piggy-back') but the size and load carried has steadily increased. A typical rail freight vehicle, which might a century ago have carried ten tons, now might carry fifty. This is not an unmixed blessing – what do you do if you have only ten tons to send?

Not only do individual vehicles have this much higher capacity, but trains also can be made up to much higher loads, carrying, perhaps, 10,000 tons instead of 200. This time the railway companies have the problem and what do they do? Wait until they have accumulated 10,000 tons for one destination and delay the traffic, or send what they have at the time and increase the cost?

Safety has been a foremost concern of railways ever since an English Member of Parliament was killed on the opening day of the Liverpool and Manchester Railway in 1830. Soon enough it was realized that something better than just the train driver's eyes was needed for these fire-chariots, when running at their mind-boggling speeds of 30 mph.

At first, policemen were appointed to signal to drivers that a preceding train had passed less than or more than so many minutes ago – time-interval working, it was called. After the invention and installation of the electric telegraph, it was possible to signal back from the

station ahead that a particular train had passed, thereby confirming the line was clear. This was called the Block System; it was installed in special places very early on and became general in the late 1800s. Also, in due time, fixed mechanical signals of various types (disc, ball, semaphore) replaced hand signals. Further development of mechanical signalling gave interlocking with points and switches, so that a signal could not show clear unless the route had been set correctly.

A device called the track circuit, which detects the presence of a train on a line electrically, led the way, first to preventing signals being put to all-clear when there was a train on the line ahead, second to putting them automatically to danger as a train went past. This has led to a large degree of automation in the signalling of trains; almost all rail routes of any importance are now controlled in this way, with human intervention at junctions, usually from remote-control locations.

A quite different philosophy of train safety still exists in many different parts of the world, notably the US although it is on the wane. It applies particularly to single lines. The basis of this system is that trains should run according to the timetable and, that the timetable should be worked out so they shall not collide with one another.

Common to all systems is the requirement

for trains to be able to stop when they need to. For this reason automatic brakes, applicable to all vehicles on a train and self-applying in the case of malfunction, are compulsory in practically all countries. A much less universal but growing contribution to safety is an automatic connection between the signals and the brakes on a train to which they apply. If a train passes a signal at 'caution', brakes are automatically applied and the driver, of course, warned.

In general, safety considerations have had precedence over financial ones, but the latter govern the continued existence of most railways. Recognizing this, people are curious to know the score and one is often asked about a particular railway, 'does it pay?' Accordingly, official figures have, wherever possible been given, expressed usually in the form of expenses as a percentage of receipts.

A warning was given earlier that official statistics of quite solid things like mileage of route and number of wagons are a trifle suspect, but when it comes to so sensitive a matter as a railway's finances, we really enter the realms of fiction. Oddly enough, capitalist-owned railways seem to give more plausible figures than ones owned by governments, which have the power to play all sorts of tricks. Subsidies for certain traffic, money lent free of interest, over-generous payments for social services may improve results; free carriage for, say, military traffic, continuance of uneconomic services for political ends, and the like may make them worse. Even so, a very good percentage figure gives some indication of a well-run railway and a very bad one an indication that the railway is one with problems.

The permanent way at the approaches to a great terminus.

Bulgaria went beyond anything normally built for the Fatherland with 4-10-0 tender and 2-12-4 tank designs. Passenger power took the form of 4-8-2s but the ubiquitous standard German 2-10-0s predominated in the later years of steam, still not quite over in 1978. Even on the 2ft 6in gauge the standard locomotives were Germanic 2-10-2Ts of Polish build. The handsome lines of all these locomotives are enhanced by a bright green livery complete with golden wings on the smokebox.

Electrification did not begin until well after World War II and accordingly, Bulgaria began by using the high voltage standard frequency AC system. Skoda of Czechoslovakia supplied the first bogie 25,000v 50-cycle locomotives. Lines with lesser traffic are being dieselized.

Train Services

One hundred million passengers are carried on BDZ annually plus 79 million tons of freight, hauled an average distance of 120 miles. The successors and the derivatives of the famous 'Simplon Orient Express' finally dwindled away in 1976 when the three-times-a-week Paris–Istanbul sleeper was withdrawn. Instead, solid trains of Soviet sleeping cars run daily from Moscow to Sofia and to the Black Sea resorts in season.

Below: A Bulgarian 2-12-4T steam locomotive hauls an empty mineral train back to the mines.

CYPRUS

See map on pages 250-251.

In the early 1900s the then-British island of Cyprus had a 67-mile 2ft 6in gauge railway which ran from Famagusta on the east coast, passed a mile or so away from Nicosia, the capital, and reached Morphou on the north coast. It was opened on 21 October 1905 and closed on 31 December 1951. Among the twelve-strong locomotive fleet were four noble 4-8-4Ts from Kitsons of Leeds. There were (possibly are) also two short private mineral lines.

Above: The main line of the Cyprus Government Railway ran from the port of Famagusta to the capital, Nicosia. This 2ft 6in gauge line tottered on into the 1950s but by then its ageing Nasmyth Wilson 4-4-0s and even its rattling railcars were anachronisms. This picture of the midday train from Nicosia was taken in April 1946.

Left: The 76cm narrow-gauge Bulgarian line to Septembri now uses smart red diesels in place of the huge green 2-10-2 tanks which sometimes ran in pairs in earlier years.

CZECHOSLOVAKIA

See map on pages 26–27.

CZECHOSLOVAK STATE RAILWAYS – CSD

*Ceskoslovenské Státní Dráhy
Příkopy 33,
Prague 1.*

Until 1918 Czechoslovakia was part of the Austro-Hungarian empire. From a railway historian's point of view, Austria and Hungary were separate entities and, accordingly, the provinces of Bohemia and Morovia should be regarded as originally part of Austria; Slovenia as part of Hungary. Since Vienna and Budapest were the respective focal points of these railways, the new republic had to alter the railway maps to suit a new country whose capital was Prague. Some 100 miles of new line were built and some 125 miles more upgraded from single-line branches to double-track main lines; in this way east-west communication was improved, in line with the new direction of political control.

All significant public railways were taken over by the new state and this involved several major privately owned concerns as well as part of the Austrian and Hungarian state railways. In gratitude to the man who helped create the nation, the centre of the new system in Prague was called the Wilson Station; under Communist rule even the most benevolent of American presidents are anathema – the central station is now called Hlavni.

One small but significant step for the new nation was to make some order out of a motive power fleet that consisted of 184 locomotive classes. Each class was allocated a number which – unlike those allocated to modern aircraft and computers – contained a code which still tells anyone with a certain mathematical ability something useful concerning the locomotive.

For a locomotive foreman with a strange engine on his hands it is important to know the maximum load on any axle, which governs the lines on which the locomotive can work: too heavy an axle-load and damage could be done to the track. If you added ten to the righthand or 'units' digit, this gave the axle-load in tons.

The centre digit gave a clue to the locomotive's maximum speed – add three and multiply by ten and there it was in kilometres per hour. The hundreds digit simply told the number of coupled axles. Hence a class 498 'Albatross'

Left: The 2ft 6in gauge 2-10-2 and narrow-gauge train on the banks of the Danube near Oryakhovo.

Above: The 498 class 4-8-2s were Czechoslovakia's pride and joy – and with good cause as they were magnificent modern machines, lasting in regular service into the mid-1970s. Here is one with the 'Saxonia Express' in July 1965.

locomotive had four coupled axles – in fact they were 4-8-2s, among the best and most modern in the world – was allowed to run at 75mph and had an axle-loading capacity of eighteen tons.

This excellent and quite unique classification system was a mere reflection of the superb quality of Czech locomotive building, which has continued (mainly through the well-known firm of Skoda) into the diesel and electric era. Steam is currently (1978) still in use but on a small and rapidly decreasing scale.

World War II came and went with much destruction, but with the Czech borders and railway system more or less as they were before the notorious Munich Pact (Hitler said 'I have no more territorial claims to make in Europe' but the German tradition of ignoring scraps of paper proved too much for him) of 1938. The system now comprises 8150 miles of standard-gauge route, 62 miles of broad (Soviet) gauge and 110 miles of narrow-gauge line. Fifteen hundred miles are electrified, most at 3000v DC, but more recently at 25,000v AC.

Incidentally, the first ever recorded railway (horse-drawn with wooden rails) occurred in what was then Hungary but is now southern Czechoslovakia. It appears as embroidery on a sacred altar cloth dating from around 1500. (Where, however, does one end in moving away from what we now know as a railway; do the grooves for chariot wheels in the stone-paved streets of Roman cities count?)

Freight traffic in Czechoslovakia now exceeds 320 million tons annually, needing a fleet of around 150,000 wagons. Passenger traffic, using a fleet of over 10,000 carriages, is three times what it was before World War II.

DENMARK

See map on pages 38–39.

DANISH STATE RAILWAYS – DSB
Danske Statsbaner
40 Solvgade,
1349 Copenhagen K.

Denmark's railway *system* began on 27 June 1847, when the locomotive *Odin* (a 2-2-2 from Sharp-Stewart of Manchester) hauled a train on the Zeeland Railway Company's line from Copenhagen to Roskilde. This was not the first railway in Denmark as then constituted, for a line was opened the previous year from Altona to Kiel in the province of Schleswig-Holstein, which in 1864 was grabbed by Prussia to form part of a greater Germany.

The original lines were privately owned, but in the later years of the century the trunk routes were taken over by the state. In 1885 the present Danish State Railways was formed; local railways remained (and to some extent still remain) unnationalized. This 'non-doctrinaire' approach, typical of the Danish way of doing things, pervades the story of Danish railways.

Denmark presented few problems to railway builders regarding hills and valleys. Her difficulty lay in the fact that the places to be linked by rail lay on several separate islands. For many years the most important routes were interrupted by train ferries: for example between Copenhagen (on Zeeland) and Esjberg (on Jutland) there were two ferry rides and, hence, a journey time of seven hours for the 194 miles. Between the wars efforts were made to fill in some of the gaps. First, in 1935, was the 0.75-mile bridge across the Little Belt, which enabled DSB to introduce diesel-electric 'lightning trains' (*Lyntog* in Danish) which reduced that seven-hour timing to four. In 1938 came the two-mile Storstrom bridge connecting Zeeland with Lolland, an island which is a stepping-stone on the route south from Copenhagen into Germany. Both these bridges are in the world class with main spans of 450ft and 722ft respectively. At the same time, the DSB still finds employment for modern ferries taking trains across the sixteen

mile Great Belt and across the Baltic and the Skaggerak to Germany and Sweden.

Danish steam was distinctive, handsome and not allowed to pass away in unwanted disrepute. Indeed, one of the last steam trains to run in Denmark was the recent funeral train of King Frederick; he was a life-long railway enthusiast and had actually specified this form of transport for his last journey. Distinction lay deeper than the band of national colours which Danish steam locomotives carried round their chimneys; older locomotives frequently had the rare Allan straight-link valve gear in full view outside the frames and later ones (such as the elegant compound 4-4-2s) had big wind-cutter wedge-fronted cabs.

Some of the 4-4-2s were rebuilt as 4-6-2s, but the most powerful Danish express locomotives, also compound 4-6-2s, actually came from Sweden, which was disposing of them because of electrification. The economics of compounding made sense in a country which had to import its coal.

There was no Gadarene rush into dieselization, which cost so many unthinking railways so much. In fact, the Danes spent over forty years on the job. Hence no scrapping of brand-new steam locomotives or, for that matter newish but unwisely ordered diesels, which characterized the process in Great Britain and other countries. Of the Western European systems, the DSB was the first to begin dieselization, in 1927 – and one of the last to complete, in 1970. In Denmark the word 'complete' is correct, as main-line electrification has not yet begun there, understandable in a country which has neither coal, water-power, nor mountain grades. There is a 1500v DC suburban electrification around Copenhagen, using 283 electric motor coaches, but elsewhere a fleet of 298 diesel locomotives and 105 railcars reign supreme.

The early amalgamation of third-class and second-class accommodation into a 'general' passenger class, anticipated similar moves in the rest of Europe by many years.

Top: The striking and unusual lines of a Danish 4-4-2 steam locomotive.

Centre and left: Over forty years ago Danish Railways were putting diesel-electric power into service. The locomotive (above left) was built in 1937 and the one on the left is a modern diesel locomotive at Jutland station.

Extreme left: The five hundredth engine, No T679, emerges from the Nové Zámky (Czechoslovakia) locomotive works on 9 July 1973.

SCANDINAVIA

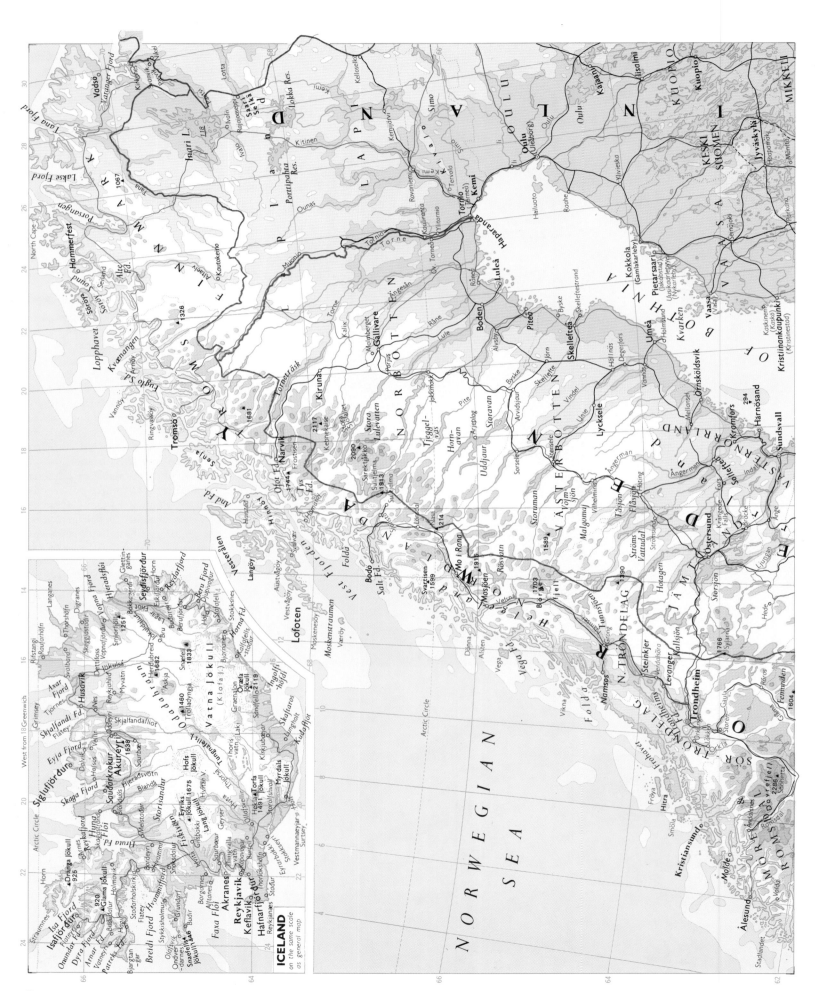

NORWEGIAN SEA

ICELAND
on the same scale
as general map

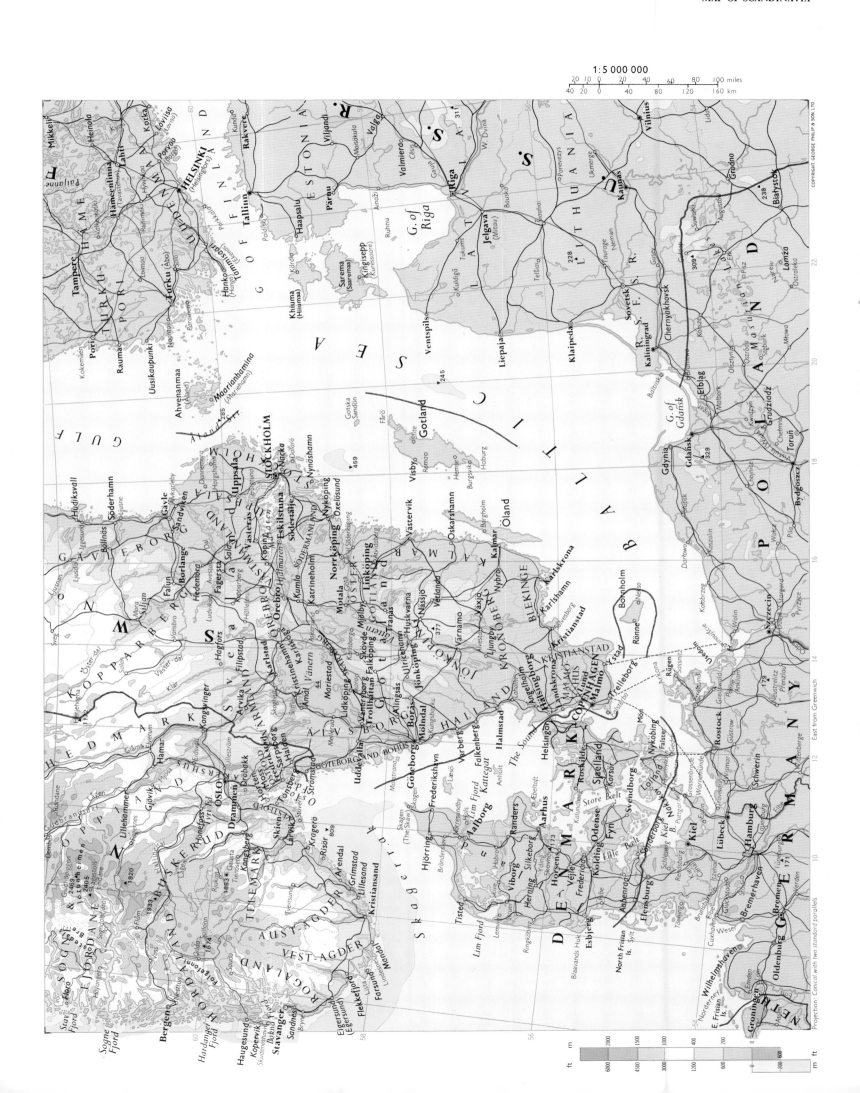

1:5 000 000

Right : A Lyntog train leaves the Great Belt train ferry at Nyborg across the channel from Korsör.

Below : The circulating area of the great hall of Copenhagen's Central Station is typical of the general Germanic design found from the Baltic to the Black Sea.

FINLAND

See maps on pages 38–39 and 118–119.

FINNISH STATE RAILWAYS – VR
Valtionrautatiet,
Vilhonkatu 13,
00100 Helsinki 10.

Finland is a land without mountains – except for some high hills in the extreme north called mountains by courtesy. However, little of it is flat; the typical landscape is of many low hills of granite, ground down by ice-age glaciers, covered by forest and many lakes, some forming large navigable systems. The south is relatively mild and fertile, but conditions get harder further north. Although the railway system does not penetrate as far as the Arctic coast, two lines go well beyond the Arctic circle.

History
Although there is a large Swedish-speaking minority, Finland was a part of Imperial Russia until it seized its independence in 1918. A large part of the east of the country was regained by the USSR through conquest in 1945, but Finland retains a genuine independence and is, in fact, the only Western democracy to have any border with Russia itself (apart from a short Norwegian frontier length in the Arctic). A legacy of Soviet dominion is witnessed by the fact that the Finnish railway system is built to the Soviet gauge of 5ft.

The first railway in Finland, from Helsinki to Hameenlinna, was opened in 1862. Connection was made to St Petersburg (Leningrad) by 1870, and construction, almost all undertaken directly by the state, continued steadily up to 1918 and thereafter. Indeed, two important new lines, improving and shortening major routes, have been opened during the 1970s, chief of which is the 75-mile Tampere-Seinajoki link. The present route mileage is 3750.

Locomotive Development
Even more than in the USSR proper, early Finnish locomotive design was much influenced by American practice. Later on, German influence predominated. Right up till the end of steam traction, woodburners outnumbered coalburners, since wood is the only home-produced fuel, and it was only after the 1920s that coalburners came to work most of the heavier duties. Designs tended to be hampered by axle-load restrictions, and conditions did not require any remarkable machines to be developed; the steam fleet consisted mainly of handsome but fairly conventional 2-6-0s, 4-6-0s and 2-8-0s, with 2-8-2s, 4-6-2s and a few US-built 2-10-0s coming in from the late 1930s onwards. Dieselization had begun by the early 1950s, but was not rushed and not completed for twenty years by which time electrification was well in hand on the busiest lines in the south. However the Finns remain nervous about the strategic 'wisdom' of dependence on imported oil or easily bombed hydro-electric complexes (with good reason in their short national history) and still maintain a large number of woodburning locomotives in reserve.

Train Services and Rolling Stock
Considering the relatively sparse population, passenger train services in Finland are very good, quite fast and frequent. To some extent this occurs because of reliance on diesel railcars, but even during the steam age the picture was much better than might have been expected. One reason might be the fact that roads are not as good as they can be in kinder climates; frost in the sandy soil tends to destroy most road surfaces unless they are very strong and expensive. Until the last decade most passenger coaches were wooden-bodied, and shared with Soviet railways a very large loading gauge giving plenty of space inside. However, heating has been by steam for many years, and the Soviet practice of having a separate coal stove in each coach is not followed. Recent coaches, railcars, and multiple units (both diesel and electric) have been in line with current European practice. The only international passenger service is from Helsinki to Leningrad, where no gauge problem arises; there is some limited use of axle-changing to accommodate standard-gauge freight vehicles at the connection with the Swedish railways at Tornio at the head of the Gulf of Bothnia, and at the ice-free port of Hangö whence a train ferry operates to the East German port of Travemünde.

Operations and Signalling
Traditional Finnish signalling is German in equipment, and somewhat American in method. Racquet-shaped upper-quadrant semaphores, with numbers of arms coding divergent routes, plus wire-worked frames and points are Germanic, and single-line working by train

order and telephone are American. More modern installations, on both single and double line, tend more to the international norm of CTC, and automatic block. One feature which remains doggedly in stations and yards is an absence of remote control of points, due to the impossiblity of keeping wires and rods clear and working during icebound weather; most points therefore had to be hand-worked and locally indicated. A few modern power-worked, propane-heated points do exist.

Administration and Finance

The Finnish State Railways is now under the control of the Ministry of Communications. Some minor railways, including several of 75cm and 60cm gauge, were privately owned, but no independent undertaking now survives. There is an annual deficit of some thirty per-cent.

Top: Diesel shunter and electric commuter trains at Helsinki. Today Finland's trains are diesel hauled and steam no longer appears on its 5ft gauge tracks.

Centre right: Further north in Finland, where the traffic is comparatively sparse, passengers are catered for in blue and cream railcars which run between wooden clapboard stations. Here is a car waiting to depart from Oulu to Kemi.

Right: More modern than their spark arresting stacks make them appear, Finland's 2-8-0 1100 class woodburners are mainly confined to shunting duties further north, where copious supplies of fuel are available for little cost. Here at Rouveniemi, No 1150 sets the coaches for the overnight train to Helsinki.

Above: A steam-hauled freight train at Esjberg in Denmark.

Above: Gare de Lyon, Paris, France.

Right: French signals glow in the night.

FRANCE

See map on pages 46–47.

Except for the industrialized belt running along the Belgian and Luxembourg frontiers from Lille towards Strasbourg, France, with a total population of 53 million, is the least densely populated country of Western Europe, excluding the Scandinavian and Iberian peninsulas. There are of course great cities, especially Paris, and industrial and mining areas, but most of the nation is farmland, forest, or mountain, so that it is not too difficult to escape from urban pressures. The largest area of flat plain lies in a great 180° arc south of Paris, to a radius of perhaps 100 miles; to the north the landscape varies from gently rolling to hilly, but with little that could be called mountainous. The southern centre comprises the Massif Central, high hills often wild and broken, showing here and there signs of volcanic origin; and along the southern and southeastern borders, facing Spain, Italy and Switzerland, are (generally) very rugged alpine areas, including the Pyrenees and the Savoy Alps themselves. In these regions the great river valleys mark the lines of communication, indeed of most development of any kind.

FRENCH NATIONAL RAILWAYS – SNCF

Société Nationale des Chemins de Fer Français,
88 Rue St.-Lazare,
75436 Paris.

Greater distances and smaller population meant that the French railway network was slower to become established than the British. Gallic logic ensured that once it was commenced, it was designed and carried out in a much more comprehensive and cohesive form; and Gallic tradition insisted that its whole philosophy and policy in every department had to spring from different roots and develop uniquely French objects and attributes. Since the seventeenth century, the French state had concerned itself with constructing the best system of roads, and later canals, in Europe; once the British had demonstrated the feasibility of a national railway system, several years were needed to work out how one could be established in accordance with French legal and political principles, although a few lines were commenced earlier by impatient small companies. The Railway Law of 11 June 1842 is probably the grandest and most ambitious programme of organization and construction ever launched anywhere, with the possible exception of the recent American Interstate Highway system.

Firstly, the 1842 Law established the basic principle that the state was to own all public railways without exception, just as it owned the roads. This fixed its right to determine what lines were built as well as to supervise their operation. However, private enterprise would be invited to work the railways under lease;

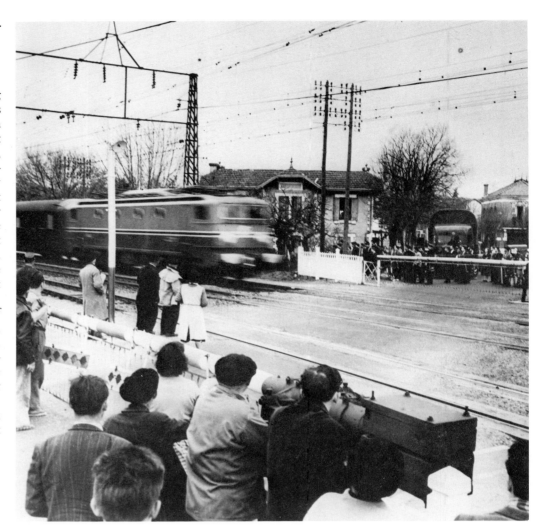

Top left: On 28 March 1955 the French Railways (SNCF) broke the World Rail Speed Record at 205 mph using electric locomotive CC.7107 – seen here during the run passing the level crossing at Labouheyre.

Left: Two of France's top expresses, 'L'Aquitaine' and 'Le Capitôle' (together with relief trains) await departure from Paris Austerlitz station on a peak traffic day.

Top: SNCF electric locomotive BB9004, joint holder with CC7107 of the World Rail Speed Record of 205 mph hauls a fast train between Paris and Savoy.

Above: A Clermont-Ferrand to Paris Express accelerates after leaving Vichy in April 1967. These superb 241P class 4-8-2s were based on a PLM design and though not so efficient as the Chapelon 240P locomotive, gave a very good account of themselves.

FRANCE

each line, once built by the state, would be put up to tender and the company offering the largest rent and the shortest lease (within a maximum of 99 years) would be given the concession.

Secondly, the 1842 scheme ordained a network of seven main lines radiating from Paris, plus two transverse routes; these still form the foundation of the system. These lines ran from Paris to Belgium via Amiens and Lille; to Marseille via Lyon; to Bordeaux and Spain via Orleans; to the Massif Central, also via Orleans; to Brittany via Chartres and Rennes; and to Normandy via Rouen. The transverse lines were to run from Bordeaux to Marseille via Toulouse and Narbonne; and from Dijon, between Paris and Lyon, to Mulhouse, Basel and Strasbourg.

As the network developed, the 1842 Plan was modified by schemes of (principally) 1859, 1865 and 1879. Ultimately the intention developed, and was almost achieved, that there should be a standard-gauge railway to every Sous-Préfecture, or roughly every town of over 1500 inhabitants, with feeders of standard or narrow gauge generously filling in the gaps (about a third of the 1914 route-mileage in France was metre-gauge). Working these rail-

FRANCE
DEPARTMENTS
1:8 000 000

1. VAL d'OISE
2. YVELINES
3. ESSONNE
4. HAUTS-DE-SEINE
5. SEINE-ST.-DENIS
6. VAL-DE-MARNE
7. VILLE DE PARIS

1 : 4 000 000

20 10 0 20 40 60 80 100 miles
20 10 0 20 40 60 80 100 120 140 160 km

CORSICA
on same scale

East from Greenwich

COPYRIGHT. GEORGE PHILIP & SON. LTD.

Below: The Mont-Doré portion of the Clermont-Ferrand to Paris Express tackles the long climb (eighteen miles at 1 in 40) to Vauriat Summit in March 1949. The engine is one of a batch built by the North British Locomotive Company in 1916/17 as class 141TA. The design was based on a very successful class built by SLM Winterthur for the Thunersee Railway in Switzerland.

Below: The Lyon–Nantes 'Corail' train on the Montciand viaduct near Arfeuilles in October 1976. This is one of the fastest cross-country services in France.

ways were private companies whose dividends were, in general, guaranteed by the state, which took in exchange for the guarantee, two-thirds of any greater profits. Some lines were, however, worked by the state itself, usually because of the failure of the original leaseholding company. After 1930 this dense railway network needed pruning as road transport developed. Almost all the narrow gauge has now gone, mainly through closure; the national route mileage has declined by about forty percent to its present figure of around 25,000 miles. Similarly, the financial difficulties which had begun to face the old companies, most of which had worked happily and uneventfully for eighty years, led to their nationalization in 1938 and formation of the present Société Nationale des Chemins de Fer Français, an act carried out by a socialist government but with a minimum of the bitter quarrelling, obstruction and disappointment which marked the nationalization of the British network ten years later.

However, since the old companies have left their mark both physically and in folklore forty years later, short accounts of the main ones are

in order. There were six of them, following an initial period of regrouping, which had settled by 1857, and they still in large part are mirrored by the six regions of the modern SNCF.

Chemin de Fer de l'Est
This company was incorporated in 1845 as the Chemin de fer de Strasbourg, when it received the concession for the Paris-Strasbourg trunk line. It changed its name in 1854 on obtaining the concession for the parallel route from Paris to Basel via Chaumont. It covered, exclusively, the eastern quadrant of the nation centring on these lines, without sending any branches out of the area, and it remained reasonably affluent throughout. The main event in its corporate history was the purchase – forced, but for real money – by the victorious Prussians after 1870, of its lines in the seized provinces of Alsace and Lorraine; on the return of these territories to France in 1919, the railways (somewhat Prussianized meanwhile and converted to right-hand running) were administered until 1938 by a separate state organization as the Réseau de l'Alsace et de Lorraine.

Chemin de Fer du Nord
This company received the concession for the line to Belgium in 1842, and prospered happily thereafter, coming to monopolize the area between the territory of the Est and the Channel coast (including but not going far beyond the Paris-Calais line). It did send one tentacle westwards for the important freight route from Amiens to Rouen. Its prosperity was originally such that not only did the company repay the whole cost of building its main lines to the government but until war came in 1914 it never had to ask the government to make up its dividend to the level of the guarantee and so never had to surrender any of its profits. Being so rich, it always had the reputation of being the best-run line with the best equipment, not unjustly.

Chemin de Fer Paris-Lyon-Mediterranée
The PLM was nearly as continuously well-off as the Nord, and arguably as well run. It was formed in 1857 as the result of a series of amalgamations of smaller companies which had not only come to own the whole of the trunk

Right: A modern compound locomotive is about to depart from Quimper in Brittany with a Paris train in June 1961.

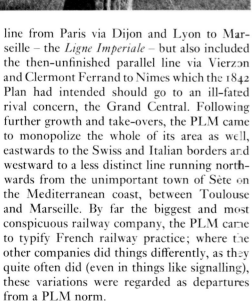

line from Paris via Dijon and Lyon to Marseille – the *Ligne Imperiale* – but also included the then-unfinished parallel line via Vierzon and Clermont Ferrand to Nimes which the 1842 Plan had intended should go to an ill-fated rival concern, the Grand Central. Following further growth and take-overs, the PLM came to monopolize the whole of its area as well, eastwards to the Swiss and Italian borders and westward to a less distinct line running northwards from the unimportant town of Sète on the Mediterranean coast, between Toulouse and Marseille. By far the biggest and most conspicuous railway company, the PLM came to typify French railway practice; where the other companies did things differently, as they quite often did (even in things like signalling), these variations were regarded as departures from a PLM norm.

Chemin de Fer Paris-Orléans

This company had been set up in 1838 to build the short line indicated by its title, but in 1842 it obtained the concession for the Paris-Bordeaux route and began to grow. Its two

principal main lines were from Paris to Bordeaux and to Toulouse (via Limoges), and it monopolized the area west of the PLM country as far as the Bordeaux main line. However, westwards of that things got a little complicated, (discussed below). Until 1934 the Orléans company also had the important line from Tours to Nantes and Quimper, and so held half the Breton peninsula, but as part of that year's rearrangements lost it.

Chemin de Fer du Midi

The only one of the major companies not to serve Paris, the Midi was established in 1852 to work the transversal line from Bordeaux to Toulouse and the Mediterranean (meeting the PLM end-on at Sète). It came to own all the other railways south of this line, but its only important venture to the north of it was the long and mountainous branch from Béziers to Neussargues, right on the PLM/Orléans borders. Always closely associated with the Orléans company, from 1934 the two railways were worked as one and the companies thus amalgamated in everything but legal form. However,

the Midi is historically important for two matters. One is that, dissatisfied with its unreal eastern terminal at Sète, it fought hard with the government for the right to build a line of its own to Marseilles, ultimately losing, and so confirming the principle of the 1842 legislation that directly parallel and competing railways would not be allowed. The other is that the Midi was the first French railway to go all-out for electrification; even by the 1920s its policy was to electrify everything, and this was largely achieved by 1934 (with the major exception of the easy Bordeaux-Toulouse main line, on which the company's steam locomotives were to serve out their time). Following 1934 the policy was taken up by the combined undertakings; although checked by the war, by 1948 a map of French main-line electrification still closely resembled a map of the PO-Midi.

And in the West

This brief account so far omits any mention of the corporate history of the railways of the western part of the country, between the Nord and the Orléans. This is because it was complicated. In the beginning were the Normandy and Brittany companies, holding the concessions under the 1842 Plan. They did not prosper and amalgamated in 1855 to form the Chemin de fer de l'Ouest which, surprisingly enough, did not prosper either. However, it struggled along from bankruptcy to reorganization and back until 1909, and contrived to operate (after some fashion) the main lines from Paris to Brest, le Havre and Cherbourg, and in the area surrounding. Much less respectable were the various small companies which maintained, in a kind of state of statutory brigandage, the majority of the lines in the area west of the Bordeaux main line and south of Nantes; ultimately during the 1870s things reached such a pass that the government cancelled their concessions and ran their lines itself.

Having just smacked down the Midi for wanting a rival line to Marseilles, the government then changed the rules in its own favour. In 1883 in an endeavour to make these lines in the Vendée pay, the government linked certain lines together with others obtained in exchange from the Orléans company, and demanded from the Ouest running powers from Chartres into Paris. It then established itself as the operator of a rival and competing main line from Paris to Bordeaux, the only example of direct mainline competition in French railway history. This continued until after 1938. The state system having thus been linked with the Compagnie de l'Ouest, when that sank into bankruptcy again in 1909 it was nationalized and the two concerns then operated as the Réseau de l'Etat. It remained something of a byword for most kinds of malpractice until finally taken in hand in the 1930s; the Paris-le Mans electrification of 1937, with its associated line and junction improvements for high speed running, set new standards worldwide.

With the 1938 unification under the SNCF, most of the old and unique legal foundation for the French railway network became of academic interest, but not all. It still colours the French official and public attitude, and in many ways they speak of 'our' railways much more meaningfully than elsewhere in Western Europe. After all, the main lines never were privately owned, and commercial motives have never been allowed to outweigh social and political ones; but yet the operator has always stood aside from politics and been firmly independent. Few other countries have managed

Bottom right: A modern stainless-steel train on the Paris Métro.

Below: French speed is electric.

this balance so well, and its roots in France lie still in the 1842 system.

Civil Engineering

Since the state undertook the original construction of the main-line networks, there is a certain consistency of style about them, particularly in the older buildings. But, although they were later relaxed when the time came to build branch lines and routes over which heavy traffic was never likely to pass, the fundamental specifications of all lines – maximum grade, sharpest curve – was decided *ab initio* and centrally, quite independently of the financial state of the company which ultimately worked the line. Nothing was therefore ever skimped, and large and expensive works were undertaken without trepidations. In the 1840s the civil engineering of French railways was much influenced by the ideas of Joseph Locke, who built several early lines including that from Paris to le Havre. Locke was much more willing to accept steep gradients (by which he meant something around 1 in 125) than his mentor George Stephenson (who liked to avoid anything steeper than about 1 in 250, or else concentrate it dramatically into a short pitch

designed for cable working). On the other hand, Locke shunned tunnels; but both engineers undertook very large viaducts and earthworks, and liked to avoid sharp curves. Locke's lines therefore tended to be rather cheaper to construct at the price of involving gradients which in steam days proved demanding against fast and heavy traffic, but yet were solid and well adapted to speeds of up to 60 or 75 mph even through fairly difficult country; and this, in effect, well describes the character of French main lines built up to about 1870. Later, more faith was put in tractive effort, and main lines built in the 1880s and 1890s, such as the direct route from Limoges to Toulouse, are quite difficult.

But state financing had its most dramatic effect on some of the spectacular engineering undertaken in hilly areas, even on lines of no great importance at all. It having been decided, for instance, that railway policy required the construction of a line from Volvic to Lapeyrouse, west of Clermont-Ferrand, it followed that the then-highest viaduct in the world was unavoidably necessary; no commercial concern would ever have built the Fades viaduct, carrying the tracks 430ft above the bottom of a

limestone gorge, but the line was felt to be needed even though little traffic would use it. Some of the other high viaducts in the Massif Central are equally impressive, both as engineering works of art and as, in some sense, sledgehammers to crack nuts. Perhaps the most remarkable example of mountain railway building never in fact got finished; construction of the line from le Puy to Lalevade d'Ardeche was suspended in 1914, never to be resumed, with the long summit tunnel at St Cirgues (two miles) finished and much else, but not the southern descent of the mountains which would have included some extraordinary gyrations inside the vast crater of a primeval volcano, involving two distinct spirals within a third; quite a unique feature.

Locomotive Landmarks

Just as the legal and political foundations of French railways were unique, so was their locomotive practice, particularly in steam days. Fundamental to their approach was the idea that a locomotive driver had to be quick, sure, and dependable, master of a complex machine, and that it was therefore a job for a young man. None of the gradual promotion through the

grades of cleaner, fireman, and passed-fireman universal elsewhere – a driver was trained directly for his job, including classes in scientific theory, and workshop practice. After twenty years on the footplate he retired on a good pension, and it was nothing to see an engine crew with the fireman twenty or thirty years older than the driver. On the other hand, discipline was strict, and no excuses acceptable; for example, if a driver passed a danger signal by mistake, he never drove again.

With men of this calibre to operate them, French steam locomotives therefore tended to be more complex and sophisticated. Elsewhere the sheer difficulty of getting crews to understand its finer points, quite as much as any question of maintenance costs, made the steam locomotive into a rather crude and simple tool. The French team made it possible to turn it into an exact instrument for extracting the last ounce of power from every ton of coal burned, and a complex system of bonuses motivated the crew to make the effort. There was, for example, a worthwhile bonus for saving fuel, but a very much larger one for making up time (within speed limits) lost for other reasons. This system reached its zenith with the big mainline locomotives of the 1920-1950 period, almost all four-cylinder compounds. On nationalization in 1938 the great André Chapelon was placed in charge of steam locomotive research and development. Unfortunately the war and postwar changes prevented him, very narrowly, from actually achieving any new construction of engines designed to take full

advantage of his ideas, but his utter transformations of older machines by rebuilding them made a series of dramatic impressions. Not least the last. In 1947 the die had already been cast in favour of widespread electrification and cessation of steam construction, and plans were almost ready to build the first series of powerful express passenger electric locomotives. Then Chapelon wheeled out his experimental 4-8-4, a rebuild of a twenty-year-old 4-8-2, which put up a dazzling performance and clearly outclassed anything that the new electric would be capable of. The modernists scurried, panic-stricken, back to their drawing boards, and the 5000hp 2D2 9100 series of electrics which ultimately emerged in 1950 had been very much beefed up as a result of this rude experience.

Steam has now gone, of course, but something of its panache remains all the same. The designers of the latest 8000hp (continuous rating) electrics, and some of the more powerful main-line diesels, have achieved the nearly impossible by producing machines which combine – almost uniquely – high performance with a distinctive and acceptable exterior styling. For all of us but the specialists, a diesel is a diesel is a diesel – unless perhaps it's French.

New Construction and Electrification
As we have seen, the Midi and the Paris–Orléans led the way in electrification before 1938, establishing the 1500v DC overhead system firmly in the south-west. The first great

postwar conversion, the Paris–Lyon–Marseille trunk route, was also carried out on this system. However, before it was completed a cheaper method had been developed by SNCF engineers, using 25,000v 50 cycles AC. This has, since 1950, covered most of the north and east of the country, with some lines also in the west and south. No DC lines have been converted to AC, as in Britain, because it was felt that this would be wasted effort; indeed DC lines are still being extended here and there in a small way. Problems at change-of-voltage points have been avoided instead by the development of adequate numbers of locomotives able to run on both systems although the majority of machines are confined to one or the other.

Electrification, coupled with more advanced signalling systems, brought about large increases in line capacity as well as average speeds. However, it has been felt that further improvements are called for, particularly on the most important main line between Paris and Lyon, where the original route of the 1840s is beset with curves through the hills of Burgundy and unsuitable for speeds over 100 mph as well as being congested with traffic. A completely new railway suitable for 170 mph is now being built between the outskirts of Paris and Lyon, cutting the 320 miles via Dijon down to about 260 miles. This is going to be a real space-age railway, the first of its kind in Europe; it is interesting to note that since modern power-to-weight ratios enable gradients of up to one in thirty or so to be used freely, vertical curvature has become as much of a consideration as

Left: The once-huge network of the metre-gauge Côtes du Nord system in Brittany had been reduced to a single branch by 1956 – that from St Brienc to Paimpol. Trains were mostly autorails (railcars) with trailer cars but on high days and holidays the maroon 0-6-0 tanks came out again. Here is one such day – an enthusiasts' excursion from England.

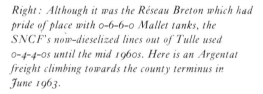

Right: Although it was the Réseau Breton which had pride of place with 0-6-6-0 Mallet tanks, the SNCF's now-dieselized lines out of Tulle used 0-4-4-0s until the mid 1960s. Here is an Argentat freight climbing towards the county terminus in June 1963.

ordinary horizontal curvature and much trouble has therefore had to be taken to ensure that there are no sudden changes of inclination. But unlike the Japanese Shinkansen lines, the nearest comparison, this new railway will form part of the national network, used by through trains to other destinations.

Train Services and Rolling Stock

For most of the steam age, distances between Paris and most provincial cities were such that there were only two times each day during which trains linking them could run; either they left quite early in the morning and travelled all day, or in the evening and travelled all night. Traditionally, therefore, the time-table shaped itself round an infrequent service of long-distance trains radiating from Paris, meeting connections at all junctions which was, of course, easier when so few main-line trains were involved. As traffic grew, to avoid disturbing this complex pattern of connections, main-line trains became extremely heavy and tended to run in 'flights', a series only a few minutes apart with long gaps between. In the last few decades of steam, faster running first made possible a midday flight of trains which could still reach their destinations before midnight, and ultimately a few extra-fast evening flyers, generally charging extra fares, were also put on (a process taken much further after electrification). The French tradition was therefore one of heavy, fast, but infrequent long-distance services, which still remains the norm to a large extent, although the need to compete with the car and the aircraft are bringing about a shift to the more usual European pattern of more frequent regular-interval services on the most important lines.

French railways were in the 1920s and 1930s among the first in Europe to standardize all-steel construction for main-line passenger stock, and the typically rather spartan but immensely strong and heavy vehicles of that era are only now being replaced by new stock, somewhat more comfortable. However, the vehicles used on the relatively few prestige trains have always been up-to-date and luxurious.

Freight services have always been efficient and relatively intensive, with modern ideas being adopted without delay. On the other hand, traditional wagonload and sundries traffics, although less profitable, have been promoted and improved just as keenly, and a real effort made to maintain freight services on a wide scale even where passenger trains have been replaced by buses.

Operations and Signalling

Traditional French signalling was radically different in conception to British, not least in making a distinction unknown to British practice, between a 'stop' signal given for the reason that there was some positive blockage or conflicting train ahead, and one given just for the reason that there was another train ahead proceeding in the same direction. In the latter case, 'stop and proceed' was the normal rule, although the distinction was made manifest by the use of a different type of signal. Modern practice has developed from this base, and has tended therefore to be fundamentally rather cheaper and simpler than the mammoth and expensive complexities of current large installations in Britain or Germany, for example. Safety, however, is maintained at a very high level by the system of monitoring and recording drivers' actions, standard for many years. For example the system makes a chart automatically of each run noting not only that the driver has obeyed all speed restrictions and signal indications, but that he has signalled in good time to the apparatus his intention to do so. Any rule-breaking or even bad habits can thus be detected and put right long before an accident results. This system is in use on all SNCF trains, on branches as well as main lines.

Administration and Finance

Looked at simply in the light of the total sum declared to be paid over each year by the French state to the SNCF, the French railways have proportionately quite a large deficit by European standards. However, leaving aside the question of whether the declared sum in France and every other country is the amount including past capital write-offs (perhaps the biggest single factor making simple comparisons of this kind wildly misleading), or indeed whether any useful point can be made by crudely comparing totally non-comparable figures just because they are called the same thing, it can be noticed that in France this total sum includes compensation to the SNCF for

many items, including subsidized charges for many disadvantaged groups, accepted as a state concern for many years. In addition, the 1842 legislation allowed for the fact that certain lines could never be commercially viable or worth building, and found an ingenious method of having them operated by successful commercial enterprises all the same, by accepting a large share of state responsibility from the outset. One can only, nowadays, judge by results; and during the last decade, passenger traffic (both long-distance and suburban) and freight traffic on the SNCF have both shown a rising tendency. There is no sign that the deficit is out of control, and indeed the state has shown its continued faith in the vitality of the railway system by funding the construction of the new Paris-Lyon high-speed line, as well as other improvements.

PARIS TRANSPORT AUTHORITY – RATP
Regie Autonome des Transports Parisiens,
53 Quai de Grands Augustins,
75271 Paris.

The most important non-SNCF railway undertaking in France is the CF Métropolitain de Paris. The original conception of the Paris Métro was much that of an underground tramway, with many routes, frequent stations, shallow tunnels or sometimes low viaducts, sharp curves, and therefore slow running. All this of course survives with great character and charm, particularly on those lines still worked by fifty-year-old trains rather than their sometimes rubber-wheeled replacements. However, the city has grown beyond its old Métro, and in the last few years a new and much grander, longer-distance system has begun to be superimposed on it, the Réseau Express Régional. The RER trains are high-speed, compatible with those on SNCF lines, and run right across the urban map. They tend to use ex-SNCF lines in the suburbs, but in the centre they run in new deep-level tunnels, laid out for fast running, and with widely spaced stations connecting with the older system. The older Métro lines are not quite the most antiquated of their kind in the world (Madrid, Buenos Aires, New York are in the running for this), but the RER is certainly the most modern.

Other French Railways

The narrow gauge is now all but extinct in France, though the SNCF still runs two electric metre-gauge lines of great scenic attraction, one in the Alps and one in the Pyrenees. A few other minor outposts survive, including much of the Corsican system. The most important of them is the last section of the old Chemins de Fer de Provence, 95 miles from Nice to Digne. Serving a spectacular part of the Savoy Alps, it still runs an efficient all-diesel passenger and freight service, under the pre-1938 rules, at the prime financial responsibility of the local authorities in fact, though in form centrally subsidized. Like the other lines mentioned, it still offers a year-round transport service so

perhaps it is remarkable not that so much has gone but that so many narrow-gauge lines still manage to perform this function.

Perhaps this is the reason why there are only relatively few narrow- (or even standard-) gauge 'entertainment' railways in France, running strictly for tourists and generally with steam traction. However, they do include perhaps the most successful operation of its kind in Continental Europe, the twenty-mile line from Tournon in the Rhône Valley to Lamastre. This is a surviving fragment of the old metre-gauge Réseau du Vivarais, which at its peak had over 120 miles of track winding and climbing over the high and broken rocky country along the watershed of the Atlantic and the Mediterranean. Resurrected in 1971, there is something very French about this railway now, for every Sunday morning a stately procession of trains, some hauled by restored ex-Vivarais 0-6-6-0T Mallets, climbs to Lamastre, a small town with more notable restaurants per cobbled street than any other in Europe.

Among the select list of railways opened in the world during 1978 was one which, although just another 'daisy-picking' line, is notable for having bumped the English Romney, Hythe & Dymchurch Railway from its position as the 'smallest (ie, having the least distance between the rails) statutory public railway in the world'. This is the 12in gauge four-mile steam-operated Réseau Guerledan at Mur-de-Bretagne near Pontivy in Brittany. Because lengths of rail had survived at level crossings, statutory powers were inherited from the old metre-gauge Réseau Breton, on whose road-bed the new line was laid.

GERMANY

See map on pages 26–27.

GERMAN FEDERAL RAILWAY – DB
Deutsche Bundesbahn,
Friedrich-Ebert-Anlage 43–45,
Frankfurt (Main).

GERMAN STATE RAILWAY – DR
Deutsche Reichsbahn
Voss Strasse 33,
108 Berlin.

Railways in Germany are said to have begun on 14 February 1834 when King Ludwig I of Bavaria gave his assent to the construction of a four-mile line between Nuremburg and Furth. Fredrich List, the 'Father of German railways', had been involved in railway development in the USA and built there a 21-mile coal-hauling line (Tamaqua to Port Clinton, Pennsylvania). He then had the idea of building railways in Germany. He opened the Nuremburg-Furth line on 7 December 1835 and, four years later, the first long-distance line in Germany, running 75 miles from Leipzig to Dresden.

The total length of railway in operation then

A West German Co-Co electric locomotive hauls a freight along the banks of the Rhine.

was a mere 92 miles, but subsequent development was rapid. By 1850 the figure was almost 4000, by 1870 over 12,000 and by the turn of the century approached 40,000 miles. The main lines were administered by five states, (Prussia, Bavaria, Saxony, Mecklenburg and Hesse), which had taken over from private companies in the 1875-1900 period, and three (Wurtemburg, Oldenburg and Baden) which had owned their railways from their inception.

After World War I, the lines (then 34,000 miles in extent) were formally unified and became the Deutsche Reichsbahn. The loss of Alsace-Lorraine in 1919 was counterbalanced by the gain of Austria in 1936. In fact, authoritarian Germany had for many years before 1920 used the railways as a single instrument to secure overriding power for the central government and, above all, to wage war.

For the Germans the availability of rail transport coincided in a remarkable way with the beginning of the series of wars of aggression which marked German history from 1860 to 1945. An attack by Prussia on Denmark in 1863, on Austria in 1866 (the Seven Weeks War) and on France in 1870 led to the King of Prussia being proclaimed Emperor of the then-enlarged German Confederation in 1871. Railways played an increasingly important part as this aggrandisement took place.

World War II found the German railways in excellent shape, well prepared for the struggle which was to put virtually the whole European railway system under German control. The use of it to transport six million non-Aryans from their homes to far-away extermination camps was a new (on this scale) use for railways. And in addition, the normal but immense military needs were satisfactorily catered for. Had the armies penetrated deeper into the USSR, supply lines would have become even longer. Plans had been drawn up for a 9ft 10in (3-metre) gauge trunk line to reduce the effort needed for mass transportation over the great distance involved.

Defeat in 1945, involving railway destruction on a vast scale, led to partition as well as loss of territory to Poland. The lines in the West became the Bundesbahnen or Federal Railways, while the railways in the Soviet Zone, now East Germany, kept the Reichsbahn title.

The first German locomotive Der Adler (the Eagle) was a standard Robert Stephenson 2-2-2 from England which arrived complete with driver. In his role as the nineteenth-century equivalent of a Concorde pilot his salary was twice the general manager's.

German locomotive practice is best known for the excellent standard range of simple locomotives – most of them of the 'world standard form', that is, two outside cylinders and Walschearts valve gear – which were produced in large numbers and in different shapes and sizes to cover all the duties on the railway. Outstanding were the Kriegslok (War Loco) 2-10-0s; 11,879 were produced in two and a half years, beginning in September 1942, by an industry already fully committed to war production, an achievement on a scale unequalled elsewhere. The same standards of

Above: Trans-Europ Express (TEE) No 10 'Rembrandt' (Munich–Amsterdam).

Left: A modern Bundesbahn electric train races along the Rhine.

Right: The new control tower outside the huge arched roof of the Frankfurt (Main) Hauptbahnhof.

Below: Eating the Mitropa way.

Right: The dining and sleeping cars on West German Railways are owned and run by the German Sleeping Car Company, DSG.

design were applied to locomotives exported to many countries, particularly those in eastern Europe. Turkey was a case in point, even after it had ceased to lie in the path of the German drive to the east.

German thoroughness ensured that the possibilities of constructing steam locomotives more thermally efficient than conventional ones, were thoroughly explored. As has been found elsewhere with less thorough investigations, the conclusion was drawn that the savings did not justify the extra cost of maintainance of such things as condensers, super-pressure boilers and compound cylinders.

Postwar practice produced few significant new developments – in fact locomotive building capacity was removed wholesale from East Germany to the USSR. In so far as there was new construction, the two administrations were careful to dovetail their numbering systems. Some steam still operates in the East. In the West it came to an end in 1977.

Electrification began early with a demonstration of the first-ever electric railway in public service at the Berlin exhibition of 1879. The inventor, Werner von Siemens, gave his name to a firm which is still a famous name in the electrical world. Some remarkable electric traction trials were carried out on an experimental line from Zossen to Marienfelde in 1901–03, when electric cars reached speeds of up to 135 mph, eclipsing steam in this regard forever. The first main-line electrification proper was completed in 1922, when 15,000v $16\frac{2}{3}$ cycles AC locomotives went into public service between Breslau and Görlitz. By 1932, 1200 miles were in operation.

The prewar total has since been well surpassed, all principal main lines (6200 miles) in West Germany now being turned over to this form of traction. In the East relatively little electrification or re-electrification has been done, in all, only one tenth of that in the West.

In talking of Germany and diesel traction it almost suffices to say that Dr Rudolf Diesel, the inventor in 1897 of the original engine of the kind that now bears his name, was a German born in Paris. Numerous experiments were necessary before his invention became adapted as a practical instrument of rail traction, but perhaps a landmark was 15 May 1933 when the diesel-electric 'Flying Hamburger' went into service between Berlin and Hamburg, scheduled to run the 178 miles in 138 minutes, an average speed of 77.4 mph. This was, at the time, the fastest scheduled run in the world and the attention it drew from the public led to a widespread consideration of the possibilities of diesel-electric traction.

Since the war, Germany has specialized in diesel locomotives with hydraulic transmission. On the face of it, it would seem that such a system – a kind of grown-up 'fluid flywheel' – would be simpler, cheaper and less prone to failure than an electric transmission system. In fact, this has not proved to be the case but, in West Germany anyway, the manufacturers have not yet given up their speciality. In the East there has been a tendency to rely on Soviet-built diesel-electrics.

Train Services and Operations
The main problem faced by the West German system is the re-orientation of traffic flows. North-south lines that were once mere cross-country routes have now become main arteries (one could add also that grass grows undisturbed on many west–east lines leading into East Germany that were once main arteries). Proposals for high-speed lines to by-pass the worst sections together with upgrading elsewhere are in hand and this should lead to very-much-reduced journey times and more frequent express services.

A feature of both DB and DR is that branch-line and local passenger services are maintained at present (though there are signs of change) to a much greater degree than, for example, in Britain or France. But, on DB certainly, the concentration of effort and investment is directed at the long-distance traveller, making what is already an excellent service (with, incidentally, particularly good restaurant car meals, very reasonably priced) even better. DB carries 632 million passengers a year, using a fleet of 17,700 carriages and 1000 railcars of various kinds. In West Germany 2600 electric and 3100 diesel locomotives provide the haulage (East Germany provides no information), covering of course, both passenger and freight traffic. As might be expected in one of the world's greatest industrial countries, freight traffic in Germany is on a vast scale; it is relatively denser in the East, no doubt because of the lesser use made of road transport in the Soviet-dominated area. The figures for 1976 illustrate the position (see page 60).

Above: A modern diesel express under the great arched roof of Leipzig station, East Germany.

Top: Hamburg station in June 1966 with an East German 01 class Pacific heading a train for Berlin. These engines were still at work in 1978.

Extreme left: Diesel express at Saalfeld in East Germany.

Left: Diesel maintenance in East Germany.

Below: A traditional steam train hauled by a class 38 4-6-0 crosses the Hohenzollern Bridge at Cologne.

Figures for 1976	DB West Germany	DR East Germany
Length of route, miles	17,980	8910
Length electrified, miles	6260	880
Tons hauled annually, millions	326	286
Average distance hauled, miles	122	108

Below: A train at Altermarkt station on the Wuppertal Suspension Railway.

A recent development on DB is the fitting of a type of automatic coupler to certain wagons in circuit service. This is the coupler which, having been chosen as the European standard, is intended to become universal in Europe in due course, replacing the primaeval and familiar side buffers and screw-couplings.

WUPPERTAL SUSPENSION RAILWAY
Bromberger Strasse 39, 56 Wuppertal 2.

In the 1960s, there was a transient fashion for promoting monorails. Conventional railways were unfashionable and schemes for promoting them had to be packaged under such names as 'duo-rail'. But very few monorails indeed have achieved any extended existence. In fact, the only significant one is an eight-mile line, suspended above the Wupper River, which has carried the citizens of Barmen and Elberfield about their business ever since 1900, except for a three-year hiatus at the end of World War II. Forty-four electric cars carry 28 million passengers annually.

GREAT BRITAIN

See maps on pages 64 and 69.

Ninety-five out of every hundred miles of railway line in Britain belong to the state railway system and of the remainder the three largest systems (Northern Ireland Railway, London Transport and the National Coal Board) are also publicly owned. Much British early railway history is also World Railway history and hence has already been mentioned in the introduction. Maybe it is a result of being citizens of a country that was the birthplace of railways that the British have such an extravagant passion for them. This is reflected in various ways. For example, the British public demands, expects and is willing to maintain a well-equipped national rail system, much larger than purely plain economic considerations should allow. The other way in which this extraordinary love shows itself is in the growth of railways built or preserved for pleasure. This has been a feature of the last twenty years and in it Great Britain has played the leading role. None of the 143 pleasure lines currently operating in the United Kingdom qualifies for inclusion here on the grounds of length – in fact a mileage even in double figures is rare – but several (Bluebell, Festiniog, Isle of Man, Middleton, Romney Hythe & Dymchurch, Talyllyn, and Volks) do so on the grounds of world 'firsts' or 'onlys' of one kind or another.

The past influence of Great Britain in the world of railways is reflected in the amount of railway material manufactured there for use in other countries. Even more important was the export of ideas; the influence of past British railway engineers and managers can be seen on many systems which have long since ceased to depend on any British-made material.

The political stability of the mainland has meant a climate in which steady development could occur, but the enforced neglect and overuse of the railways in two world wars have been setbacks, the effect of which can still be felt. As regards the Republic of Eire (Southern Ireland), which ceased to be part of the United Kingdom in 1921, the railways there had always been independent of those in England, Scotland and Wales. Accordingly this event had little effect on the railway map.

BRITISH RAILWAYS – BR

222, Marylebone Road,
London NW1.

The 11,000-mile network of British Rail routes interconnect the larger towns and serve the basic industrial customers. During the last twenty years, BR has, on the whole, withdrawn from serving smaller towns and villages as well as the less concentrated industries. At the same time every aspect of railway operation has been transformed; the complete elimination of steam (except for one tiny line), multi-aspect colour-light signalling on most main routes, continuous welded rails, new and faster diesel and electric trains, computer control of freight

Formation of the Principal pre-1923 Railway Companies

Company name	Date of formation	Constituents on formation	Opening date of first section
Great Western	1835		1838
		London & Southampton	1838
London & South Western	1839	Birmingham & Derby Junction	1839
Midland	1844	North Midland	1840
		Midland Counties	1840
			1846
North British	1844		1848
Caledonian	1845	Liverpool & Manchester	1830
London & North Western	1846	Grand Junction	1837
		London & Birmingham	1838
Great North of Scotland	1846		1854
London, Brighton & South Coast	1846	London & Brighton	1841
Great Northern	1845		1850
Furness	1846		1846
North Staffordshire	1846		1846
Lancashire & Yorkshire	1847	Manchester & Leeds	1841
Glasgow & South Western	1850	Glasgow, Kilmarnock & Ayr	1840
		Glasgow, Dumfries & Carlisle	1843
North Eastern	1854	York, Newcastle & Berwick	1839
		York & North Midland	1841
		Leeds Northern	1849
Great Eastern	1862	Eastern Counties	1839
		Northern & Eastern	1842
		Eastern Union	1846
		Norfolk Railway	1846
Cambrian	1864	Llanidloes & Newton	1859
		Oswestry, Ellesmere & Whitchurch	1863
		Newton & Machynlleth	1863
		Oswestry & Newton	1864
		Aberystwyth & Welsh Coast	1864
Highland	1865	Inverness & Aberdeen Junction	1858
		Inverness & Perth Junction	1863
Great Central	1897	Manchester, Sheffield & Lincolnshire	1841
South Eastern & Chatham	1899	South-Eastern	1842
		London, Chatham & Dover	1859

operations and many new or refurbished stations, have combined to give BR a completely new ambience and image. Regretably, this modernization has been accompanied by a fairly steady deterioration in railway finances, but it would appear that the British people, on the whole, are prepared to underwrite their affection for railways by putting their hands fairly deeply into both their fare-paying and their tax-paying pockets. The result, even if expensive, is good. While a few countries have trains as fast and as comfortable, very few indeed have them as frequent.

History and Development

Early British railway promotors, far from being encouraged by the government and establishment, had to fight every sort of opposition, reasonable and unreasonable, legal and illegal, in order to obtain the right to build their lines. The outcome was a fairly haphazard kind of development, but by 1850, as shown on the map on page 64, virtually all the principal cities were linked to the capital by rail. By 1860 the majority of the great railway companies (until the government-dictated 'grouping' of 1923) had already emerged by name.

The Great Western company was the first

(and, as we shall see, the last), having been incorporated as early as 1835, but its 118-mile 7ft ¼in gauge main line from London to Bristol was not completed until 1841. By this time the original 1830 inter-city route between Liverpool and Manchester had, in 1836, been joined to Birmingham, by the first main line, known as the Grand Junction Railway and in the following year, the first 100-mile plus line in Britain, the London and Birmingham, opened to traffic. The table above shows how the old companies emerged.

Big profits made by the early companies led in the 1840s to an excessive amount of railway promotion – a period known as the 'Railway Mania' – but the subsequent 'crash' did not slow things up for long. As the century progressed the network was completed not only by the construction of lines competing for traffic between most important places but also by the building of comprehensive networks of country branches. With the completion of a competitive main line known as the Great Central from Nottingham to Marylebone station, London in 1899, new main-line railway construction in Britain came to an end. The Great Western Railway (then known as the 'Great Way Round') still had a few corners to cut off, and

*A British Railways' country station on the
Dolgellan–Llangollen line which is now closed. Note
level crossing gates shut across the line.*

Inset, bottom right : A British Railways express on the London–Edinburgh route, hauled by a 'Deltic' diesel-electric locomotive.

Way out

there was some suburban and rapid transit work to do, but otherwise, the show was at an end. In seventy years 20,000 miles of railway had been laid and few places, however small, failed to have a railway station.

Rural railways in Britain (with a few honourable exceptions) were operated by the big companies. Often, a branch line would be sponsored and financed locally but, once built, a wise management would make arrangements for the main-line company to work it for, say, a percentage of the receipts. In due time the shares of the little company would be exchanged for shares in big brother and what had then become a mere paper existence would finally be extinguished. A few bold spirits decided to go it alone, but often their fate was that of the Culm Valley Railway in Devon. This line, after a few unhappy years on its own, was taken over by the Great Western for a price that was 'the best that could be expected between a seller that had to sell and a buyer who did not want to buy' as the GWR's official history put it. In other cases the big companies did it all. But however they came into being, the rural railways of Britain were, it must be said in salute to their memory, a particular delight, from the polished levers in the signal boxes to the roses in the flower-beds.

One of the reasons for this attractiveness was their solid main-line construction; they had to be built, manned and signalled to very expensive full main-line standards, when low speeds and infrequent trains would have made something simpler more appropriate. In 1898 the Light Railways Act was passed, which allowed local railways contemplated after the turn of the century to be promoted more easily – without a private Act of Parliament – as well as built to less exacting standards and thus much more cheaply. Fifty years before, this Act would have been of great use; fifty years later, as we shall see, it was.

Incidentally, one effect of this application of main-line standards to branch-line railways was that narrow-gauge lines were very rare in Great Britain except in one specific area, North Wales. Here, in fact, the worldwide use of narrow gauge for public railways was pioneered.

All the 'golden age' companies except one came to the end of the line in 1923, when by an Act of Parliament they were grouped into four big groups; the London Midland & Scottish, the London & North Eastern, the Southern and the Great Western but only the latter kept its name and entity.

The purpose of the 'grouping' was to strengthen the weaker companies, which had

British railways built up to 1841 ——
British railways built up to 1850 ——

been badly affected by over-use and enforced neglect during the 1914–18 war, by amalgamating them with the stronger ones. The main constituents of each group appear below.

All these pre-'grouping' railways had their own ways of doing things and their own designs for everything from uniform buttons to steam locomotives. Replacement by new and (in some cases) rather brash styles was a sad blow to those who took pleasure in such matters,

although much pre-'grouping' railway material is still in use over fifty years after the event and even more is now housed in sixteen railway museums, working and stationary (see table opposite).

The 'grouping' may have helped some weaker lines to survive, but the burdens came near bankrupting the stronger ones. Ordinary railway shares (previously the safest 'widow and orphan' investment) quickly fell into the wall-

The 'Grouping' of 1923

London, Midland & Scottish	London & North Eastern	Southern	Great Western
London & North Western	Great Northern	South Eastern & Chatham	Great Western
Midland	Great Eastern	London, Brighton & South	Cambrian
Lancashire & Yorkshire	Great Central	Coast	South Wales
Caledonian	North Eastern	London & South Western	'pit-to-port' lines
Glasgow & South Western	North British		
Highland	Great North of Scotland		
Furness			
North Stafford			

Principal Museums with Major Railway Exhibits

Name & Location of Museum	Speciality
National Railway Museum, York*†	
Steamtown, Carnforth, Lancashire*†	International
Cranmore, Near Shepton Mallet, Somerset*†	—
Great Western Society, Didcot, Oxfordshire*†	Great Western
Birmingham Railway Museum, Tyseley, W Midlands*†	—
Dinting Railway Centre, Near Manchester*†	London, Midland & Scottish
Bulmer's Railway Centre, Hereford*†	Great Western
Scottish Railway Preservation Society, Falkirk*	Scottish Railways
Science Museum, London	Early locomotives
Great Western Museum, Swindon, Wiltshire	Great Western
Bressingham Hall, Diss, Norfolk†	—
North of England Open Air Museum, Beamish, County Durham†	North-Eastern
Darlington North Road Railway Museum, Co Durham	Stockton & Darlington
Quainton Railway Society, Near Aylesbury, Buckinghamshire†	—
Birmingham Museum of Science & Industry	London, Midland & Scottish
Glasgow Museum of Transport	Scottish Railways

* operation facilities on BR   † facilities for steaming and demonstration

paper category – except inevitably those of the Great Western, in whose re-structuring there had been the smallest element of political meddling. The sixteen lean years until 1939 passed in absorbing the stresses of this enforced reorganization. Such modernization as was done had largely to be carried out with government assistance.

The 1939-45 war brought even severer strains on the railways of Britain and so, perhaps inevitably, it was followed in 1948 by nationalization, thereby bringing the United Kingdom into step with virtually all countries outside North America. With 650,000 staff and 6000 stations, 18,000 miles of route, 19,000 locomotives and over a million carriages and wagons, British Railway was a vast and even more indigestible meal for the administrators. After a long and costly process of trial and error on its part, today's smaller system (200,000 staff, 2000 stations, 11,000 miles of track, 4500 locomotives and 250,000 cars) meets the present-day demand for a lesser quantity but a higher quality of rail transport.

On the whole the stations and lines that

The main west-coast line from London to Scotland had two major obstacles to surmount – Shap Fell in Westmorland and Beattock, just over the border into Scotland. Now that this line has been electrified they pose no problems to trains but in steam days, locomotives were hard pressed, often needing banking assistance, as is the case with this LMS 'Patriot' class 4-6-0 heading a fast freight.

Above: A train leaves Porthmadog Harbour station hauled by Fairlie articulated locomotive along the narrow-gauge Festiniog Railway.

closed were rural, but some duplicate main stations and main lines went as well. Included was the last to be built, the Great Central line of 1899 from Nottingham to London.

Not all the 7000 miles of closed railway line were abandoned. Scattered about the country and aggregating almost 100 miles are a dozen or so sections of line which groups of enthusiasts, semi-professionals and businessmen have restored to run old-fashioned steam trains. They obtained powers to do so under the handy provisions of the previously little-used Light Railways Act of 1898. One can journey back into nostalgia, travelling not only in early BR and post-'grouping' style but also in that of the old pre-'grouping' companies, in trains which use their locomotives, their coaches, their tracks and their stations. In rural England, this is the new railway age. The pioneer was the Bluebell Railway, which is separately described; the complete list is as follows:

British Rail Lines Restored as Museum or Pleasure Lines

Re-opening date	Name and Location	Length (miles)	Old Company
1960	Bluebell; Sheffield Park, Sussex	4.5	London, Brighton & South Coast
1961	Welshpool Llanfair; Llanfair Caerenion, Powys	5.5	Great Western
1968	Keighley & Worth Valley; W Yorkshire	5	Midland
1969	Dart Valley; Buckfastleigh, Devon	7	Great Western
1970	Severn Valley; Bridgnorth, Shropshire	12.5	Great Western
1970	Lochty; near Ardeer, Fife, Scotland	1.5	North British
1971	Torbay & Kingswear; Paignton, Devon	6	Great Western
1973	Lakeside & Haverthwaite; Newby Bridge Lancashire	3.5	Furness
1973	North York Moors; Pickering, N Yorkshire	18	North Eastern
1974	Kent & East Sussex; Tenterden, Kent	4	Kent & E. Sussex
1975	Wight Locomotive Society; Haven St., Isle of Wight	2	Isle of Wight
1976	Great Central; Loughborough, Leicestershire	6	Great Central
1976	North Norfolk; Sheringham, Norfolk	4	Great Eastern
1977	Strathspey; Aviemore, Scotland	4	Highland
1977	West Somerset; Minehead, Devon	5	Great Western
1977	Mid-Hants; Alresford, Hampshire	3	London & S.W.
1977	Nene Valley; Peterborough, Cambridgeshire	3	London & N.W.
1978	Midland Railway; Butterley, Derbyshire	3	Midland

Civil Engineering

In Britain the task of constructing 20,000 miles of railway in a short seventy years was made easier because during the previous seventy years many miles of canal had been built, involving the solution of many similar problems. In fact the name 'navvy' given to the men – and later to the machines – who built the railways, derives from the term 'navigator' which was first applied to those who built the canals.

Bridges and viaducts made of stone or iron were entirely familiar to the engineers of the time and such problems as did arise occurred largely because of an increase in scale. Nothing like the bridge on the Irish Mail route across the Menai Straits with its two iron box-girder spans of 460ft each had been made before. (The Admiralty were unhappy about the obstruction which would have been caused by a bridge with many short spans, well within then current technology.) Robert Stephenson's ability as an engineer is well illustrated by the fact that the bridge lasted, carrying the much heavier trains of later years, until, in 1970, some small boys destroyed it by setting light to timbers

inside. Still existing today and younger by nine years is Brunel's Royal Albert Bridge of 1859 across the River Tamar at Saltash near Plymouth. This ingenious combination of the arch and suspension bridge principle crossed a similar water gap with two spans of almost identical length, but at a cost per track of thirty percent less.

Since 1859 there has been a requirement for only one large-span railway bridge on the scale of these two; this is the Forth Bridge between Edinburgh and Dundee with its two cantilever spans of 1710ft, which of course completely eclipses both Menai and Saltash.

Locomotive Landmarks
Steam

In a country where dozens of workshops have built hundreds of thousands of locomotives for hundreds of customers at home and abroad, it is impossible to single out individual landmarks of design. One can only look at families of design.

In the nineteenth century the typical British locomotive was a six-wheeler, either 2-4-0, 2-2-2, 0-6-0 or occasionally 0-4-2. It had two

Above: Built to the design of Robert Stephenson, the Britannia tubular bridge linked the island of Anglesey with the mainland of Wales. The weight of each of the four large tubes was 1800 tons and the smaller ones 1000 tons.

Top: The Forth Bridge on the railway connecting Edinburgh with Aberdeen.

inside cylinders and valve gear (Stephenson or Joy) out of the way between the frames. It was considered indecent to expose the works.

A landmark event occurred at the turn of the twentieth century when there came to one of the sleepiest and most conservative of companies a *volte-face* that fixed the layout of most British locomotives for their last fifty years of domestic steam construction. Locomotive superintendent Churchward of the Great Western Railway introduced 4-6-0, 2-8-0 and 2-6-2T types of advanced design, incorporating a combination of the best US and British practice.

They were respectively for express, freight and suburban trains; fifty years later locomotives of similar appearance and layout (but not quite so much brass and copper decor) were still handling most of Britain's rail traffic in these different fields.

Another great landmark was the introduction of the big (for Britain) engine with the wide firebox. Ivatt of the Great Northern produced his 4-4-2 'large Atlantic' in 1905. His successor Gresley in 1922 developed this idea with the first of the famous LNER family of 4-6-2s, a type that was also introduced by the LMS and SR companies, as well as British Railways to the tune of, in all, fifteen designs.

Apart from two experimental Gresley wide-firebox 2-8-2s built in 1925, the big freight engine had to wait until 1952, when the famous '9F' 2-10-0 was introduced. Steam construction on BR came to an end (saving a replica for the Liverpool & Manchester's 150th anniversary in 1980) in 1960 when *Evening Star* of this design was put into service.

Of main-line locomotive types, the one which was both the most numerous and the last steam survivor was the LMS company's legendary 'Black Five' 4-6-0. The 842 examples of the class were equally satisfactory on passenger trains at 80+mph as on slow and heavy freights.

No one could describe steam designers as unadventurous – twentieth-century British locomotive history was remarkable for many brave but unavailing attempts to improve the poor thermal efficiency of the Stephenson type steam engine, by using the greater range of temperatures and pressures typical of those found in steam plant in ships and power stations. Compounding was tried by many and even adopted by a few of the companies in the 1880–1914 period, but only the Midland (and its successor the LMS) persevered for more than a decade or so. Perhaps the LNER *Hush-Hush* compound 4-6-4 No 10,000, completed in 1929 with a Yarrow water-tube boiler pressed to 500lb/sq in, was the bravest among some twenty major attempts by private firms and by the main-line railways. But none, in any sort of overall sense, approached the economy of the simple Stephenson type.

Diesel

Diesel traction on British Railways and its predecessors began in the 1930s on a very small scale by first developing a low-power diesel shunting locomotive and then proceeding to

greater things. The first serious order for more than one or two main-line prototypes was placed with British manufacturers in 1957 but, before a reasonable time for evaluation had passed, the then-BR management unwisely decided to ignore their engineers' advice and proceed with large production orders. During the painful and expensive process of turning the resulting fleet into one on which the operators could rely, the reputation of the railways fell to a low ebb, which recent developments, such as the 125-mph high-speed train (HST), are at last beginning to retrieve. Currently there are 3500 diesel locomotives (including the single-unit Deltic diesels with individual horsepowers as high as 3300) and a large fleet of self-propelled diesel trains.

Electric

Electric locomotives were a rarity on the constituents of British Rail; in fact, at nationalization in 1948 only six were active. On the other hand, electric motor coaches from multiple unit sets numbered almost 5000 including such rare designs as the powered Pullman parlour cars of the 'Brighton Belle'. All the grouped railways except the Great Western had electric trains of their own design.

There was also great experience with electric traction in the export field and when the time came to go ahead with long-distance electrifica-

Top: Another form of large-span bridge – this time a combination of the arch and suspension principles – the Royal Albert Bridge links Devon with Cornwall over the River Tamar at Saltash. Designed by Isambard Kingdom Brunel and completed in 1859, it is still extant in its original form.

Centre: One of the larger signal boxes of semaphore days is Preston No 1 of the London Midland and Scottish Railway.

Above: The modern train control power box at New Street Station, Birmingham.

Right: A map of the British Railways system at its greatest extent in the 1950s.

An electrically hauled freight threads the English countryside.

Left: An electric express on the London–Glasgow route.

Right : A diesel-electric High Speed Train at 120 mph on the London-Bristol route.

tion schemes, few difficulties were experienced in putting into service an electric locomotive fleet now numbering 350, most of which operate at 25,000v AC on the London to Glasgow main line which also serves Birmingham, Liverpool and Manchester.

In the south, British Rail inherited a third-rail 750v DC electrification from the old Southern Railway (the largest suburban electric system in the world) and this has been extended. It now connects London with Bournemouth, Portsmouth, Brighton, Dover and Margate and serves a maze of lines in between. Two interesting features are rare enough to mention. First, the locomotives are fitted with auxiliary diesel generators which permit slow movement in unelectrified sidings, as well as enabling a locomotive which has come to rest on one of the inevitable gaps in the third rail, to re-start. Second, the majority of powered units on the Southern region are arranged to run in multiple with each other; that is, a train formed of, say, a diesel locomotive, an electric train and a diesel train can be worked from any of the cabs of any of the units.

Operations and Services

Passenger services in Britain have for many years been remarkable for two things; first the frequency with which they operate, and second, that the lowest class of passenger has been admitted to virtually all the trains – including the fastest and best – that run. One compares, for example, fast hourly two-class service between London and Newcastle (268 miles) with, say, that between Paris and Lyons (320 miles) where intervals of as much as $2\frac{1}{2}$ hours exist between successive trains during the day and the best ones are first-class only. The new High Speed Train services, currently being introduced, follow these two excellent traditions and, what is new, provide standards of speed and comfort (but not of cuisine) that have few rivals worldwide. Some 715 million passengers are carried annually in 23,000 passenger carriages.

Freight operations on BR suffer fundamentally from the fact that (equally fundamentally) they are confined within a small island. Hence, the average length of haul (73 miles) is not sufficient for it to be worthwhile making up the long trains that take full advantage of the potentialities of rail. Nevertheless, 176 million tons of freight is transported, handicapped by the strange anachronism that many of the 220,000 wagons are not fitted with continuous brakes. On the other hand, the reliability and economy of BR's freight service is greatly enhanced by the use of a sophisticated freight-movement computer control system known as TOPS, based on that developed by the Southern Pacific railroad of America.

International Standard containers are moved in Britain by specially built unit trains of fixed formation known as freightliners. In this way the railway can effectively be brought to any small factory or farm.

Safety has always had a high priority (over convenience and economy) in Britain and the methods of train signalling evolved there are

Above: Preston, on the west-coast line from London to Scotland appears much the same in this 1965 photo as it was in the Edwardian era.

Top: Barmouth Bridge, the Cambrian Railway trestle and swing bridge, fords the Mawddach estuary. Originally constructed to safeguard river traffic, the swing section was little used as the railway down the side of the river effectively killed this mode of transport.

Centre, above right: New Street Station, Birmingham, after rebuilding in 1967 and electrification.

widely used in the world. Specially characteristic is the method of signalling trains on single lines by a physical token (staff, key or tablet) which must be in the driver's possession when he enters the single-line section. The system is arranged so that a second token is not available from the instruments at either end of the section until the first one has been put back, also at either end. An objection is that all crossing places on single lines need to have staff in attendance even when very few trains are run, but the safeguard of having to be in possession of a physical object before proceeding is a very sure one.

In addition to trains British Rail operate a large fleet of ships (most sea-going), ferries and hovercraft. They are large hotel owners and have a multitude of road vehicles.

The Pullman Car Company

Pullman of the USA operated in Britain as the Pullman Palace Car Company from 1874 until 1907, providing both the first dining-car service in Britain – *Prince of Wales* on the Great Northern in 1879 – and, in 1881, the first electrically lit carriage in the world. This was *Beatrice* running between London and Brighton. Sleeping cars were provided for a time on the Midland and East Coast routes to Scotland, as well as on the Highland Railway. When, in 1907, the HR followed the example of the others and replaced the cars with its own; the last Pullman *sleeper* service in Europe had ended, but *parlour* cars continued.

Also in that year, G M Pullman's executors sold out to an Englishman called Davidson Dalziel (pronounced 'DL'), who quickly put into service the first daily all-Pullman train, the famous 'Southern Belle' – later the 'Brighton Belle'. The first British-built Pullman cars were made for this train.

In general, the arrangements were that Pullman provided the cars, staffed them, maintained them above the underframes and collected the supplements as well as anything paid for meals. The railway companies hauled them, maintained the running gear and took the basic fares. The extra comfort and superb service made it worth people's while to pay the extra, except where the standard of ordinary service was particularly high.

After 1922, of the 'big four' companies, only

Left: This evocative photograph shows the famous (or infamous) 1-in-37.7 Lickey Incline on the old Midland Railway main line from Bristol and Gloucester to Birmingham and the North. In steam days, every train needed banking assistance using one, two or even three helper engines. This is an example of how an early saving on capital cost can result in years of heavy running expenditure.

Above: The reconstruction of New Street Station, Birmingham, 1965-67.

Top: Diesels at Bristol's Temple Meads station in March 1978. On the left is a west to north express and on the right the 125 mph High Speed Train is leaving for London (Paddington).

the LNER and the Southern were consistently happy to run Pullmans. It was possible to travel from Bournemouth to Glasgow by all-Pullman train – except for crossing London. (Pullmans did, in fact, run on the London Underground, but not to connect the 'Bournemouth Belle' with the 'Queen of Scots'.) The electrified 'Brighton Belle' entered service in 1933; the naming of cars marked a change, in tune with the times, from high-born ladies like the *Duchess of Connaught*, *Lady Dalziel* and *Zenobia* to ordinary and probably nicer ones like *Audrey*, *Gwen*, and *Hazel*.

The Pullman Car Company was bought by British Railways in 1952 and a brief flare-up of expansion took Pullmans (of a kind) to Swansea, Birmingham, Liverpool and Man-

chester. Alas, the beautiful brown and cream lined-out livery, many of the trains and much of the standard of service, disappeared, like many other good things, after a few years of nationalization. In 1978 only the Manchester, Liverpool and Hull services still run, although some purveyors of nostalgia can offer vintage Pullman travel.

BRADSHAW'S RAILWAY GUIDE

From 1841 until 1961 there appeared a monthly publication whose fame was such that its name became part of the English vocabulary.

Bradshaw's Railway Guide gave the reader details of all the passenger trains on all the railways in the British Isles. From 1839 to 1841 it came out intermittently. However, glancing at the centenary issue for July 1939, one finds a small fat volume of 1300 pages with peculiarly Bradshavian numbering (for example, page 182 ran from 182a to 182f, while 296 to 315 was all one). Bradshaw, a Quaker, disapproved of pagan names for the months and all issues prior to 1939 referred to them by number, *viz*: 7th. Mo. (July). Every table is festooned with pointing hands and references to complex tables of notes, such as 'U-runs alternate Mondays and cattle sale days at Wadebridge only' or 'b-stops to take up for beyond Montrose or to set down passengers holding ordinary return', 'm-monthly return tickets for Edinburgh, Glasgow or beyond who may wish to break their journey' and so on. Nine thousand stations are included in the index and one can plan, say, twenty different journeys between the five stations at Oldham (Clegg St, Mumps, Glodwick Road, Werneth and Central) or, perhaps, one from French Drove and Gedney Hill to Fleur-de-lis Platform. Bradshaw puzzle enthusiasts suffered a great sense

of loss when his guide ceased publication. Until 1939 there was also a *Bradshaw's Continental Guide*. Reprints of selected issues of the time-table are available.

BLUEBELL RAILWAY LIMITED
Sheffield Park Station,
Uckfield, Sussex.

In 1960 a group of amateurs made world history when they took over and began to run a length of full-size standard-gauge railway as a tourist attraction. Previously this had only been done with narrow-gauge lines. The line in question connected East Grinstead and Lewes in Sussex and has always been known as the Bluebell line. A 4.5-mile section between Horsted Keynes and Sheffield Park was chosen as the path for this live rural railway museum. Seventeen steam locomotives, mostly survivors from the Southern Railway and its constituents, have been acquired although only one at a time is normally needed for operation. Vintage carriages offer nostalgic vintage transport to passengers, who have kept coming in sufficient numbers for the line to survive, greatly to the surprise of sceptics and professionals, especially in the early days. With a minimum of paid staff, the Bluebell Railway is a complete pleasure railway; not only do its travellers travel for pleasure but most of its workers work for pleasure too. The style was set for many other full-size preserved railways in Britain and elsewhere in the world.

FESTINIOG RAILWAY COMPANY
Harbour Station,
Porthmadog, Gwynedd.

Although only thirteen miles long, the Fes-tiniog Railway has its place in railway history

Above: British Railways' only steam-operated line is the 1ft 11½in gauge section from Aberystwyth to Devils Bridge in Wales. Three 2-6-2 tank locomotives are used to work this summer-only passenger service.

Top centre: This rather rare photograph shows an ex-Great Central Railway 'Director' class 4-4-0 Gerrard Powys Dewhurst on the old Great Northern Railway line. The train is the Harrogate Pullman – note somersault signals.

Left: One of the diminutive London Brighton & South Coast 'Terrier' 0-6-0T locomotives in use on the Bluebell Line.

75

as the pioneer of steam traction, passenger-carrying and common-carrier operation on a narrow gauge, in this case as little as 1ft 11½in. Opened in 1836 as a tramway for slate transport (gravity downhill, horse traction uphill) the historic metamorphosis into a full railway came in 1864.

After a period of disuse following World War II, it was restored (an operation in which volunteers played a significant part) progressively from 1955 to 1979 as a steam pleasure line. The route from Porthmadog to Blaenau Ffestiniog in North Wales is superbly scenic. On a 2.5-mile deviation opened in 1978 to avoid a new reservoir, there is not only a new 330-yd tunnel but also the only railway spiral in Britain.

The locomotive fleet in use includes one of the original 1865 locomotives – 0-4-0T *Prince* – and, uniquely in the world, two Fairlie articulated double engines. Both of the latter were built in the line's own Boston Lodge works and completed in 1879 and 1979 respectively. Currently in use are six steam and two diesel locomotives.

Passengers carried (most of whom travel in July and August) amount to some 400,000 annually and, in the peak period, trains are run at half-hour intervals. Buffet and observation cars are usually present.

Above: Double Fairlie locomotive Merddin Emrys *negotiates the new deviation line on the Festiniog Railway in June 1978. The old course of the line is now engulfed by the waters of the reservoir seen in this picture.*

Top right: Middleton Railway – locomotives at the depot in Leeds.

Below: One of London Transport Metropolitan Railway's dark red Bo-Bo electric locomotives on the Baker Street to Aylesbury line.

ISLE OF MAN RAILWAY
The Railway Station,
Douglas.

The Isle of Man Railways have few rivals in maintaining almost continuous passenger service with the same steam locomotives for more than one hundred years. The first route of this 3ft-gauge network was from Douglas to Peel, a distance of 11.5 miles, and was opened in 1873.

An inspection train prior to the opening was hauled by the Beyer Peacock 2-4-0 locomotive *Sutherland* which was derailed while running round the train at Peel. Despite this inauspicious beginning *Sutherland* is still hauling trains of tourists on the line to Port Erin. This 15.5 mile route was opened in 1874 and *Loch*, one of the locomotives delivered for that new service, is still in use.

In 1879 a separate company built a 16.5-mile railway from Ramsey to connect with the Douglas–Peel line at St Johns. Finally, the 2.5-mile branch from St Johns to Foxdale was opened in 1886. Although this was primarily for freight traffic from the lead and silver mines in the area, it also provided a regular passenger service until 1942. In 1961 the whole of the Foxdale branch was still in position although scarcely used and while the rest of the network was still in use it was with a much reduced level of service. This year also saw delivery of the last new rolling stock – two second-hand diesel railcars from County Donegal. By this time the major traffic was summer tourists and from the autumn of 1965 the railway closed for the winter. The railway did not re-open in 1966 but services were resumed during the summer of 1967. In 1969 the lines to Peel and Ramsey were finally closed.

Now only the Port Erin line remains with two of the centenarian locomotives, assisted by the Septuagenarian *Maitland* and the diesel railcars, gamely maintaining a service for the summer visitors – an eloquent demonstration of the lasting quality of Victorian engineering design and construction.

LONDON TRANSPORT
55 Broadway,
London SW1H 0BD.

The original section of the Metropolitan Railway (now part of the Metropolitan Line), the first underground city railway in the world, was opened in January 1863 in London from a junction with the Great Western Railway at Paddington to Farringdon (now Barbican) via Euston Square and King's Cross. It was steam operated, originally on the 7ft-0¼in gauge (apparent very clearly if one looks carefully at the tunnels on this section of line) and almost wholly in cut-and-cover tunnel, that is, just below street level. With surface extensions the 'Met' and its slightly younger companion the 'District' now cover 99 miles. Electrification began in 1890; the last steam-operated section from Rickmansworth to Amersham was electrified in 1960. Steam was used for works trains until 1970.

The deep level tubes began with the City

and South London Railway in 1890 and their extension is still in progress. The name 'tube' arose from the small-diameter circular tunnels, cut in the London clay, in which the trains ran. An extension of the C & SLR, called the Northern line, includes the longest railway tunnel in the world, seventeen miles from Archway to Morden. To permit running in the small tube tunnels, tube trains are only 9ft 6in in height, although standard gauge.

The system has been unified since the formation of the London Passenger Transport Board in 1933 and the total length of line now operated is 236 miles, making it the largest rapid transit system in the world. The great days of Pullman-car trains have now passed, and the 600 million passengers carried annually are now transported in elegant one-class aluminium-coloured electric multiple-unit trains.

In the sulphurous days of steam underground, the mainstays of the services were Beyer-Peacock condensing 4-4-0Ts. Handsome 4-4-4Ts handled trains on the fifty-mile open-air extension to Verney Junction via Aylesbury.

Trains for this outpost of empire left London behind handsome electric Bo-Bo's bearing names such as *Sherlock Holmes* whose lodgings at 221B Baker Street would (had they existed) have overlooked the Metropolitan's station and headquarters on the opposite side of the road. From 1920 to 1939 Pullman cars *Mayflower* and *Galatea* ran on these trains.

Steam locomotives were fortunately unknown in traffic in *deep level* tube lines such as the Central London Railway. Known in its early years as 'the tuppenny tube' – on account of a uniform fare – it had, to begin with, some noble electric locomotives. Their vibra-

tions were the cause of complaints and claims from property owners above and lighter self-propelled trains soon replaced them.

An American called Samuel Yerkes had a good deal to do with the London systems and his influence can still be felt in the use of such terms as 'westbound' and 'eastbound' instead of the more usual British 'up' and 'down', and also in the early adoption of open cars in place of compartment carriages on the District, Inner Circle, and the tube lines. Compartment stock remained on the Metropolitan line until 1960.

The last complete new tube, the Victoria line from Brixton to Walthamstow, opened in 1965. A new feature was the automatically controlled train; the train-man needs only to initiate the start. The most important recently opened station is Heathrow (London Airport), to which the Piccadilly line was extended in 1977. Just completed is the first stage of the Jubilee line from Baker Street to Charing Cross; this new tube is intended to relieve congestion.

MIDDLETON RAILWAY
Garnet Road,
Leeds LS11 5JY.

Although very short, this railway was old when the Stockton & Darlington was new; now in its 222nd year, it was running steam locomotives commercially when the battle of Waterloo was fought in 1815. A group of enthusiasts centred at Leeds University rescued the three-mile line from oblivion in 1958 and it is now run partly for freight and partly (at weekends) as a pleasure line. Of ten industrial steam locomotives and four diesels, all standard gauge, none actually is original MR, but all are representative of factory and works power.

Above: Steam in the Isle of Man. Now a government-sponsored tourist line and using only a truncated section of its original network (Douglas–Port Erin) this 3ft 0in gauge railway has always been unique. Its locomotives, all 2-4-0 tank engines (bar one), were built by Beyer Peacock of Manchester and a typical example of that firm's Victoriana; its coaches were equally ancient. Today these museum pieces travel the tracks during the summer as part of the Island's holiday attractions. This photograph was taken in 1956 and shows the terminal station at Douglas when trains ran to Port Erin, Peel and by the circuitous route to Ramsey.

Right: Of all Ireland's broad-gauge (5ft 3in) railways the Great Northern was probably the finest. Its main line ran from Belfast to Dublin and to Londonderry, its express engines were painted in sky blue and scarlet (and named) and its coaches were finished in varnished teak. Here is a Belfast to Londonderry express at Dungannon in the Six Counties (Northern Ireland) in 1957.

NORTHERN IRELAND RAILWAYS COMPANY LIMITED – NIR
1 York Road,
Belfast, BT15 1NG.

The Northern Ireland Railway is a 225-mile remnant of three companies which thirty years ago operated 900 miles of broad (5ft 3in) and forty miles of narrow (3ft) gauge within the province. Apart from a few container trains, nowadays only passenger traffic is handled, the majority by means of a fleet of 132 diesel rail-cars and trailers. In very few countries has such wholesale slaughter of railway facilities taken place.

When Ireland was partitioned in 1921, the railways north of the new border were not affected regarding ownership. The major system wholly within the province was the 120-mile Northern Counties Committee (NCC) Railway owned by the Midland Railway of England, shortly to become the London Midland & Scottish. The efficient Great Northern Railway of Ireland had one half of its 617 miles of route north of the border and there was also a small system, local to the capital, called the Belfast & County Down (B&CDR).

On nationalization of the LMS in 1948, the NCC was incorporated, together with road transport interests, in the Ulster Transport Authority. When the Great Northern ran out of revenue in 1955, the portion north of the border came into the UTA as did the B&CDR in 1950. The present company was formed in 1967.

The NCC ran charming broad-gauge Irish versions of standard Midland and LMS trains; they just had less distance between their terminals, and more between the rails. On the narrow gauge, delightful two-cylinder compound 2-4-2 tanks handled the traffic, including corridor boat trains out of Larne.

The GN was another fine concern dating from 1862 – lovely sky-blue 4-4-0s were its pride and joy. Its trains had, even as late as the 1950s, a completely Edwardian aspect once one was away from the Belfast-Dublin main line; they had Edwardian virtues such as comfort and convenience also.

The Belfast and County Down was not an Edwardian but a Victorian survivor when most of the system was closed down in 1950, leaving one dieselized run out of Belfast to Bangor, County Down.

POST OFFICE RAILWAY
King Edward Building, Newgate Street,
London, E1.

Under the streets of London for a distance of 2.5 miles runs a railway with ten stations which is thought to be unique in that its trains are not only driverless but also crewless. Work began in 1913, but was suspended in World War I. During that war the tunnels were used for storing national treasures. The line opened in 1927 and currently the fleet of thirty 2ft-gauge electric units run 1.75 million miles each year carrying mail. The techniques used, with some updating, make a nationwide unmanned

freight transport system an economic and practical possibility. But alas, no politician is prepared to tell one of the most powerful trade unions in the country, that their members' services are no longer required and, accordingly, the proposals have foundered.

ROMNEY HYTHE & DYMCHURCH LIGHT RAILWAY COMPANY
New Romney Station,
New Romney, Kent.

The fifteen-mile 15in-gauge Romney, Hythe and Dymchurch Railway is, by a substantial margin, *the longest miniature railway in the world* and until 1978 was the only such railway with statutory or common-carrier status. The gauge is 1ft 3in and all nine steam locomotives built for the line since it opened in 1927 are still in use there (plus one other steamer).

Double track from Hythe to New Romney facilitates the operation of a half-hourly service. A buffet car is provided on some trains and, in all, some 300,000 passengers are carried each year; most take the journey for pleasure, but a school train service is also included.

TALYLLYN RAILWAY COMPANY
Wharf Station,
Tywyn, Gwynedd.

Although a mere eight miles long, this 2ft-3in-gauge railway made history in 1951 when, 86 years after it had opened, it was taken over by a group of volunteers called the Talyllyn Railway Preservation Society. They have run the

Above: Post Office Railway's engine and trucks in a tunnel at Western District Office, London. The Railway runs by remote control for over 6.5 miles across central London, seventy feet below ground, at a speed between stations of 35 mph. Over 40,000 bags of mail are carried each day.

Top: A Romney, Hythe & Dymchurch train enters Dymchurch station.

This photo of the Talyllyn Railway taken in 1951 during the first year of enthusiastic operation shows 0-4-0T Dolgoch *crossing the brick viaduct over the Dolgoch Gorge.*

line as a tourist attraction ever since and this was the first time that amateurs successfully managed to take over the running of a railway.

Both the original 1865-built steam locomotives are still in use, supplemented by four more acquired elsewhere. One hundred thousand passengers are now carried each year, involving (in the peak period) twelve trips each way daily.

The TRPS inspired many other amateur take-over operations all over the world, including standard-gauge lines, where the problems are considerably more daunting. (The premier British ones are referred to in the British Rail entry.)

VOLK'S ELECTRIC RAILWAY
Marlborough House,
Old Sterne, Brighton.

Least in length of the independently worked lines described in this book, but one of the greatest in its significance to world railway development is the 2.5-mile 2ft-8½in-gauge Volk's Electric Railway on the sea-front at Brighton. This is because it is the *oldest electric railway in the world* and was the first to achieve any sort of permanent existence. There are nine electric cars, run singly or in pairs, providing a frequent service in the summer season. The line is now owned and run by the Brighton Corporation.

GREECE

See map on pages 86–87.

HELLENIC RAILWAYS ORGANIZATION LIMITED

1 Karolou Street,
Athens 107.

Civilization in Greece stretches back 2500 years, yet main-line railways did not appear until the twentieth century. The first railway, between Athens and the port of Piraeus, was a local concern and opened in 1869. The six-mile line was electrified in 1904 and still remains outside the state system.

The first section of what was to become the Hellenic State Railways standard-gauge network, eventually to connect Athens with the rest of Europe, was French owned. It was not opened until 1904. The actual link at Salonika (now Thessaloniki) was made in 1916, at a time when through running involved trespassing on the battlefields of what is now northern Greece but which before the war was Turkish territory. The State Railways were formed in 1920, when three French companies were absorbed. A long line runs eastwards through Macedonia to a much-disputed point where Bulgaria, Turkey and Greece meet.

South of Athens a separate metre-gauge noose-like system serves Peloponnesus, home of an even more ancient civilization than that of Greece, and technically an island since 1892 when the four-mile wide Isthmus of Corinth was cut through by a canal. These lines were absorbed into the state system after World War II.

At present there are 1000 miles of standard-gauge and 600 miles of metre-gauge line, on which run 188 diesel locomotives, 480 passenger carriages (only six restaurant cars) and 11,000 freight wagons.

Not all the narrow gauge was in the south; there were both metre and 1ft 11½in gauge lines north of Athens. All three gauges met in the town of Volos, where there was an interesting (and possibly unique) stretch of triple mixed-gauge track.

Much heavy civil engineering characterizes the railways of Greece; there was also much destruction in World War II and the troubles which followed it. For some years after the war trains in the Peloponnesus pushed mine-exploding wagons in front of them and moved only in the daytime.

As the railway north from Athens came nearer to becoming a trunk route, the Greeks in 1914 did what they should have gone on doing and ordered some down-to-earth American 2-8-2s from the American Locomotive Company of Schenectady. Commonsense did not, however, prevail and over the years the system accumulated the products (in some cases, the discarded products) of Germany, Austria, Britain and Italy as well. Steam is now virtually at an end.

Athens is the starting point for several international trains. Destinations include West Germany and Turkey; through sleeping cars have ceased running to Paris but have begun running to Moscow by two routes. The annual carriage of passengers is twelve million, while four million tons of freight is hauled an average distance of 230 miles by Hellenic Railways trains.

Bottom: Bralos viaduct on the Athens to Salonika main line of the Greek State Railways.

Below: A Peloponnesian Railway train leaves Patras behind a 1952 postwar Italian-built 2-8-2 locomotive built by Breda, as one of a class of reparation engines.

Above: The Peloponnese Express at Corinth.

Top right: A diesel-electric locomotive backs down onto its train at Waterford, Ireland.

HOLLAND
See Netherlands

HUNGARY

See map on pages 26-27.

HUNGARIAN STATE RAILWAYS – MAV
Magyar Allamvasutak,
Népköztársaság Utja, 73-75,
1940 Budapest, VI.

At the time modern railway history opened, Hungary was a reluctant partner in the Hapsburg Austro-Hungarian Empire, although there are records (the earliest known) of railways with wooden rails in the gold and silver mines of Upper Hungary, now part of Czechoslovakia, as early as 1500, before the Turkish invasion of 1530 and well before the Hungarian throne fell to Austria.

Shortly after the first section of the Budapest–Vienna railway – the first steam railway in Hungary – was opened in 1846, the Hungarians rebelled once again against foreign domination. Although the Austrians (like the Russians 110 years later) put it down with ferocity, they took a more enlightened view in the long term and gave Hungary internal self-government in 1867; Emperor Franz Josef of

Austria was crowned King of Hungary. This was the signal for the state to begin constructing new lines and taking over old ones. The present MAV initials first appeared in 1869, though an additional adjective, *kiralyi* (royal) was included until 1914, in the full title. In that fateful year there were almost 14,000 miles of railway in Hungary, but the fully independent republic set up after the war contained under 6000 miles because so much territory was lost to newly independent Czechoslovakia and Yugoslavia, as well as to Rumania. A small amount of territory was temporarily regained between 1938 and 1942, but the present frontiers of the country remain virtually the same as imposed in 1919.

The Hungarian Railways, Ganz of Budapest and electrical engineer de Kando were jointly responsible in 1933 for the very first main-line high-voltage industrial-frequency alternating-current electrification – the present world standard. Convertors – rotary ones in those days – on the locomotives converted this type of current supply to more digestible form (initially this was three-phase AC) for the traction motors. The location was the 120-mile Budapest to Vienna main line, as far as the Austrian frontier station of Hegyeshalom. Since 1954, a further 700 miles of railway have been electrified on the same system, but using locomotives of more conventional type with static convertors to convert AC to DC.

Hungarian steam locomotives have always

Above: Eight of the ubiquitous class 424 4-8-0 locomotives await their turns of duty at Budapest in 1967.

locomotives. The famous 424 class 4-8-0s handle heavier assignments – some of these were built as late as 1959. They have been exported to Czechoslovakia, Yugoslavia, the USSR and either China or North Korea (there are conflicting reports).

Present-day Hungary is easy locomotive country, but mountain territory now ceded to others, bred, in 1914, a sixty-strong class of 2-6-6-0 Mallet articulated locomotives, the most powerful ever to run in Hungary.

On the diesel side may be noted locomotives of Soviet, American (via the Swedish firm NOHAB) and homemade origin. Electrification has so far not proceeded far enough to relegate diesel traction to a secondary role.

A feature of Hungarian passenger operations is the use of locomotives on long push-pull trains, controlled from a cab on the leading coach when the locomotive – which can be electric, diesel or steam – is pushing. Common elsewhere with electric traction, it is rare to find this arrangement with diesels and virtually unique today with steam.

Currently there are 4870 miles of railway in Hungary, including 175 miles of 2ft 6in gauge and 23 miles of Soviet broad gauge on a connecting line near the frontier. Almost 133 million tons of freight are carried an average distance of 110 miles per year as well as 320 million passengers.

been distinctive (at times hideously so). Today they are distinctive by merely remaining in well-cared-for existence, backing up electric and diesel operation in an economical way.

Very old but entirely serviceable 0-6-0s and 0-6-0Ts of early standard MAV design survive on station pilot duties. For secondary lines there are Edwardian 2-6-2s and on the branch lines 2-4-2s and two sizes of 2-6-2 tank

Above: Budapest West station in 1974 with one of the frequent suburban push and pull sets passing the signal box at the platform's end. At that time these services ran partly by steam (424 class) and partly by electric locomotives but the service is now all electric and the whole station (bar the façade to the street) is being rebuilt.

Right: A 424 class 4-8-0 locomotive with a fast train at Budapest East station in 1967.

IRELAND

IRISH TRANSPORT COMPANY – CIE

Coras Iompair Eireann,
Houston Station,
Dublin 8.

The first railway in Ireland ran from Dublin to Kingstown (now Dun Laoghaire) and was opened on 17 December 1834. Development proceeded piecemeal but once one route had been built there was no reason, in a sparsely populated land, to build a competitive one. Originally the separate lines were built to several separate gauges. A Royal Commission decided that the best way to settle the matter without fear or favour would be to take the average – hence the gauge of 5ft 3in. In the remoter districts, construction took place under government subsidy or profit guarantee. At the time of independence from Britain – in 1921 – four major companies existed. The Midland and Great Western radiated from Dublin to Sligo and Galway; the Dublin & South Eastern went to Rosslare, Waterford and Wexford; the Great Southern & Western served Cork and Killarney. One could travel across the new border by Great Northern to Londonderry and Belfast.

Once the Civil War of 1923–24 ('The Troubles') was over, the government rationalized the situation by grouping all the lines wholly inside the border into a new company, the 2200-mile Great Southern Railways. In addition to those already mentioned several small lines, including several of local interest built to 3ft gauge, were included in the new company.

Until 1950 the railways of Ireland presented an incredibly fascinating and varied spectacle, quite out of proportion to the small scale on which their operations were conducted. For example, there were 143 different types of locomotive among the 700-strong fleet. These varied from the superb 'Irish Queen' 4-6-0s *Maedb*, *Macha* and *Tailte*, as modern and up-to-date as any steam locomotives in Europe, down to surviving 2-2-2 single drivers on the Waterford and Tramore line. The Londonderry and Lough Swilly line had narrow-gauge tank locomotives which were the only 4-8-4s in the British Isles and faithful hay-burners still plodded their way along the GN's horse-operated Fintona branch until the 1950s. One might also cite such delights as Limerick Junction (nowhere near Limerick) where no train could leave without reversing or the Tralee & Dingle narrow gauge which only ran trains once a month in connection with the cattle fairs.

Full nationalization came in 1950 (the change of title from GSR to CIE came in 1944) and included integration with road and water transport. Other closures followed – nationalization meant a 35 percent reduction in mileage – including the eclipse of all the narrow gauge – and then came modernization involving the early replacement of steam (and horse) traction by diesel. The present system is as efficient as it can reasonably be, but it is not possible to run at a profit nor, alas, has it been possible to retain the particular charm of the old days.

County Donegal Railways' diesel railcar climbs through the Barnesmore Gap, Ireland in 1952.

ITALY
& THE BALKANS

SWITZERLAND

Lyons
Villeurbanne
Geneva
Grenoble

DAUPHINÉ

Marseilles
Nice
Cannes
Avignon

PROVENCE

LIGURIAN SEA

CORSICA

Ajaccio

PIEDMONT
Turin
Torino

LOMBARDY
Milan
Milano
Como
Bergamo
Brescia
Novara
Pavia
Alessandria

Genoa
(Genova)
La Spezia
Carrara
Pisa
Leghorn
(Livorno)

TUSCANY
Florence
Firenze
Siena
Arezzo
Perugia

G. of Genoa

Parma
Reggio
Modena
Bologna
Ravenna
Forlì
Cesena
Rimini

EMILIA ROMAGNA

Ferrara

Mantua
Cremona
Piacenza

Verona
Padua
Venice
(Venezia)

VENETO
Vicenza
Treviso

Gulf of Venice

Trieste

TRENTINO ALTO ADIGE
Bolzano
Trento

FRIULI VENEZIA GIULIA
Udine

SLOVENIA
Ljubljana
Klagenfurt
Maribor

CROAT
Zagreb
Rijeka

ADRIATIC SEA

Pula
(Pola)

Pesaro
Fano
Ancona

MARCHES

UMBRIA
Terni
Ascoli Piceno
Pescara

ABRUZZI
L'Aquila
Chieti

BOSNIA
HERCE
YU

Split

ROME

MOLISE
Campobasso
Foggia
Barletta
Andria
Bari

CAMPANIA
Naples
(Napoli)
Salerno

BASILICATA
Potenza
Matera
Taranto

TYRRHENIAN SEA

SARDINIA
Sassari
Cagliari

G. of Oristano
Oristano

G. of Cagliari

Cosenza
Catanzaro

CALABRIA

Palermo
Trapani
Messina
Reggio

Str. of Messina

SICILY
Mt. Etna
3340
Caltanissetta
Catánia
Siracusa
(Syracuse)
Ragusa

G. of Taranto

Crotone

MEDITE

S.E. EUROPE
POLITICAL
1:25 000 000

FRANCE
SWITZ.
Bern
Vienna
AUSTRIA
HUNGARY
RUMANIA
Budapest
Bucharest
Belgrade
YUGOSLAVIA
BULGARIA
Sofia
ALBANIA
GREECE
ITALY
ADRIATIC SEA
AEGEAN SEA
TURKEY
Istanbul
Athens
MEDITERRANEAN SEA
Crete
MALTA
Sicily
U.S.S.R.

MEDITERRANEAN SEA

MALTA
Valletta
Gozo
Comino

Projection: Conical with two standard parallels

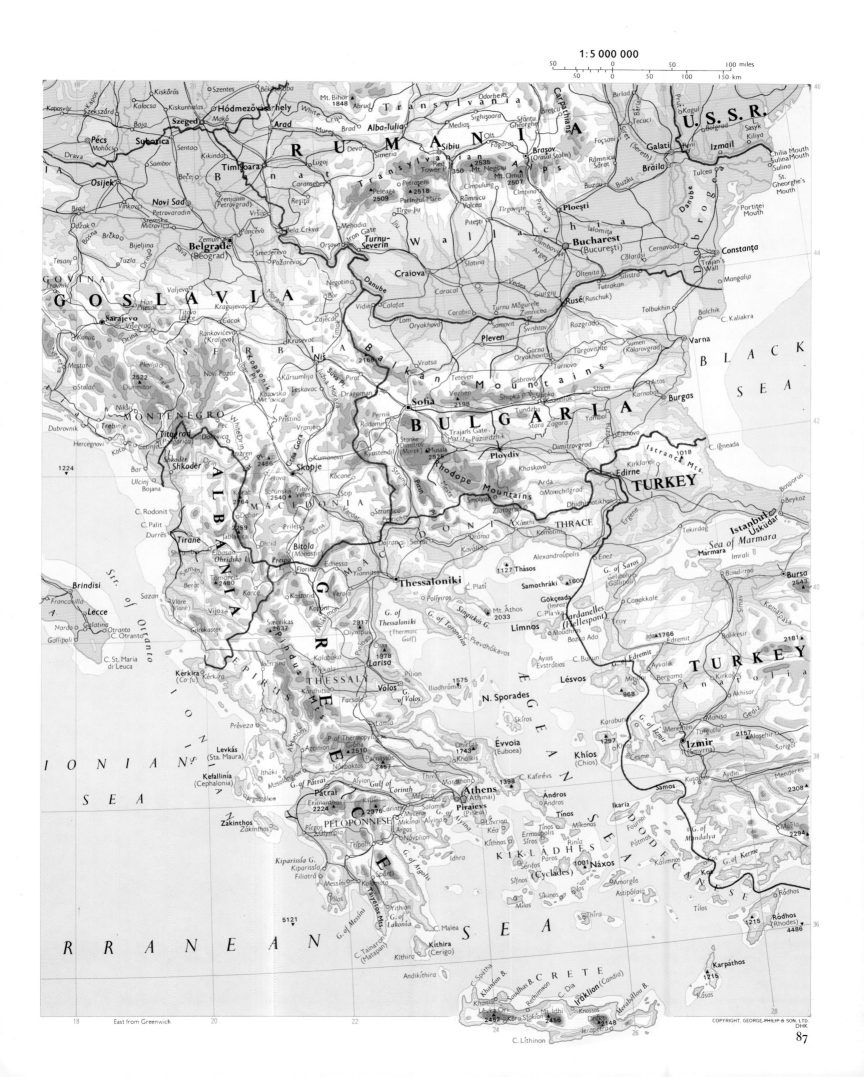

Initial dieselization came to Ireland in 1931 on the Donegal narrow-gauge lines. The reduction in expenses by some pioneer light-weight bus-type railcar units made this system into the only profitable line in the Republic – and it was half owned by the British government as successors to the London Midland & Scottish Railway. The LMS had been joint owners with the Great Northern of Ireland.

Currently the CIE owns 221 diesel locomotives and 39 railcars, 582 passenger and 8599 freight cars plus 3500 road vehicles. In 1974 it carried 190 million passengers and 5.4 million tons of goods. The expenses represented 125 percent of the receipts.

IRISH PEAT BOARD

Bord na Mona,
28 Upper Pembroke Street,
Dublin 2.

The peat bogs of Ireland have in recent years been developed as sources of mechanically dug fuel, mainly for electric power stations. Trucks are not too satisfactory when used on the bogs so 3ft gauge railways are used for transport. The fleet of 250 diesel locomotives exceeds in number those in the national railway system. The 600 miles of track that exists also exceeds the amount of public narrow gauge that ever existed in Ireland. Numerous experiments were made on burning peat in locomotives, both on the peat railways and on the main lines, but with no lasting success. During World War II, it had to be used, but steam production was very uncertain.

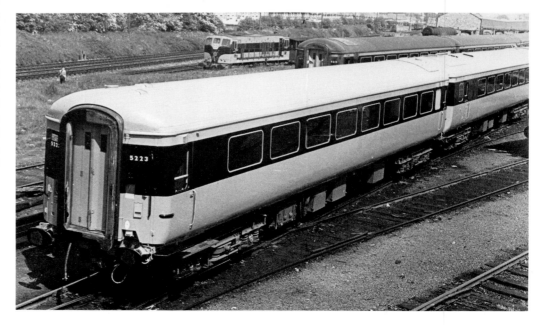

Top: The Valencia Harbour branch of the old Great Southern & Western Railway was Ireland's most westerly 5ft 3in gauge line. This photograph was taken around the turn of the century.

Right and above right: New coaches for a new image on Ireland's diesel-hauled express.

ITALY

See maps on pages 86–87.

ITALIAN STATE RAILWAYS – FS
Ferrovie dello Stato,
Piazza della Croce Rossa,
Rome.

When railways first became a practicable proposition, back in the 1830s, Italy was not a political entity but a collection of kingdoms, states and areas under foreign (Austrian) domination. The first one to have a railway was the Kingdom of Naples, in which a line, five miles long from Naples to Portici, was opened on 3 October 1839.

The first inter-city main line was completed in 1854. It ran from Turin to Genoa in Piedmont under the joint encouragement of King Victor Emmanuel and Prime Minister Cavour. Five years later these two were to embark on the hazardous venture of freeing the whole of Italy from foreign domination and unifying the country. By then Piedmont had over 600 miles of railway (nearly half the Italian total) and this enabled the Piedmontese army and its French allies to concentrate against the Austrians. The Austrian army lacked a well-developed railway system and could not be deployed in the same rapid manner. Accordingly, they suffered decisive defeats at Magenta and Solferino.

The price exacted by the French for their support was the transfer to France of the Piedmontese provinces of Nice and Savoy. One consequence was that the Mont Cenis tunnel project, under way since 1860, became a joint French and Italian one instead of being purely Italian.

Subsequently Parma, Modena and Tuscany all agreed to join a united kingdom of Italy, while Garibaldi sailed from Genoa with a thousand men to win over Sicily and Naples. He was so welcome in the south that he was actually able to enter Naples by train, well ahead of his army.

King Victor Emmanuel and his new Italian government encouraged railway construction, mainly by means of generous concessions to private companies. By 1866 it was possible to travel by train between every Italian city, except a few in the far south, to this day an impoverished area. By 1871 Rome had become the capital, the 8.5-mile Mont Cenis tunnel leading into France was open, the Austrians had been driven out of the northeastern province of Venetia, and the Pope's once-vast temporal domains had shrunk to that of the Vatican City in Rome.

In addition to the unification of the country, successive steps were taken towards the unification of the main-line railways, under laws promulgated in 1865, 1885 and 1905 respectively. The last of these provided for the formation of the present state railway system, the Ferrovie dello Stato or FS, which came into being on 1 July 1905, with almost 7000 miles of route. Numerous lines of local interest remain

outside the FS network, which currently extends to 10,000 miles.

Volta, of 'volt' fame, was an Italian and, if one notes the fact that the tricky arithmetic of justifying electrification was particularly favourable in coal-less Italy, it is not surprising that electric traction there went ahead very rapidly and very early.

Early electrification was three-phase AC, very simple electrically, but involving fixed running speeds and two contact wires. This was particularly complicated at junctions. The first line was converted from steam traction in 1900 and by 1928, when the more flexible 3000v DC system was adopted for new work, over 1600 miles had been converted. This was by far the largest and the longest lasting application of the three-phase system – it did not finally disappear until 1971. After 1928 DC electrification was pushed ahead very rapidly (remember this was the reign of Mussolini who

Above: The inaugural Italian Direct Current train arrives at Genoa. Locomotives were fitted with a special pantograph to collect current from what had once been three-phase double overhead equipment.

Top: The Franco-Crosti boiler gives some Italian steam locomotives an appearance that takes some getting used to.

Above: The station concourse at Rome, Italy is spacious and always clean.

Right: An exterior view of the Rome Terminus. The building is not only a pleasure to look at but is functional as well.

'made the trains run to time'). By 1939 it was possible to travel 690 miles from Bologna all the way to Reggio di Calabria in the toe of Italy by electric train. Currently electric traction extends 5230 miles, all the original three-phase sections having been converted to DC. Nineteen hundred electric locomotives handle the bulk of Italy's rail traffic.

Italian steam locomotives, which still exist to the tune of 600 or so but perform only reserve duties, are very distinctive. There are some with the strange looking Franco-Crosti boiler and others with inside cylinders but outside valve chests and valve gear. Because of the electrification programme, virtually no steam locomotives were constructed after 1925.

Diesel traction also came early to coal-less Italy, in the form of railcars (there are currently 1500 in service) and this experience has led to complete self-sufficiency in diesel traction, although this form is, on the whole, confined to lines of secondary importance. There are almost 1000 diesel locomotives at present in service.

Italian trains are also very fast, frequent, cheap and comfortable – and well filled too, one might add, reflecting a level of fares that only bring in just over half the cost of running them. Their Achilles heel is punctuality. Before European railways began running almost identical carriages, the wise traveller on an international train would choose an Italian vehicle in preference – and not only for the charming stained-glass windows in the lavatories. Luxury electric trains such as the 'Settebello' with observation saloons front and rear, set new standards for other nations to follow.

FS is carrying annually, with its fleet of 16,000 passengers and 120,000 freight vehicles, almost 400 million passengers and sixty million tons of freight. The latter is hauled an average distance of 200 miles.

During the interwar period, huge efforts were made to complete one of the greatest-ever feats of railway engineering, the Bologna – Florence *direttissima* ('most direct') railway, which had been begun in 1908. The Great Apennine Tunnel – only one of the great artifacts on this line – opened in 1934, was then as now the second longest mountain railway tunnel in the world, and because of the nature of the ground encountered, one of the most difficult to bore. The distance between the two

Above: Carrozza Ristorante – *eating the Italian way on an Italian TEE internal train.*

Left: View of the recently completed new Rome-Florence direttissima *railway.*

than half were standard gauge, the remainder narrow. There were small amounts of respectable 3ft 6in and 1ft 11½in (600mm) but most were three Swedish feet, that is 2ft 11in or 891mm.

Since that time SJ has gradually taken over the more important private lines and many of the others have been allowed to die. Currently only three are left, although the memory of the remainder is kept green by four vestigial remnants operated as steam pleasure or museum lines. Accordingly, SJ's mileage since 1930 has increased to 7300, including just over 100 miles of 2ft 11in gauge.

Sweden's railways were fairly easy to build – the only problems were the many river crossings but these were not of excessive size. There is a 48-span 2815ft-long bridge across the Göta near Göteborg which is the longest in Sweden. The longest tunnel is the 'Gardatunneln' of 1.3 miles near Göteborg.

The modernization which has become so necessary in recent years on most of the world's railways as a desperate last-ditch defence

Right: A standardized electric I-C-I locomotive at Åre on the Storlien train in Sweden.

Below right: A modern Bo-Bo electric locomotive hauls a Swedish express passenger train.

Extreme right, top: A freight train approaches the corkscrew alignment at Giornico on the southern ascent of the Gotthard main line, Switzerland.

Below: Sweden had two gauges below standard, 3ft 6in (mostly in the south) and the odd gauge of 2ft 11in. At one place, Växjö (below), there was even a small section of four rail track!

against extinction, has in Sweden been a steady and continuous process. Electrification, based on water power, began with the Lapland Iron Ore line from Lulea to the Norwegian border; this occurred in 1915 when most industrial countries were otherwise engaged. This northern line was completed in 1922. When, twenty years later, the Göteborg-Stockholm trunk railway was electrified, one could, for the first time in history, make a journey of more than 1000 miles by electric train, from Malmö in the south to Riksgransen east of Narvik, in the north. Currently 5000 miles are electrified, handling 90 percent of all rail traffic and using the 15,000v low-frequency AC system. There are 757 electric locomotives plus 170 railcars and motor-coaches. The technology which has resulted from this extraordinary achievement on the part of such a small nation is now a

major export, and the performance of the superb railway system is one of the major factors which has given Sweden one of the highest standards of living in the world. Sixty-five million passengers are now carried annually and 54 million tons of freight are hauled an average distance of 175 miles.

Steam traction in Sweden was not specially remarkable, except that most of it was home-made. One recently absorbed constituent of SJ, the ore-hauling Grängesberg (near Ludvika) – Oxelösund Railway made railway history by using a fleet of steam turbine locomotives in normal service; this was both the first and the only such use in the world. Steam power was held in reserve in Sweden until around 1970; up to that time it had only seen marginal use.

A more imitated innovation was the privately owned Mallesta & Södermanlands Railway's

introduction, in 1913, of the first diesel-electric vehicle to run in regular public service. Diesel traction has a secondary role to play in Sweden; there are 690 locomotives and 180 railcars in use.

Swedish railway carriages and trains are exceptionally comfortable; this is mainly due to the extraordinary width (11ft 2in), one foot wider than allowed in Europe generally. The high standard of cleanliness and small amenities such as drinking water and ladies' retiring rooms play their part. When Europe had three classes of travel, Sweden was for many years the only system to provide sleeping accommodation in third class as well as first and second. More modestly dimensioned vehicles, including USSR sleeping cars from Moscow, enter Sweden on board train ferries from East Germany or Denmark.

SWITZERLAND

See maps on pages 26–27 and 46–47.

The Swiss Railways system is notable not only for an efficient intercity service, but for a remarkably comprehensive inter-village one as well. No other country in the world even begins to offer its remote corners such a magnificent service of fast and frequent electric trains. In other aspects of service, Swiss trains also have few peers; their safety, comfort, convenience and cleanliness all rate among the world's best.

Two reasons for this fortunate state of affairs must be noted: stable government and long-standing neutrality in war. The Swiss Confederation dates from 1815, well before the coming of railways. Since that time political changes have been minimal, in spite of the four language groups – German, French, Italian, Romansh – into which the population is divided.

The way in which the railways have become organized has also played its part. The Federal railways, with centralized control, are confined to the main trunk routes, while most regional needs are met by independent and provincially minded local companies – often described as private but in most cases and in truth public. Only 2934 of the miles of railways in Switzerland belong to the Swiss Federal Railways, the remainder being divided among 127 other administrations. Many of the minor railways are narrow gauge.

Although this fragmentation allows for local control, it is not allowed to invonvenience the passenger or trader. One ticket will cover a journey over two or more railways, and baggage checked through can be relied on to arrive simultaneously with the traveller, even after several changes of train.

SWISS FEDERAL RAILWAYS – SBB/CFF/FFS
Schweizerische Bundesbahnen – Chemins de fer Fédéraux-Ferrovie Federali Svizzera, Hochschulstrasse 6, CH 3030, Bern.

Left: Swiss mountain engineering is well illustrated by the bridge over the Bietschtal gorge between Brig and Irandersted.

Above: A Swiss inter-city express features the latest type Bo-Bo electric locomotive.

Above: A typical wayside station in the Swiss Alps.

Centre top: A Furka-Oberalp Railway steam train runs through a snow cutting in Switzerland higher than its chimney.

Centre: One solution to the snow problem is the steam rotary plough used here on the Bern–Lötschberg–Simplon Railway.

Right: A 6240 HP Bo-Bo locomotive handles 600 tons on a 1 in 38 gradient on the Bern–Lötschberg–Simplon Railway.

Extreme right, top: This railway map of Switzerland was drawn in 1958 but the routes have remained almost unchanged.

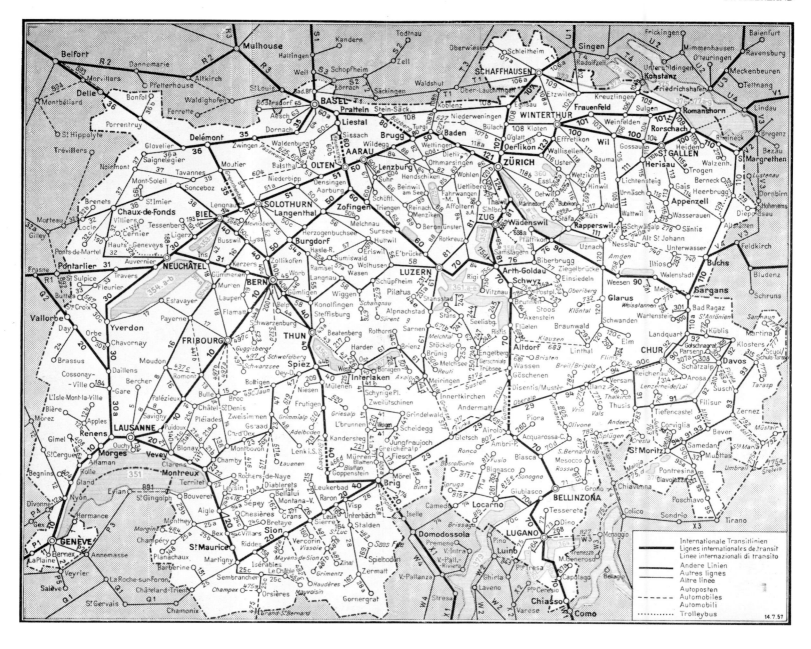

History and Development

The first railway to open in Switzerland – apart from the tip of a French tentacle which reached Basel in 1846 – was a line from Baden to Zurich which opened in 1847. It got to be known as the 'Spanish Bun Railway', from one of its original staple traffics. As was common in Europe, subsequent development took the form of private concessions rather than free-for-all competition. In this way the trunk railway system was developed by a number of companies. Three of them, the Swiss North-Eastern, the Weiss Central and the Swiss United, were incorporated into the Swiss Federal Railways in the year 1901. The Jura-Simplon followed in 1906 and the Gotthard in 1909; the only trunk route to escape nationalization was the Bern-Lötschberg-Simplon railway, which was not opened until 1913.

Belonging to a country without indigenous fuel supplies, Switzerland's railways suffered serious problems during World War I and, accordingly, immediately the conflict was over, electrification was undertaken. By 1925 on the SBB, only secondary routes remained. The SBB became totally electrified in 1965 and in fact today, only four short private lines remain in the hands of other forms of traction.

In recent years much effort has been put into re-aligning and doubling sections of trunk route that were originally single and so sharply curved as to preclude fast running. Having regard to the terrain, this has involved very heavy expenditure.

Civil Engineering

The task of laying out a main-line railway system in country that would daunt a mule-train, has given Switzerland some of the world's greatest railway engineering, including the longest mountain railway tunnel which joins Brig in Switzerland to Domodossola in Italy. Strictly speaking the Simplon is two tunnels, the first single line bore being completed in 1906 and the second in 1912. It is 12.25 miles long. The double track 9.3-mile Gotthard tunnel, the previous longest, was built between 1880–1889.

As remarkable as the long tunnels are the helicoidal ones used to overcome height differences while still keeping the gradient down to an acceptable figure. The four double-track ones on the approaches to the Gotthard tunnel are specially notable – and quite bewildering to the traveller.

The bridges and viaducts in the Swiss Alps are, as might be expected, also remarkable; particularly elegant are the arched masonry structures typical of construction in the days before 1914. The Swiss were among the pioneers in the use of reinforced concrete and structures built in connection with doubling and re-alignments – no new main lines have been built since 1913 – and have made much use of this method of construction.

The extensive use of steel sleepers is an unusual feature (for Europe) of Swiss railway track, although practice regarding renewals is now more in line with the rest of Europe. In either case the Swiss love of order and tidiness is reflected in a permanent way that can only be described as manicured.

Locomotive Landmarks

The Swiss developed their own school of locomotive design, influenced at the start by that of their larger neighbours, France and Germany. Until 1875 most Swiss locomotives were built abroad, but in that year the Swiss Locomotive Works of Winterthur, directed by an Englishman called Charles Brown, supplied its first main-line engine. This was a 2-6-0T for the North Eastern Railway. It is interesting to note that, having Walschearts' valve gear and two outside cylinders, this machine had the exact mechanical layout of the steam locomotive in its final form of a century later – well in advance of world thinking at the time. Most subsequent Swiss locomotives were constructed by the firm. A short flirtation with the Mallet principle for sharply curved mountain lines left little mark – the conclusion reached was that the complications were not worthwhile.

French influence was felt with the introduction of four-cylinder compounds from 1901 onwards. A long series of such 4-6-0s were built for the youthful Swiss Federal Railways. The culmination of Swiss main-line steam were the 2-10-0s of 1913-17. A 2-10-0 and a 4-6-0 survive in working order and are occasionally run.

Since World War I construction has been virtually confined to electric locomotives with specialist firms like Brown-Boveri and Oerlikon supplying electrical equipment. Originally construction followed steam principles with the wheels driven via coupling rods; the famous 'crocodile' articulated 1-c-c-1s for the Gotthard line were specially notable.

Although a few rod-drive locomotives still survive, the fleet built for general main-line electrification during the 1920s had (mostly) individual motors for each driving axle. The 2-Do-1s and 2-Co-1s supplied then, still give good service although more conventional Bo-Bos and Co-Cos are now the front runners. Powers as high as 1000hp per axle were pioneered in Switzerland during the 1950s.

Incidentally, the Swiss call a 2-Do-1 an Ae4/7 and a 1-C-C-1 a Ce6/8. The first letter is an indication of the maximum permitted speed, A being fast, C being slow, etc; e means electric; 4/7 means four axles driven out of seven. Hence, the steam 4-6-0s were B3/5 and the high speed Bo-Bos are Re4/4, R being chosen because there is no letter before A in the alphabet. Switzerland is the only country in the world which opts out of internationally recognized classifications for motive power types.

One form of Swiss traction, unique to the world, was a wartime expedient whereby an 0-6-0T shunting locomotive was fitted with electric heating elements and a pantograph collector. With almost all the electricity used coming from water power (many of the generators are over fifty years old and still efficient) this was not so extravagant a proceeding as it might otherwise seem.

Operations and Services

The amazing frequency, comprehensiveness, comfort and cleanliness of Swiss passenger train services has been mentioned. In statistical terms 210 million passengers are carried annually in a fleet of 3600 carriages.

Freight operation is dominated by Switzer-

land's position as the 'Turntable of Europe' and the consequent great flows of traffic over major international arteries such as the Gotthard line. Although such 'bridge route' operations are intrinsically profitable, there is another side to the coin; international trade can fluctuate enormously and cause such *debacles* as a fall from 46 million tons of freight carried in 1974 to 35 million carried in 1975. How can Switzerland's 26,400-strong wagon fleet be utilized efficiently in the face of such variations as these?

Although the fascinating giant signalling bells of the SBB are now history, Swiss signalling is still distinctive. Notable are the square distant or warning signals which indicate messages not only by colour but by the pattern of the lights. One-man locomotive operation has been a feature for many years; the safety precautions include not only the usual 'dead man's handle' but also a vigilance button, which the driver has to press at prescribed intervals to indicate his continuing awareness.

BERN-LOTSCHBERG-SIMPLON RAILWAY – BLS
11 Rue de Genève, Bern.

Although working in close association with the Federal Railways, the Bern-Lötschberg-Simplon Railway is notable because it is the only section of the European trunk network not to be owned by a national government.

Of the main-line railways of the world, the Lötschberg, when it opened in 1913, was the first to be built as an electric railway from end to end. It was also among the very earliest to be worked electrically. The conception of the line resulted from the fact that Bern, the capital of Switzerland, was a railway cul-de-sac, whereas Geneva, Lausanne, Lucerne, Zürich, Basel and other places all lay on the great through routes that got Swiss rails known as the 'turntable of Europe'.

Getting no satisfaction from central government the citizens of Bern set out on their own to drive a main-line railroad, 75 miles long, through the Bernese Alps to reach the Simplon main line at the north end of the great tunnel. They raised the money and work began in 1902. The main task was the 9.1-mile Lötschberg tunnel and here for once the mountain gods decided to show who was master. An unsuspected cleft in the terrain was pierced and 25 men working at the tunnel face perished in the deluge – a mile of completed tunnel had to be abandoned and three curves introduced to form a wide kink in the alignment to avoid the trouble area.

The BLS also financed a cut-off line, which includes the 4.5 mile Grenchenberg tunnel, to shorten communication between Bern and the North. This, however, is only used by Swiss Federal Railways trains.

High-voltage single-phase AC electrification had then barely emerged from the laboratory and when electric trains began to run there were major difficulties with unexpected surges of power. Lots of volts and amps would

then go the wrong way – with dire results. Experience was quickly gained and the little Lötschberg railway was the pathfinder for the great Federal Railway electrifications of the 1920s. Rod drive 1-E-1 (2-10-2) locomotives were supplied first, supplemented between the wars by great articulated 1-Co-Co-1 machines. In 1947 the BLS pioneered a plain double-bogie locomotive with 1000 horsepower per axle, an amazing figure for the time; in due course the rest of the world followed.

Forty-five electric locomotives, 130 passenger carriages and 310 wagons are the main items in the rolling stock fleet. The last figure bears no relationship to the role of the BLS as an international carrier of five million tons of traffic; eight million passengers are also conveyed, expenses being 89 percent of receipts.

Independent Swiss Railways

This railway feat-of-arms, unparalleled elsewhere in the world, putting almost every Swiss hamlet and mountain top on the railway map, deserves a closer look. In the lowlands the independent lines tend to be a hybrid between a street tramway and a country branch line and are electric. The first Swiss electric line was the two-mile line from Grütschalp to Mürren, opened in 1891 and the first electric local (as opposed to mountain) railway was the three-mile line from Orbe to Chavornay, opened in 1893. Typically, the trains start from a tram stop in the street outside the main station, but take to their own right-of-way outside towns. Again typically, they are of metre gauge but standard-gauge freight cars can be hauled on transporter wagons. This is a type of railway which has almost disappeared from the rest of the world.

But Switzerland's mountain railways are what the country is famous for. Now there are four ways of climbing a mountain by rail. The

first way (for very steep inclines) is to haul one car at a time with a cable. Such funicular railways are outside the scope of this book. The second way is to use a rack-and-pinion arrangement, a cog railway as it is sometimes called. The third way is to avoid 'artificial' aids and make the climb more gradual by extending the distance, either by making U-turns on steep mountain sides, or by building spiral tunnels inside them. The second and third ways can be combined to produce a railway that works by the rack on very steep sections and by adhesion elsewhere. Descriptions of outstanding lines in all these categories follow. And because it is Switzerland under discussion, outstanding means outstanding in the world.

WENGERNALP RAILWAY – WAB
Wengernalpbahn,
Interlaken.

The largest purely rack railway in the world (by a substantial margin) is the twelve-mile 2ft 7½in gauge Wengernalp Railway in the Bernese Oberland. It runs in full view of some of the greatest *Viertausender* (13,100+ft) peaks in the Alps. The line was built for sightseers in 1893 – winter opening for skiers was an after-thought which did not occur until over ten years later and in due course brought English names like 'The Bumps', 'Mac's Leap' and 'Slip Cartilage Corner' to certain points in WAB terrain.

The WAB is quite a complex system with junctions and elaborate station layouts. The arrangements at points whereby, since the motive power has no adhesion drive, the rack is kept continuous are fascinating to see. Steam ruled on grades up to one in four from the opening in 1893 until 1908, when electrification at 1500v DC was carried out. Separate loco-motives were universal until after World War

Top centre: A steam tourist train crosses the stone arches-on-an-arch bridge at Wiesen near Davos on the Rhaetian Railway.

Above: Jungfraujoch station on the Jungfrau RW.

Top right: A train en route to Zermatt ascends a 1 in 8 rack section near Tasch, Switzerland.

II; since then the ubiquitous power car has taken over. Trains are limited to two bogie vehicles and one four-wheel ski-and-luggage truck. Currently there are 24 railcars, eight locomotives, forty trailers and fifty goods vehicles; 2.3 million passengers are carried annually. Connection is made at the WAB's lower termini and (oddly enough) also at its highest point with metre-gauge rack-and-adhesion lines. Thus Kleine Sheidegg, altitude 6260ft, is connected by an extraordinary line – the Jungfrau Railway – which runs mainly inside the Eiger mountain, to the highest point (11,800ft) reached by rail in Europe.

RHAETIAN RAILWAY – RhB
Rhätische Bahn – Chemin de Fer Rhetique –
Ferrovia Retica – Viater Rietica,
CH-7002, Chur, Graubunden.

In saying that the Rhaetian Railway system in southeast Switzerland is justifiably world-famous in many ways, one must add that it is no more so than the country in which it was built. The canton of Graubunden (the 'Gray Leagues') was once ruled by a Prince-Bishop at Chur, but is now the largest canton of the Swiss Confederation. In deference to the locally spoken ancient Romansch tongue, the Rhaetian

Railway spells its name in that tongue as well as in German, French, Italian and English.

The RhB began life in 1889 as the Landquart-Davos Railway, bringing passengers from the main line up the Pratigau Valley to Klosters and Davos. In those days most visitors were connected with the tuberculosis sanitaria at Davos, but among them must be included early skiers who found a way down from the mountains above Davos to Küblis and for whom the Parsenn funicular was later built. Even now, Davos' winter holiday season is busier than its summer one – the RhB peak month is February.

The problems of climbing up to Davos (5280ft) were overcome (and rack sections avoided) by steepening the gradient to 1 in 22.5 (45 per thousand) but when the time came a few years later to connect world-famous St Moritz (altitude 6180ft) to the outer world by train, the traffic anticipated suggested the easier figure of 1 in 29 (35 per thousand). The penalty was civil engineering on an altogether different scale with breathtaking bridges and viaducts, four spiral tunnels (two placed one directly above the other) and finally the 3.7-mile Albula tunnel under the pass into the Engadine, the high valley in which St Moritz lies.

Extensions followed; the one in the so-called Lower Engadine, leading to Schuls-Tarasp on the Austrian border, was interesting in that it was completed in 1913 as an electric railway. It became a prototype for electrification of the whole Rhaetian system, which was completed in 1923. The low frequency AC system was used, with 11,000v (nominally) at the contact wire. Trains could descend the long inclines using their motors as dynamos to give braking and return power to the system; provision had to be made for disposing of surplus power (the hydro-electric power supply system was originally self-contained) when all trains on the railway were running downhill!

After an early affair with articulated Mallet locomotives, the RhB settled in steam days for a fleet of 29 noble 2-8-0s, two of which survive for the pleasure of rail fans. Their replacement in the 1920s with only fifteen equally noble C-C 'crocodile' electrics tells its own tale. More conventional bogie locomotives now haul the dining car expresses and most other trains.

Signalling on the RhB is particularly delightful; the passage of trains is marked by sonorous notes struck on giant block bells standing like enormous toadstools on station platforms. The original revolving disc signals have now nearly all been replaced by coloured lights.

Currently there are sixty electric locomotives, forty electric railcars, 300 passenger cars and 1100 freight cars. These carry 7.5 million passengers and 750,000 tons of freight annually on the 244-mile system.

USSR

See map on pages 118-119.

USSR RAILWAYS
Novo Basmannaya 2,
Moscow 10714.

The railways of the Soviet Union form by far the largest single system in the world. Having 85,700 route miles, they are well over twice as large as any other and extend over 6000 miles from west to east and over 3000 from north to south. The first public railway in the land was opened in 1837 between St Petersburg (now Leningrad) and the royal resort of Tsarskoye Selo, fifteen miles. The first trunk line over the 400 miles separating St Petersburg and Moscow opened on 13 November 1851. This is the line where the Czar, asked to choose the route, sent for a ruler and drew a line; fortunately the country is flat!

The privately owned railway systems did not cope well with the demands of the Crimean War of 1877–78 and the government set about nationalizing them. One third had been acquired by 1900 and two thirds by 1914. The state also set up factories to make the USSR self-sufficient regarding locomotives and rolling stock. Standard designs were also adopted.

Much has been written of the crossing of other continents by rail but the construction of the 5900-mile trans-Siberian railway surely eclipses them all. The dates are rather complicated:

1891 The enterprise is approved. Tsarevitch Nicholas inaugurates construction at Vladivostok.
1903 The line is complete, except across Lake

Left: A traditional Soviet station, Rostov-on-Don.

Extreme left: The cab of a Soviet P36 class 4-8-4.

Above: A modern Soviet station, Sverdlovsk.

Top: Modern motive power in the USSR.

Extreme right, centre: The magnificent control station of Maiakovskaia on the Moscow Metro.

Below: Soviet FD class 2-10-2s double-head a freight, which can now be seen in China.

Extreme right, top: A Moscow Metro train at an outer terminus.

Right: Crowds throng the suburban platforms at the Kazan station in Moscow.

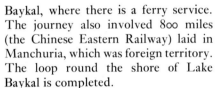

Baykal, where there is a ferry service. The journey also involved 800 miles (the Chinese Eastern Railway) laid in Manchuria, which was foreign territory.

1905   The loop round the shore of Lake Baykal is completed.

1915   The line north of the Chinese Border – the Amur River – is completed, giving a continuous railway on Russian soil from Moscow to Vladivostok.

When revolution came in 1917, half the present network had been completed, although the emphasis was much more in the European part of the USSR than in the Asian. The latter with two-thirds of the land area had less than one-fifth of the mileage.

The new regime made tremendous efforts, at considerable sacrifice, to improve and extend the system. All vehicles were fitted with air brakes and converted to automatic coupling before 1939. No doubt the fact that the Soviet gauge of 5ft 0in differed from that of all her neighbours except Finland, probably helped by minimizing the problems of interchange. Lines laid with weak track were strengthened and many new ones were built, particularly in Asia. Others, including the trans-Siberian from end to end, were doubled. Today the trans-Siberian line is having to be duplicated, on a new course further north.

The devastation in areas overrun by the Germans in World War II was on a colossal scale, but it was usually possible for most of the rolling stock and even workshop equipment to be evacuated in time. After the war, once the destruction had been made good, the strides made were even more remarkable. Thirty thousand miles of new route have been built, steam has been almost eliminated and

electrification of 25,000 miles of line has meant that over half of Soviet rail traffic is hauled electrically.

Civil Engineering

In addition to being the world's biggest system in the operational sense, the USSR has the biggest railway rolling stock, 17ft 2in in height and 11ft 2in wide. For many years these magnificent dimensions were not matched by track strong enough to carry a corresponding load. Locomotives with, say, a twenty-ton axle-load found themselves with a very limited territory in which to work.

Although the great rivers of the USSR intersect the railways at numerous points, no bridge is recorded as being longer than a mile. Similarly, there are no tunnels of world class in the USSR. The longest one is, as one might expect, in the Caucasus mountains. This is the Suram Tunnel, 2.5 miles long, on the Baku-Poti line.

Locomotive Landmarks

The first steam locomotive in the USSR ran on an industrial line in the Urals. M Cherepanov built it in 1833 following a visit to England. Locomotives for the first Soviet lines were imported from Britain and elsewhere, but indigenous production began in the early 1840s at St Petersburg under the supervision of Ross Winans of the Baltimore & Ohio Railroad in America.

The steam period in the USSR is remarkable mainly for the exceptional amount of standardization that was achieved both before and after the 1917 revolution, as well as for its extraordinary continuity across that watershed in history. The basic simplicity and, in later years, Soviet duplication of North American designs served

as recognition of what best suited Soviet conditions rather than inability to comprehend or design anything else; in the USSR, the academic foundation of and experimentation into possible improvements to the steam locomotive were carried further than anywhere else.

Two projects suffice to illustrate this point. In 1934, in order to provide a big pull on lightish rails, a fourteen coupled 4-14-4 locomotive was built, the longest non-articulated locomotive ever constructed. In the event, interaction between the track and the 33ft rigid wheel-base caused problems that were never surmounted.

A little later, attempts were made to develop a type of locomotive known as the Teploparovozy. This was a combined steam-diesel machine, which used steam for starting (remember that a diesel gives no push when stationary) and diesel plus steam for running; the steam was generated by waste heat from the diesel cylinders. Theoretically there is a promise of thermal efficiency better even than a diesel, as well as there being no need for the complications of electric or hydraulic transmission. Three attempts were made, two before and one after the 'Great Patriotic War' but in the end success remained elusive. Yet the promise remains.

Out on the line could be found the 'E' class 0-10-0, the most numerous locomotive class ever built. Thirteen thousand of them were made between 1912 and 1947. In the 1920s a batch was hurriedly ordered from Nohab of Sweden; they were loaded onto a Soviet ship which promptly unloaded gold bars on to the quayside in payment.

The standard passenger locomotive, the 'S' 2-6-2, the most numerous passenger class in

the world, was built to the tune of 4000 or so, over an even longer period, from 1910 to 1951. Some 2-8-4s and finally 4-8-4s (the latter of a particularly handsome design) supplemented the 2-6-2s on the heaviest duties.

Freight movement was dominated by 13,000 2-10-0s and 2-10-2s of only three classes, supported by 2000 2-10-0s captured from the Germans. For light shunting, industrial and pilot duties the 'O' (for 'principal') 0-8-0, the first Soviet standard design of 1891, survived almost until the end of steam, an event which in 1978 has not yet been confirmed.

At its maximum in 1957, the steam fleet of 35,000 was easily the world's biggest. Ten classes accounted for over 30,000! In that year steam construction was halted without warning and Kaganovitch, the Commissar of Transportation who favoured continuance of steam, almost certainly liquidated.

The Soviet school of design had little effect on the world's locomotives outside the mother country – except in China, where it has been total.

In spite of the commendable efforts that were made, reliable diesel locomotives were not produced in the USSR before 1945 but, influenced by some American units that arrived during the war, production began in earnest afterwards. The earliest ones were conservatively rated at around 1000hp for each unit. A 2000hp unit was not out of the prototype stage in 1956 when the political decision to get rid of steam meant that the new design had prematurely to be put into mass production. The next step up, which led to 3000hp per unit was taken sensibly and slowly. In this way success was achieved. The size of the present fleet remains a state secret but is no doubt in the region of 10,000.

The USSR's electric locomotives are not specially remarkable, except that there are a lot of them and all are of the bogie type. A long series of designs with three-axle trucks were developed from some prototypes supplied by GEC of USA in 1929. Other prototypes have been supplied since the war by France, Germany and Sweden and production units from Czechoslovakia; the bulk, however, are homemade, both for 3000v DC and 25,000v AC. A common design is a permanently-coupled twin unit, with four two-axle trucks.

Train services

Freight dominates rail operations; the two million ton-miles produced annually by the railways is not only the greatest on any system in the world but is more than *ALL* the rest of the world's railway traffic put together. This is a figure so big as to be meaningless, but if one considers the overall tonnage handled per year (3600 million) one gets a figure perhaps of 250,000 loaded wagons dispatched each day. A typical freight train will weigh in the region of 3000 tons.

Passenger trains are in general timed to keep up with freight – but no more – and in consequence are not fast. The 'Russia' (the correct name for what is usually and incorrectly known as the 'Trans-Siberian Express'), for example, averages 30 mph on its 5900-mile journey from Moscow to Vladivostok. The standards of amenity and cleanliness are high; each coach has two attendants to keep it clean and heated, with the samovar on the boil. The premier Communist country can hardly have classes, so there are soft and hard cars. In spite of its taking second place to freight, the passenger count amounts to 3500 million each year, second in the world.

MOSCOW METRO
Moskovski Metropolitana Imeni V.I. Lenina,
5 Kolokolbnikov Street,
Moscow 103045.

The first section of the Moscow Metro was one of the great show-pieces of the revolution although built using compulsory labour. The magnificent stations in the central area would more aptly be described as palaces. The first line opened in 1934. Since then further lines have been built (three transverse, three radial and one circular), making a 103-mile system. The gauge is the Soviet standard of 5ft and the current 825v DC with third rail. The Metro's annual traffic of 1800 million passengers is by far the heaviest traffic handled by any city underground railway.

USSR

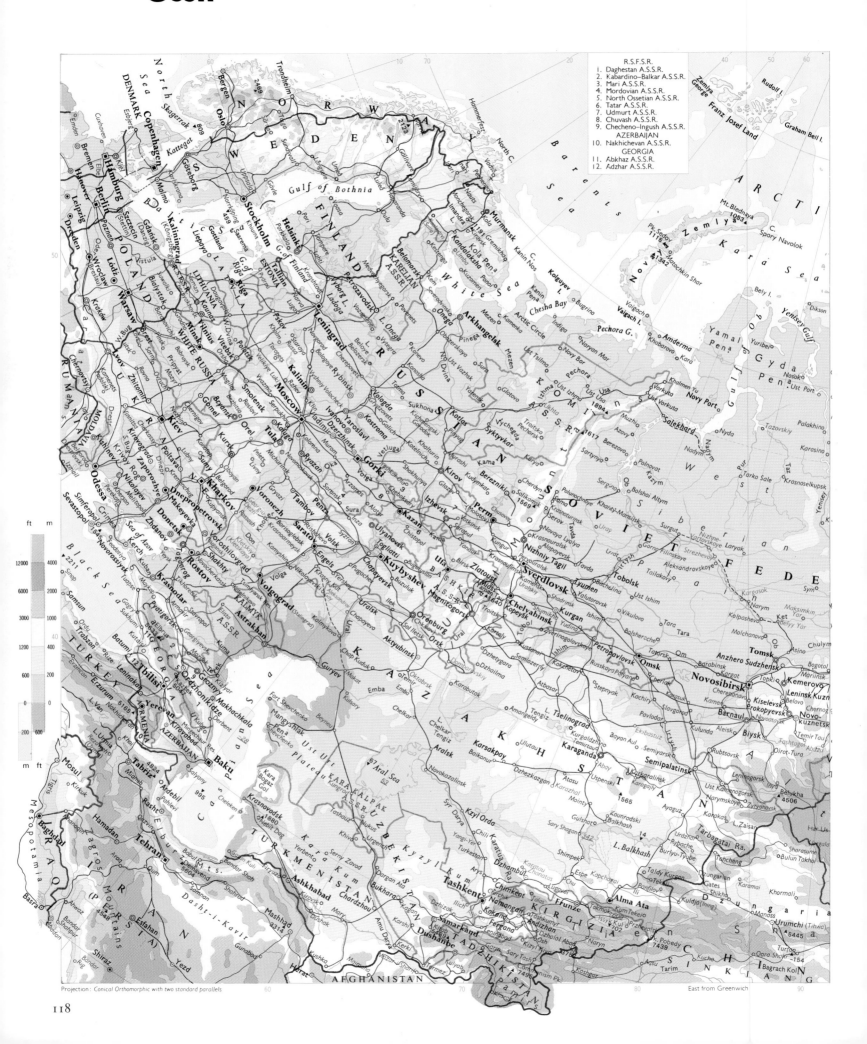

R.S.F.S.R.
1. Daghestan A.S.S.R.
2. Kabardino–Balkar A.S.S.R.
3. Mari A.S.S.R.
4. Mordovian A.S.S.R.
5. North Ossetian A.S.S.R.
6. Tatar A.S.S.R.
7. Udmurt A.S.S.R.
8. Chuvash A.S.S.R.
9. Checheno–Ingush A.S.S.R.
AZERBAIJAN
10. Nakhichevan A.S.S.R.
GEORGIA
11. Abkhaz A.S.S.R.
12. Adzhar A.S.S.R.

Projection: Conical Orthomorphic with two standard parallels

East from Greenwich

1 : 20 000 000

100   0   100   200   300   400   500 miles

100   0   200   400   600   800 km

	Boundaries of U.S.S.R.
	Boundaries of S.S.R.
	Boundaries of A.S.S.R.

COPYRIGHT GEORGE PHILIP & SON. LTD.
DHH

─── YUGOSLAVIA ───

See map on pages 86–87.

YUGOSLAV RAILWAYS – JZ
Jugoslovenskih Zeleznica,
Nemanjina 6,
Belgrade.

Yugoslavia was another country created by the Allies in 1919, partly from the dismemberment of the Austro-Hungarian Empire, but including most of the territory of the former Kingdoms of Serbia and Montenegro. The first railway in what is now Yugoslavia was a section – between Maribor and Ljubljana – of the Austrian main line from Vienna to Trieste, then an Austrian port. It opened in 1849. Steady extension took place in the area controlled by Austria. In 1878 the Austrians invaded Bosnia and Herzogovinia (then under Turkish domination), and during this campaign laid narrow-gauge military railways. This system remained after the Turks were driven out; its main line connected Sarajevo, Mostar and Dubrovnik with the rest of the country and involved major engineering works as well as sections of rack-and-pinion operation.

The Kingdom of Serbia had both standard and narrow-gauge railways. Basically, the former applied on the plains and the latter in the mountains and the system penetrated to the Bulgarian and Turkish borders as well as to the Aegean Sea at Salonika. The narrow gauge

reached Uzice (now Titovo Uzice), twenty miles distant across the mountains from the Bosnian border.

Croatia was part of Hungary, and the Hungarian MAV system owned the trunk line from Budapest via Zagreb to Fiume (now Rijeka). All these areas became part of the new Kingdom of Yugoslavia after World War I.

There was great destruction of railways in World War I. The Serbian system (740 miles of standard gauge and 500 miles of narrow gauge) was almost totally destroyed.

After that war, the newly independent Kingdom of Yugoslavia restored the railway system, first bringing the Simplon-Orient Express route from Italy via Belgrade to Bulgaria up to international main-line standard. A new narrow-gauge link, involving some magnificent spirals in the mountains and the mile-long Sargan tunnel, was opened in 1925. It joined Visegrad to Uzice (now Titovo Uzice) and thus connected the Serbian and Bosnian systems. After a connecting line into Belgrade had been built in 1928, through running – of a dubious kind – was possible between the Serbian capital and the Adriatic at Dubrovnik. Before the war, Salonika was the main Serbian port.

In World War II, from all accounts, it was trains and the people in them which got destroyed, rather than the railways themselves. Four million out of sixteen million Yugoslavians died, but they took a proportionate number of the enemy with them. The survivors gained a strength of purpose from these sacrifices which enabled them not only to drive out

the Germans but to resist Soviet domination as well. Few visitors were allowed into the country in the first years after the war but Laurence Durrell (who served in the British Embassy then) writes a hilarious account of Yugoslavian rail travel in his book *Esprit de Corps* – in English in spite of its title – telling something of the happy-go-lucky air of those days, no doubt a reaction from the terrible years that had gone before.

The Communist government of Marshall Tito, in spite of many other calls on its meagre resources, then embarked on the greatest railway project to be constructed in Europe since the war. It was undertaken in order to provide Belgrade with an outlet to the sea, a mere 200 miles away across the mountains, but 470 miles by the meandering course of the narrow-gauge railway already discussed. The 26-hour journey, involving such fascinating but time-wasting delights as rack-and-pinion working south of Sarajevo, was definitely for enthusiasts only.

The new line, which was to run to the port of Bar rather than Dubrovnik, had been planned before the war. Construction started in 1952 and after a little go-stop-go in the early years, was opened throughout on 27 November 1975. It is 298 miles long; some idea of the work involved may be judged from the fact that 72 miles are in tunnel, the two longest, Sozina and Zlatibor, both being 3.9 miles in length. Two hundred and fifty others average 450 yards each; 234 bridges aggregate to nine miles and include the Mala Rijeka Bridge, 613ft high

1518ft long with a 460-ft central span. Electrification is in progress.

In the meantime, work had been initiated on the less spectacular task of transforming the original system, which had previously consisted of 4500 miles of standard gauge and over 2000 miles of narrow, into one of 6500 miles of standard gauge and a few stubs of narrow. The 65 miles of electrification (DC), inherited from the Italians in the north, have become 1650 miles; most of this is wired at 25,000v AC. Incidentally, the Bosnian-Herzegovinian 2ft-6in gauge mountain network, with 650 locomotives was, until conversion and abandonment took hold in the 1960s, the largest in the world laid to a gauge as narrow as this.

The locomotive power which Yugoslavia inherited came mostly from Austrian and Hungarian sources, but mechanical engineers in both these countries had a tendency towards complications as a means of solving difficult traction problems. It is significant that the new administration adopted straight-forward Serbian designs (2-6-2s, 2-8-0s and 2-6-0s) for stop-gap construction, following this with some very simple and handsome two cylinder 2-8-2s, 4-6-2s and 2-10-0s with interchangeable components for the main lines. The ruggedly basic Bosnian 0-8-2s went on being built for the narrow gauge. Such extravagances as 2-6-6-0s or 0-10-2s with flexible wheel-base (on the Klose system) and many other curiosities were not duplicated, although – to the regret of the mechanical department but to the pleasure of ferro-equinologists – had to con-

tinue in use for a long time because the country lacked the resources to replace them.

In traffic terms JZ is a busy railway, annually hauling eighty million tons of freight an average distance of 180 miles as well as carrying 130 million passengers. The amount of equipment is (unusually for a Communist country) given as 550 steam, 320 electric and 800 diesel locomotives, 3400 passenger cars and 52,000 wagons. The steam locomotives are mostly in reserve.

—VATICAN CITY—

VATICAN RAILWAY

The shortest railway system in any sovereign state is the final half mile of what is effectively an Italian State Railways siding leading into the Vatican City. Iron sliding doors shut off the rails in the Holy see from the secular ones outside. Provision is made for special passenger trains, although these have been almost non-existent in recent years.

Above: Until well into the 1970s sections of the once huge 2ft 6in gauge network in Yugoslavia continued to function – often by steam. This section of the Austria–Hungarian empire used 0-8-2 and 2-8-2 steam locomotives, ran buffet cars and had rack sections. Here is a typical train on the line from Hercegnovi to Uskoplje behind double-headed 83 class 0-8-2s complete with spark arresters on their chimneys.

Top left: The new Yugoslavian line from Sarajevo to Ploče is electrified.

North America
The Official Guide

Canada
Canadian National Railways – CN
Canadian Pacific Limited – CP RAIL
Cartier Railway Company
Other Canadian Railways
   Algoma Central Railway
   British Columbia Railway
   Ontario Northland Railway
Quebec, North Shore & Labrador Railway
White Pass & Yukon Corporation Limited

Mexico
National Railways of Mexico

United States of America
The Pullman Company
Alaska Railroad
Amtrak – National Rail Passenger Corporation
Atchison, Topeka & Santa Fe Railway

Autotrain Corporation
Bay Area Rapid Transit – BART
Black Mesa & Lake Powell Railroad
Boston & Maine Corporation
Burlington Northern Inc.
Chessie System Inc.
Chicago, Milwaukee, St Paul & Pacific Railroad – The Milwaukee Road
Chicago & North Western Transportation Company
Chicago Transit Authority
   Chicago, South Shore & South Bend Railroad
Conrail – Consolidated Rail Corporation
Cumbres & Toltec Scenic Railroad
Delaware & Hudson Railway
Denver & Rio Grande Western Railroad
Detroit, Toledo & Ironton Railroad
Edaville Railroad
Florida East Coast Railway
Illinois Central Gulf Railroad
Long Island Rail Road
Maine Central Railroad

Other US Railroads
Mount Washington Cog Railway
New York City Transit Authority
New York, Ontario & Western Railroad
Norfolk & Western Railway
Ponce & Guayama Railway (Puerto Rico)
Port Authority Trans-Hudson Corporation – PATH
Seaboard Coast Line Industries Inc
Southern Pacific Transportation Company
Southern Railway System
Southwestern US Railroads
   Missouri Pacific Railroad – MoPAC
   Chicago, Rock Island & Pacific Railroad – Rock Island
   St Louis – San Francisco Railway System
   Missouri – Kansas – Texas Railroad – Katy
   Kansas City Southern Railway
Strasburg Rail Road
Union Pacific Railroad
Western Pacific Railroad

Inevitably the railways in North America are dominated by those in the United States, but it is pleasing to note, that, in sharp contrast to those of other continents, railroad cars can and do circulate over virtually the whole of the mainland portion without any significant technical or political problems. Compatible couplers and brakes as well as an identical rail gauge (except where the spikes have worked loose) assist the former, commonsense and restraint – the rarest of all human qualities, especially among governments – the latter.

Having recently won independence from Great Britain, the USA, when railways first came to North America, chose to call *their* lines, rail*roads*, although some companies continued to use the British 'rail*ways*'. The term railway is fairly universal in Canada.

THE OFFICIAL GUIDE
424 West 33rd Street,
New York, New York.

No treatise on the North American railroad scene could avoid mention of one great institution – the once-monthly Official Guide of the Railways and Steam Navigation Lines of the United States, Porto Rico [sic], Canada and Cuba. Taking April 1949 as an example, we find a modest 1504 page volume, listing the services offered at 138,000 railway stations from Aaron, Georgia via (the writer is interested to see) Hollingsworth, Louisiana, to Zylonite, Massachusetts. The 730 railroads listed begin with the Aberdeen and Rockfish and end with the Yuma RR in Arizona. Vanished delights such as the 'California Zephyr', the 'Orange Blossom Special', not to mention the 'Twentieth Century Limited', abound in its pages. With the virtual extinction of passenger service in the USA on the part of individual railroads, *The Official Guide* has now become smaller but remains full of interest.

as well as to enforce better standards of safety. By the turn of the century the USA rail network was approaching completion and the scene seemed set for a golden age of railway progress and development. But clouds, as yet almost unnoticeable, appeared over the horizon. First, Henry Ford was beginning to mass-produce cheap automobiles; second, the brothers Wright flew an aeroplane for the first time.

Competition from other modes of transport was something new for the railroads; competition among themselves was something they understood, but this was different. The first lines to go were the local electric passenger railways, the inter-urbans as they were called. These had only entered the field in the 1890s but developed so quickly that by 1916 there were 25,000 miles of them. By 1925 only a handful were left.

Long-distance passenger operations were affected, but more slowly. Better roads and better motorcars made steady encroachment – except during World War II – until in the 1960s the jet airliner delivered the *coup de grâce*.

In 1977 the US government's expensive rail passenger holding operation known as AMTRAK carried only one out of every one hundred inter-city travellers – true revival must await the end of easily available motorcar fuel. The bus and aeroplane also remain minority carriers with five percent and eleven percent respectively; the vast majority of people travel in their own cars.

As a typical example of how passenger operations have declined, Union Station at St Louis had 276 arrivals and departures daily before World War I; 128 at the start of World War II; and a mere eight today. The greatest factor in this decline is the wealth and industrial strength which the railroads helped to create, permitting, in its turn, near-universal car ownership.

The typical American small town grew up around the railroad depot, the railroad track itself often forming a convenient line of demarcation between the areas where lived the 'haves' and 'have-nots' respectively – hence the expression 'the wrong side of the tracks'. Alas, this centre-of-town station is no longer used – in contrast to still well-used European ones built as an afterthought well outside a typical town.

Regarding freight, a titanic struggle against other modes of transport has ensued and is still being raged. The outcome is far from clear and it must be said that, while the railroads now carry over twice as much freight as they did fifty years ago, the trucks particularly have a proportionally much larger share of the market.

The normal tactics of commercial competition, such as labour-saving investment, the closing down of unprofitable operations, and price adjustments, are largely denied to the railroads because of government regulation and trade union pressure – hence, the poor financial record of the majority of lines. Mergers, on the other hand, have been allowed to take place; during the last fifteen years they have been on a scale unknown since the turn of the century.

However, profits also took precedence over safety. While no system of transport – walking included – can ever be entirely without risk, trains in the nineteenth century were not nearly as safe as they could and should have been. Brakes were inadequate and not fail-safe. Timber-built cars splintered to matchwood or went up in flames in accidents that occurred far too frequently.

In 1887 the Interstate Commerce Commission was set up to curb the rate-fixing and monopoly-forming tendencies of the railroads,

Accordingly many famous old railroad names have disappeared, as follows:

Alton – (to Gulf, Mobile & Ohio 1947) now Illinois Central Gulf

Akron, Canton & Youngstown – Norfolk & Western since 1964

Atlanta, Birmingham & Coast – (to Atlantic Coast Line 1945) now Seaboard Coast Line

Atlantic Coast Line – Seaboard Coast Line since 1967

Baltimore & Ohio – Chessie Systems since 1963

Central of Georgia – Southern Railway since 1962

Central of New Jersey – Conrail since 1976

Chesapeake & Ohio (Chessie) – Chessie Systems since 1963

Chicago & Eastern Illinois – divided between Louisville & Nashville and Missouri Pacific 1969

Chicago, Indianapolis & Louisville (Monon) – (to Louisville & Nashville 1971) now Seaboard Coast Line

Chicago, Burlington & Quincy ('Q') – Burlington Northern since 1970

Chicago Great Western (Corn Belt Route) – Chicago & North Western since 1968

Delaware, Lackawanna & Western (Lackawanna) – (to Erie-Lackawanna 1967) now Conrail

Erie – (to Erie-Lackawanna 1967) now Conrail

Great Northern – Burlington Northern since 1970

Gulf, Mobile & Ohio – Illinois Central Gulf since 1972

Illinois Central – Illinois Central Gulf since 1972

Lehigh Valley – Conrail since 1976

Louisville & Nashville – now Seaboard Coast Line

Minneapolis & St Louis – Chicago & North Western since 1960

Nashville, Chattanooga & St Louis (The Dixie Line) – (to Louisville & Nashville 1957) now Seaboard Coast Line

New York Central – (to Penn Central 1968) now Conrail

New York, Chicago & St Louis (Nickel Plate) – Norfolk & Western since 1964

New York, New Haven & Hartford (New Haven) – (to Penn Central 1972) now Conrail

New York, Ontario & Western – abandoned

Northern Pacific – Burlington Northern since 1970

Penn Central – Conrail since 1976

Pennsylvania (Pennsy) – (to Penn Central 1968) now Conrail

Pere Marquette – (to Chesapeake & Ohio 1947) now Chessie Systems

Reading – Conrail since 1976

Rutland – abandoned 1963 with some local take-overs

St Louis South Western (Cotton Belt) – now Southern Pacific

Seaboard Air Line – Seaboard Coast Line since 1967

Spokane International – Union Pacific since 1958

Spokane, Portland & Seattle – Burlington

Northern since 1970
Texas & Pacific now Missouri Pacific
Wabash – Norfolk & Western since 1964
Western Maryland – now Chessie Systems
Wheeling & Lake Erie – (to Nickel Plate 1947) now Norfolk & Western
Virginian – Norfolk & Western since 1959

Many further mergers are under negotiation.

In spite of poor financial performance, the railroads do an immense haulage job on their 210,000-mile network. Each day 90,000 railroad cars, carrying a mean 58 tons of cargo set out on a journey which averages 500 miles. The average train is 65 cars long and weighs 5000 + tons.

Regarded as one system, the US railroad network is easily the largest in the world.

Its agencies are as follows:

ASSOCIATION OF AMERICAN RAILROADS
1920 L Street NW,
Washington, DC 20036.

DEPARTMENT OF TRANSPORTATION
400 7th Street SW,
Washington, DC 20590.

INTERSTATE COMMERCE COMMISSION (ICC)
12th Constitution Avenue NW,
Washington, DC 20423.

Locomotive Landmarks
The first locomotive to run on rails in America was a demonstration model built to the design of a certain Colonel John Stevens – the Father of American Railroads – of Hoboken, New Jersey in 1826. *Stourbridge Lion* of the Delaware and Hudson came from Foster, Rastrick & Company of Stourbridge, England in 1829 and was the first attempt to use steam traction commercially. The first American-built steam locomotive of the basic form which we know today was the 2-2-0 *Old Ironsides* built by a mechanic called Mathias Baldwin in 1831 for the Philadelphia, Germantown & Norristown RR. Baldwin and the works he founded at Philadelphia went on to produce 60,000 more over the next 125 years. In 1836 the first 4-4-0 was built for the same railroad by another Philadelphia builder, James Brooks. The 4-4-0s were supplied by numerous builders to virtually all the US roads; 20,000 in all were made during the next sixty years. Not for nothing was the type known as American standard, being essentially simple, with the mechanism easily accessible, rugged and eminently suitable for the light rough tracks of a pioneering land. The military railway operations of the Civil War and the building of the first transcontinental lines were monopolized by these locomotives.

In the latter half of the century, other wheel arrangements such as 2-6-0, 2-8-0 and 4-6-0 became common, under the names *Mogul*, *Consolidation* and *Ten-wheeler*. The fact that these and other types are to this day known

worldwide by these American names reflects the influence which the US school of locomotive design had upon the world.

Around the turn of the century the American steam locomotive was brought rapidly to its final form, all the remaining elements being introduced in quick succession between 1895 and 1905. The typical 1895 locomotive had a narrow firebox of limited power-producing capacity between the wheels, slide-valve cylinders, Stephenson's valve gear also between the wheels and used unsuperheated steam.

Ten years and 40,000 locomotives later, the industry was producing wide-firebox superheated locomotives, with trailing trucks, piston-valve cylinders, and accessible Walschearts valve-gear in full view. Mechanical stoking was also introduced during this period. A whole series of new wheel arrangements resulted; 4-4-2, 4-6-2, 2-6-2, and 2-10-2. The 2-8-2 or *Mikado* type (so called because the original examples went to Japan) was, in the end, built in the largest numbers – 14,000 in America alone. The period was also notable for much experimentation with and the discarding of multi-cylindered compound designs.

The forty years that remained for steam development were largely devoted to perfection of detail and the building of ever-more powerful locomotives. Even by 1905, North America had steam locomotives more powerful than any built elsewhere in the world subsequently and in the end America had ones which led the world by at least fifty percent on all size and power counts.

Articulated locomotives – that is, those with a hinge in the middle – which also appeared during this turn-of-the-century period, eventually took weights up to 550 tons, grate areas to over 180 sq ft and tractive efforts above 175,000lb. Even straight two cylinder ones reached 400 tons, 122 sq ft and 97,000lb respectively.

Detail improvements were aimed mainly at reducing maintenance cost. Frames, cylinders and other detail were cast as a single monobloc casting; roller bearings replaced plain ones and so on.

In 120 years of steam in the USA, approximately 175,000 locomotives were built and of these the American Locomotive Company and its constituents built 78,000. Baldwins produced 59,000 and various US railroads 13,000 in their own shops. The remainder were built by smaller firms. Around 37,000 were exported and countless others (notably in the USSR and China, but in Germany, Great Britain and many other countries also) were built to US or US-like design.

In spite of early promise and no lack of know-how, electric locomotives were used very little in North America; the only two electrifications of any size were on the Chicago, Milwaukee, St Paul & Pacific and Pennsylvania railroads. On the other hand, the story of the diesel-electric locomotive (which in real truth is an electric locomotive which carries its own generating station) in the USA is also the story of the diesel locomotive in the world.

The US diesel locomotive is a proven, rugged

and relatively simple machine, whose weight and size allow it to go anywhere a freight car can. It also allows as many locomotive units as are required to provide power for any given haulage task to be plugged in together and the whole handled and controlled as a single locomotive. The only limit is the strength of the couplings and even this can be overcome by having radio-controlled slave units cut into the *middle* of the train, instead of the head.

Most of the credit is due to the conglomerate, General Motors, who, through their subsidiary Electromotive Diesels (EMD), offered a production unit for passenger service as early as 1938. Electromotive had cut its teeth on gas- and diesel-electric cars and trains, but it is a long stride from such things to work-horse locomotives.

Operations and Services
Pullman sleepers, in the days when trains were the only way to travel, were not for the majority of Americans. They had to make do with plain sit-up coaches, but most of the 200,000+ miles of railroad had passenger service, even if it was only a rickety combine car at the end of the daily freight. Fifty years ago the railroad carried 600 million passengers a year – now this figure has fallen to 270 million, mostly commuters in and out of New York City and Chicago: passenger trains now only serve a mere 30,000 miles of route, with 5400 cars in use.

Viewed as an entity, the US railroads, in spite of all that is wrong, haul vast amounts of freight: in specific terms 450 million tons a year, hauled an average distance of 530 miles in trains with an average pay-load of 1400 tons. There are over 500,000 freight cars. Although still a very small proportion of the total, two types of freight movement are growing. The first one is known as TOFC/COFC (Trailer On Freight Car/Container On Freight Car); in this way the economy of road transport for local collection and delivery can be combined with the economy of rail for the long haul. The second growth area is in the use of what are called unit trains, carrying bulk materials from one source to one destination – a flow of coal from a mine to one large consumer is an example. In extreme cases – for example, with the aid of automatic loading and unloading – the utilization of expensive gondola or hopper cars is improved from so many days per trip to so many trips per day. The current fleet of 27,000 diesel and 150 electric locomotives are almost wholly engaged in freight-train operation; the twelve steam locomotives still on the books are confined exclusively to pleasure use.

The traditional US method of ensuring safety of operation, which has spread widely around the world, is based on the timetable, employees' watches and the superiority or inferiority of particular trains. One train can be inferior to another by direction, or class, or both; it is the duty of an inferior train to keep clear of a superior one when it is due, by entering a siding. A gentleman called the dispatcher (in whose infallibility it is necessary to have an almost religious faith) is in charge of each section of the railroad and he is empowered to issue orders, normally by telegraph or telephone, which vary the timetable and the rights of one train over another.

Although many miles of lines worked this way still remain, the normal thing now for any route of importance is for all movements to be fully signalled, all switches to be interlocked and the presence of trains detected by continuous track circuiting. Control of a whole route can be concentrated in what under the traditional system would have been the dispatcher's office. In this way signalling practice approaches worldwide standardization.

THE PULLMAN COMPANY
165 North Canal Street,
Chicago, Illinois 60606.

Born in 1831, George Mortimer Pullman produced his first sleeping car, by converting a Chicago & Alton RR day coach, in 1859. His first luxury sleeper was the *Pioneer* of 1864. Recognition came when *Pioneer* was used to convey President Lincoln's funeral party from Chicago to Springfield, Illinois. In 1867 the Pullman Palace Car Company was formed, with the intention of providing hotel comforts for railway travellers. His first dining car, the *Delmonico*, entered service in 1868. By the turn of the century, most of his competitors had been taken over or put out of business. At its peak before the crash of 1929, Pullman had 9000 sleeping cars, parlour cars and diners in operation on the majority of the railroads in North America. Pullman day coaches, known as parlour cars, ran on short runs and it was the parlour car which became known as a Pullman in Europe.

In contrast to Europe, where transverse beds prevailed, the standard arrangement of Pullman sleeping berths was longitudinal, with wide lower and narrower upper berths in each section. Privacy was assured by heavy curtains, drawn at night along either side of the central aisle.

Later came Pullman cars with rooms or compartments, some of which had transverse berths. The luxuries and the comforts of most of those world-famous trains upon which individual railroads so prided themselves were almost all provided by Pullman.

Every imaginable frill could be found on the cars of the fleet. Observation cars of course, club cars, bars and lounges, master bedrooms, even a choice of fresh- or salt-water baths, library cars, radio and telephone rooms and so on. But even the humblest sleeper had a name. Pullman names ranged from *Eva*, through conventional *Hickory Creek* and *George Washington*, to exotic *Quantzintecomatzin*.

Pullman cars were built and overhauled in an immense works in the company town of Pullman near Calumet, Michigan and there was also a nationwide organization to maintain and run them. 'Pullman' deserved its reputation – success was due to applying the highest possible standards in all things.

With the usual 'un-wisdom' of political organizations, in 1940 the US government brought an anti-trust suit against Pullman.

Top: This Alaska Railroad steam engine is no longer in active service but does provide an educational 'toy'.

Above: Wagons are unloaded from SS Alaska at Whittier, Alaska.

Seven years later, after protracted legal proceedings, the company was forced to dispose of the operating side of its business to a consortium of 59 user railroads. The construction side still trades as a railcar builder under the name of Pullman Standard.

AKRON, CANTON & YOUNGSTOWN RAILROAD
See Other US Railroads

ALASKA RAILROAD
Federal Railroad Administration,
Anchorage, Alaska 99510.

See map on pages 126–127.

The Alaska Railroad began in 1903 as the privately financed Alaska Central Railway, to run from the port of Seward to the gold fields at Fairbanks. It was a financial disaster and only one sixth of the distance was completed when construction ceased *circa* 1910. The US government then took over and in 1914 passed an Act authorizing construction using Federal funds. The line was completed in 1923, but since the combined population of the three towns the railroad served was under 6000, it is not surprising that heavy losses were incurred. World War II caused an explosion in traffic demand, and since that time the railroad has succeeded in balancing its books.

Fifty-four locomotives, 1606 freight cars and 38 passenger cars are used to haul 800,000 passengers and 1.9 million tons of freight annually over the 525-mile line which includes spectacular scenery and some quite heavy engineering works.

UNITED STATES OF AMERICA

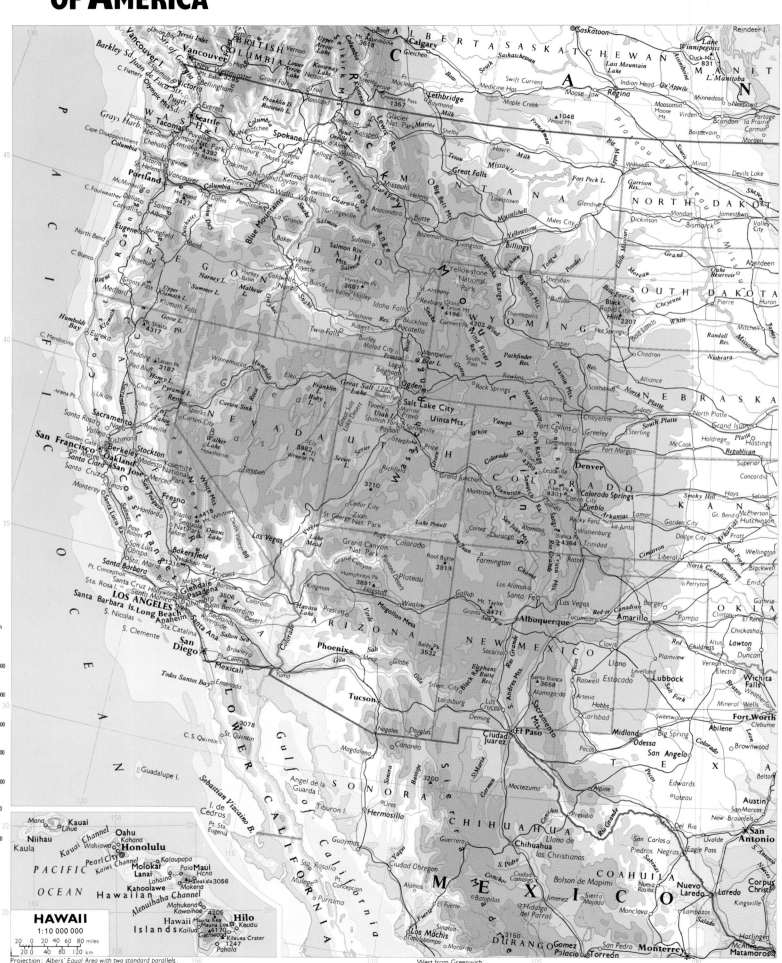

HAWAII
1:10 000 000

Projection: Albers' Equal Area with two standard parallels.

West from Greenwich

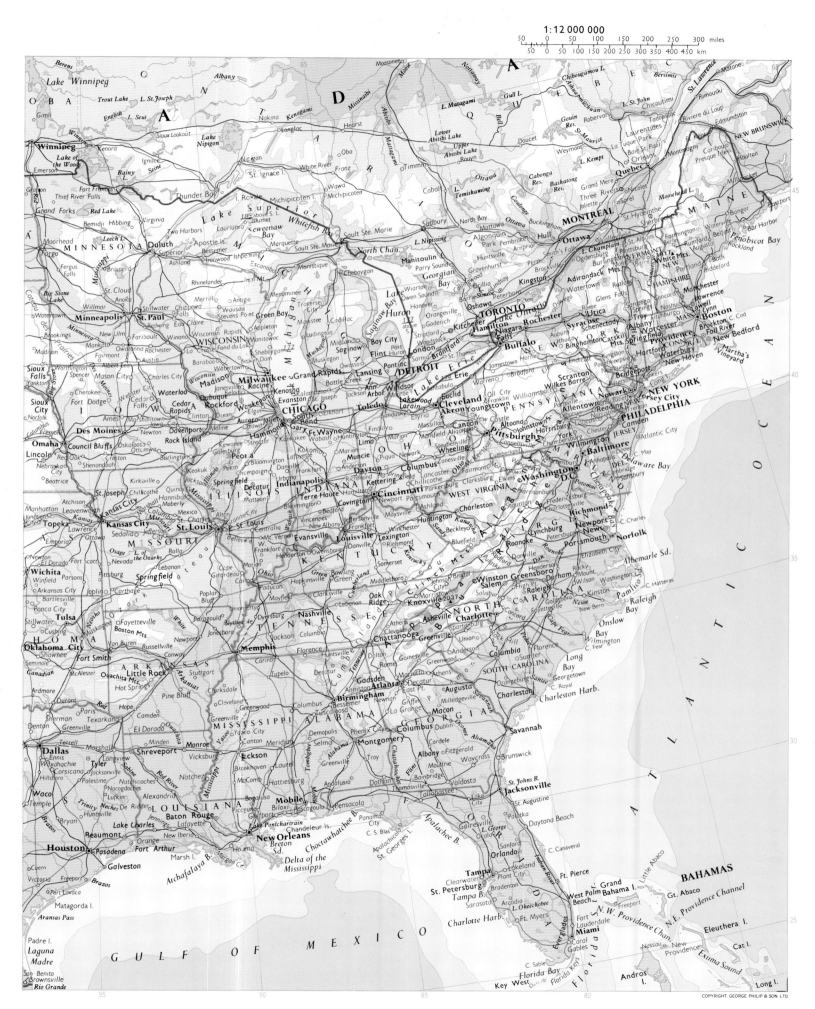

1:12 000 000

Left: Typical of the new equipment that dominates Amtrak's Washington to Boston Northeast Corridor is this Amfleet-equipped train at Elkton, Maryland.

Below left: Track crews and highly specialized equipment have begun the major task of upgrading Amtrak's Washington to Boston Northeast Corridor. The $1.75 billion programme will result in 120 mph speeds throughout the corridor by 1981.

AMTRAK – NATIONAL RAIL PASSENGER CORPORATION

400 N Capital Street NW, Washington, DC 20001.

The National Rail Passenger Corporation (Amtrak for short) was formed by Act of Congress in 1970 in order to provide long-distance inter-city passenger transport in the USA. For some time this had been a loss-making operation for the railroads and, while the government had powers to compel them to continue running passenger trains, the service given under such forced circumstances was not all that could be desired – with a few honourable exceptions. It was a voluntary deal (certain roads opted out) which involved handing over passenger equipment to Amtrak in return for no longer having to bear passenger-train losses.

The 26,000 miles of route served by Amtrak

trains are only sixty percent of those operating just before the take-over and serve a mere thirteen percent of US mileage as a whole. Most Amtrak trains are now hauled by Amtrak's own 370-strong locomotive fleet and a high proportion are equipped with new (post-1970) 'Amfleet' cars. Since the Penn Central debacle and the formation of Conrail, Amtrak has completely taken over the Washington–New York–Boston 'northeast corridor' tracks – this was the only predominantly passenger inter-city line in the country. Overall expenses are currently over twice the receipts and it is necessary to go cap-in-hand to the government each year to make up the losses; all this in aid of one percent of inter-city travel. There are 2015 passenger cars; almost twenty million passengers are carried annually.

The service which Amtrak offers its customers is on the plain and simple side and should

not be confused with the service provided by the now-legendary luxury trains of the past. One of the selling points to Congress for the Amtrak operation was low vulnerability of rail travel to interruption in bad weather. Alas, experience, particularly in the bad winter of 1976–77, has shown Amtrak to perform poorly in these circumstances; it almost had to close down in February 1977.

Most of these shortcoming are not fundamental to rail but arise directly or indirectly from a shortage of funds; there is little doubt that it is sound national policy to keep a vestigial rail passenger service in being until, as anticipated, it becomes the major mode of travel of the early 2000s. Outside the Boston–New York–Washington 'corridor', on which a frequent service is maintained, the principal long-distance passenger trains are listed on the following page.

Right and below right: Two views of piggy-back trains hauled by a three-unit diesel through the Cajon Pass, California.

Below: Amtrak's 'Broadway Limited', en route from New York and Washington to Chicago, rounds Pennsylvania's Horseshoe Curve, a section of track cutting through the Appalachian Mountains.

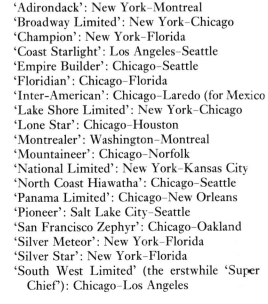

'Adirondack': New York–Montreal
'Broadway Limited': New York–Chicago
'Champion': New York–Florida
'Coast Starlight': Los Angeles–Seattle
'Empire Builder': Chicago–Seattle
'Floridian': Chicago–Florida
'Inter-American': Chicago–Laredo (for Mexico
'Lake Shore Limited': New York–Chicago
'Lone Star': Chicago–Houston
'Montrealer': Washington–Montreal
'Mountaineer': Chicago–Norfolk
'National Limited': New York–Kansas City
'North Coast Hiawatha': Chicago–Seattle
'Panama Limited': Chicago–New Orleans
'Pioneer': Salt Lake City–Seattle
'San Francisco Zephyr': Chicago–Oakland
'Silver Meteor': New York–Florida
'Silver Star': New York–Florida
'South West Limited' (the erstwhile 'Super Chief'): Chicago–Los Angeles

'Sunset Limited': Los Angeles–New Orleans – (New York)

ANN ARBOR RAILROAD
See Other US Railroads

ATCHISON, TOPEKA & SANTA FE RAILWAY – Santa Fe
80 East Jackson Boulevard, Chicago, Illinois 60604.

It is fitting that the first major railway in the North American section of this Atlas is also one of the greatest; it even has the rare distinction of being immortalized in song. It is the only line whose metals run all the way from Chicago to California and is currently among the few US railroads in excellent physical and financial shape. To this, a remarkably high average length of haul for freight (655 miles), a passenger-carrying count of zero and a certain diversification into non-railway activities, combine to contribute.

The first sod was turned by Colonel Cyrus K Holliday at Topeka, Kansas in 1872 and by 1887 Los Angeles had been reached. A quirk of its development was that the name-towns of this huge transcontinental concern are three places of relatively modest importance and not very far apart in the southwestern USA; only two are on the present main line. In the west the route followed the approximate line of the old Santa Fe covered-wagon trail.

Later on, tentacles of the system reached Oakland on San Francisco Bay and the Gulf of Mexico at Galveston, Texas, but the spread was always oriented towards what railways best provide, *viz*, mass long-distance transportation–hence, prosperity in good times and survival in bad ones, such as the present.

Extreme right, top: An Atchison, Topeka & Santa Fe switch engine at Stockton, California.

Extreme right, bottom: An aerial view of Santa Fe Railroad's computerized classification yard at Barstow, California.

Right: Amtrak's 'Broadway Limited', en route from New York to Chicago.

Bottom: Amtrak's 'North Coast Hiawatha' which runs from Chicago to Seattle.

Below: Amtrak's Los Angeles–San Diego train shows Amfleet cars running alongside the Pacific Ocean.

A brief marriage with and divorce from what is now the Frisco (St Louis and San Francisco RR) in the early years of the century caused a 'hiccup' in this continuing satisfactory state of affairs; but in general Santa Fe has managed to please both its patrons and its stockholders.

At the present time Santa Fe's 1686 blue and yellow diesel locomotives haul 77 million tons of freight annually an average distance of 655 miles. The annual expenses of 1.1 million dollars are 81 percent of the receipts from railway operations on the 12,000-mile system.

The Santa Fe chose a fairly easy route across the US, but two notable river crossings were unavoidable, namely that across the Mississippi at Fort Madison and across the Missouri at at Sibley. The Fort Madison bridge is 3347ft long with 24 spans including one of 525ft which opens to river traffic; at Sibley the structure is 4034ft long and has 39 spans. There is a 225ft high bridge across the Canyon Diabolo (Devil's Gulch) in Arizona. The summit of the system is the 7590ft Raton pass in Colorado, approached by long 1 in 33 gradients. The longest tunnel, situated in Pittsburg, California, is only just over a mile long.

The quality of Santa Fe's permanent way (as well as the state of its finances) is reflected in a permitted speed as high as 90 mph and the use of rail up to 136 lb/yd, carrying axle-loads as high as thirty tons. Such a combination is not paralleled elsewhere in the railway world.

Among the particular characteristics of the Santa Fe's steam motive power fleet (the majority of which came from Baldwin's) was early experimentation – and early disenchantment – with Mallet articulateds, including some amazing 2-10-10-2s with (believe it or not) a hinge in the boiler. The road gave its name to the 2-10-2 type, introduced in 1902, but it is better known perhaps for 4-8-4s, coal-fired like most AT&SF steam power, that ran without change from Kansas City to Los Angeles, a distance of 1780 miles. Sixteen wheel tenders, holding 19,600 gallons of water and 5600 gallons of oil were provided on these locomotives and on their freight equivalents – magnificent 2-10-4s with big 74in driving wheels. Extensible chimneys were a feature, erected for running over the many miles of overbridge-free territory in order to keep smoke clear of the cabs. The last steam locomotive was retired in 1959.

Santa Fe was a pioneer of dieselization, purchasing its first units (for the 'Super Chief') from General Motors as early as 1935. Freight diesels came in 1941. During the war the government controlled and rationed the supply of diesel locomotives. However, because of the need to haul in water to the desert areas in the southwest for steam operation, Santa Fe was able to obtain priority and, accordingly, pioneered the dieselization of two complete divisions in 1943.

Throughout its 85-year period as a transcontinental passenger carrier, the standards set by Santa Fe were a byword for excellence. For example, the classic Chicago–Los Angeles 39½-hour 'Super Chief' became a legend. The 'Super Chief's' predecessors, the all-Pullman 'Chief' of 1923, the 'De-Luxe' (limited to sixty passengers, extra fare $25 in the dollars of 1910) and the 'California Limited' of 1897 were equally notable. Coach-class passengers were not neglected and they had their own Chicago–Los Angeles streamliner 'El Capitan' from 1938 onwards.

A superb standard of meal service both in the stations and on the trains was also a feature; in the early days in the pioneer West, it was of unheard-of quality. Surprisingly, an Englishman called Fred Harvey was responsible, obtaining the catering concession from the Santa Fe in 1869. Not only were his food and his restaurants respectable but also his waitresses. Until then and elsewhere the ladies who served in the eating houses of the West had a certain 'reputation'. The Harvey girls' respect-

ability was, however, not at the expense of their charm, because among the good things that Fred Harvey offered his customers should be the thousands of his girls who married and settled in Santa Fe territory.

The present Santa Fe, of course, answers a laconic 'none' when asked how many passengers it carries. Freight is the lifeblood and its flow at say, Winslow, Arizona is as remarkable a sight as that of the nearby Grand Canyon of the Colorado River. The procession of mile-long 80 mph trains on the double track main is a tonic to any observer suffering from the pessimism which inevitably follows a close study of the railroad problem in many other parts of the USA.

ATLANTA AND WEST POINT RAILROAD
See Other US Railroads

AUTOTRAIN CORPORATION
1801 K Street NW,
Washington, DC 20006.

'Depend upon it, sir, when a man knows he is to be hanged in a fortnight, it concentrates his mind wonderfully.' Dr Johnson's saying is appropriate to the US organization Autotrain, the only long-distance passenger rail service on the American continent to be run commercially, that is, if it does not make a profit, it does not run. Autotrain covers the 856-mile route from Lorton, fifteen miles south of Washington, to Sanford in Florida and provides a superior version but the *only* example in North America of a kind of service that has developed extensively into a network of 135 routes in Europe. Travellers who sample Autotrain's standard of service report favourably on the effect of its unsubsidized condition. Extension is, alas, precluded by Amtrak's monopoly of passenger movement on most rail routes in the USA.

Autotrain have a fleet of twelve diesel locomotives, 182 passenger and 315 auto-carrying

cars. About 250,000 passengers are carried annually.

BANGOR & AROOSTOOK RAILROAD
See Other US Railroads

BAY AREA RAPID TRANSIT – BART
800 Madison Street,
Oakland, California 94607.

No more vivid illustration of the current move back to railways – and also of the extravagance of ever having moved away – exists than that of the San Francisco Bay Area Rapid Transit. A comprehensive electric railway system was dismantled in the 1930s and effectively replaced by the private car. Soon hideous road congestion, in spite of a vast motorway construction programme, made the citizens return to thoughts of a railroad.

Immediately after World War II, proposals were made to build a new electric railway network. Serious studies began in 1957 and ground was finally broken – by President Lyndon Johnson – on 19 June 1964 for a three-pronged 72-mile system; the shank of the trident was to cross the bay by means of a tunnel formed of prefabricated sections lowered onto and buried in the sea-bed. In spite of the advanced technology used, the legal obstacles put in the BART Authority's way far exceeded any engineering ones, but finally on 16 September 1976, trains began running under the bay, almost thirty years after the project was mooted. Thirty-four stations are now served by a fleet of 450 cars, characterized by a remarkably high running speed of 80 mph and an average one of 50 mph. Extensions are planned.

Equally remarkable and equally a *stupor mundi* is the cable worked San Francisco municipal tramway system connecting with BART at the Powell St station and running up and over the hill to two termini in the Fisherman's Wharf area. The vintage cable cars manage only one-eighth the speed but offer

eight times the thrill.

BESSEMER & LAKE ERIE RAILROAD
See Other US Railroads

BLACK MESA & LAKE POWELL RAILROAD
Page, Arizona.

In the world at large, electric traction is regarded as the only possible long-term solution to the railway problem. This is not the case in the USA where it has been one of the greatest non-events of railroad history. Brand-new American railroads have also been rare recently. On both counts, therefore, the brand-new (1973), all-electric Black Mesa & Lake Powell RR deserves notice – although it is not a common-carrier, is not 100 miles long and has only one train, hauled by a single three-unit electric locomotive.

The isolated BM&LP was built to carry coal dug in northern Arizona to a power station which needed to be situated eighty miles away, near Lake Powell's supplies of Columbia River cooling water. It is equally remarkable as it is free of both ICC regulation and trade union featherbedding. Each time the train makes a loaded trip it conveys 9000 tons of coal – the hopper cars are loaded and unloaded automatically. The original proposal was for train movement also to be handled automatically but this seems to have foundered. Even so, only two operators are needed as opposed to a minimum of five for a similar unit train movement on a common-carrier US railroad; this modest amount of staff and equipment carries almost three million tons of freight per year. Hopefully, it is a signpost to the future.

BOSTON & MAINE CORPORATION
150 Causeway Street,
Boston, Massachusetts 02114.

The Boston & Maine Railroad is the largest of the New England Railroads, serving Maine, New Hampshire, Vermont, Massachusetts and New York. It was formed by mergers over the years of nearly one hundred other railroads, the earliest of which was the Andover and Wilmington which was chartered in 1833 and commenced operation in 1836 between Massachusetts and Maine. The peak year for miles-of-line-in-operation was 1922 when Troy in New York, Bellows Falls and White River Junction in Vermont, Groveton, Berlin, Intervale, and Lincoln in New Hampshire, and Portland, Maine were all on B&M track. This covered 2248 miles of route and with trackage rights on other railroads you could ride on a B&M train to Montreal, Quebec or Bar Harbor in Maine. From that peak there has been a slow decline in mileage until today the railroad covers about 1700 miles.

Although small when compared to the vast railroads in the west, the B&M still holds an important place in American railroad history. It has several notable items in its past, in its plant, in its motive power, and in its services. For example, in western Massachusetts there

was a need for a rail route between Greenfield and the large cities in upstate New York. The Berkshire mountain chain stood squarely across the path of this extension, so in the 1850s a start was made on what was to become the Hoosac Tunnel. Completed in 1876 this was the longest tunnel in North America. It was 4.75 miles in length, bored through solid granite for its entire length and still handles all B&M traffic to the west. Until the end of the steam era electric locomotives were used to pilot trains through this bore. A train arriving at either portal would have its fire banked, the electric engine would couple on ahead and take the whole train, steam engine and all, through to the other side of the mountain. Once through, the steam engine would again assume control.

Bottom left: A BART train approaches Rockridge Station with the Bay Bridge, San Francisco skyline and Mount Sutro in the background.

Bottom: Boston & Maine Railroad's sorting yard at East Deerfield, Massachusetts.

Below: A Boston & Maine RR's Portsmouth to Boston passenger train in the street of Salem, Massachusetts.

As to rolling stock, the B&M was a conventional New England railroad in large part but they did possess some unusual equipment. In recent times they were the first railroad east of the Mississippi River to try a lightweight diesel-electric articulated train. This was called the 'Flying Yankee' and its arrival on the property in 1934 was a bold and innovative step. It was a three-car single-ended streamline train, built of stainless steel by The Budd Company.

The B&M even owned a narrow-gauge line for a short period of time. This was a 3ft gauge branch line which was located in the Franconia Notch region of New Hampshire and served the resort hotels in this scenic mountain area.

As to standard gauge stock, there were in later years two or three notable classes of steam locomotives. One was the T-1 class Berkshire 2-8-4 freight locomotives with their unique Coffin feedwater heater mounted outside the smokebox front, which gave these locomotives a formidable and unmistakable countenance. These were among the first super power classes of freight locomotive built by Lima in 1929.

The last and largest steam power purchased was the R1 class of Mountain 4-8-2s. These dual purpose engines, with fourteen-wheeled centipede tenders, were the last word in modern steam power when delivered by Baldwin Locomotive Works between 1935-41. The handsome appearance of these eighteen engines was enhanced by each one of the class carrying a large name-plate on each side of the running board. The names were chosen from ones submitted by school children and lent a 'touch of class' not often seen on American railroads.

Some of these name-plates are now in museums but none of these locomotives was preserved. There are however, three steam engines still extant: at Edaville tourist railroad along with the 'Flying Yankee' is a 2-6-0; at Science Park in Boston is a latter-day 4-6-2; and at a city park near White River Junction in Vermont is a 4-4-0, built in 1892 by the Manchester Locomotive Works.

In its heyday B&M had an impressive roster of passenger services with named trains such as the 'Bar Harbor Express', the 'East Wind', and the 'Pine Tree Limited' with parlour, sleeper, and dining cars from Boston serving Portland, Maine; Montreal, Quebec; and Bar Harbor, also in Maine. In addition, Boston & Maine participated in through-services between New York and Canada's Maritime Provinces.

The railroad's major passenger terminal was North Station in Boston, which now handles only commuter trains each day, but in the 1930s its 24 tracks were in constant use accommodating the many local trains for eastern Massachusetts as well as the named trains which were arriving and departing for Portland, Halifax, Montreal, Troy and Albany New York, and the west.

The B&M in 1978 is still an independent railroad, not part of the Conrail system, nor a subsidiary of some larger corporation. Its business is now freight only, but it does operate the rail commuter lines for the Massachusetts Bay Transportation Authority. Although not the most prosperous road in the country, it still does the job that was started by the Andover and Wilmington Railroad 140 years ago.

BURLINGTON NORTHERN INC – BN
BN Building, 176 East Fifth Street,
St Paul, Minnesota 55101.

The first section of what is now the Burlington Northern received its charter in 1849 and was completed the following year. It connected the town of Aurora – a suburb of Chicago – with another line leading into that city. The present BN was formed as recently as 1970 (at which time it was the longest railroad in North America) by the merger of three major lines: first, the Chicago, Burlington and Quincy, which served the area west of Chicago ('Everywhere West' was its slogan) and reached out to Denver, Omaha, Kansas City and in particular the seven cities, St Paul–Minneapolis; second, the Northern Pacific (NP); and third, the Great Northern (GN). Both NP and GN connected the twin cities with the Pacific north-west.

NP received its charter by act of Congress over President Lincoln's signature in 1864, only two years after the Union Pacific's (with whom the CB&Q also connected) was granted. The usual land grants and subsidies were offered for a line to follow the route originally explored in 1804 by the famous pioneer travellers, Rogers and Clark. Even so, progress was slow and the financial crash of 1873 brought construction to a halt for six years. Movement of troops to put down the Sioux rising of 1876 was greatly aided by the existence of the railroad, while the NP people found, rather to their surprise, that, with the spur of military expediency, it was quite possible to operate in 45°F below zero temperatures and several feet

Top left: A pair of new diesel locomotives for the Boston & Maine RR.

Top: A Burlington Northern train on the Gasman Coulee Bridge in North Dakota.

Centre left: A Burlington Northern coal train at Cordero Mine, Wyoming.

Centre right: A typical Burlington Northern freight train hauled by a four-unit diesel.

Left: The Great Northern Railway's 5000 hp electric locomotive, takes a freight train through the Cascade Mountains near Leavenworth, Washington. Although this was a modern electric locomotive, the need for this relatively short electrified section came to an end with the advent of powerful diesel traction.

of snow. The settlement induced by the pacification of the country and the existence of rail transport led, in 1879, to an upsurge in confidence and a resumption of progress. The golden spike was driven in the presence of President Ulysses Grant on 21 April 1883. The second transcontinental line was complete.

The GN was a very different and more personal affair. Its driving force was a certain James Jerome Hill. Without government assistance and in the face of universal prognostication of disaster he built his Great Northern Railway through to the Pacific in three years. The last spike (an iron one this time) was driven without ceremony on 18 September 1893 – even Hill himself was not present. No doubt he had set his sights on a great day a short ten years ahead when his steamship *Minnesota* would carry the GN flag on to China, connecting with his all-Pullman 'Oriental Limited' from Chicago.

The route taken by the GN was well to the north of the NP, in fact close to the Canadian border. The line was well-engineered and soundly constructed; very little rebuilding has been necessary since. JJ avoided financial disaster by making immense efforts to develop agriculture in the lands opened up by his line and appeared, unlike most of his contemporaries, to put the long-term benefits to his

Above: Burlington Northern's daily fast freight from Galveston, Texas, heads for its Seattle terminus headed by three 3600 hp diesel electric locomotives. This train, shown in the spectacular Wind River Canyon, Texas, moves shipments from the Gulf Coast to the Pacific northwest.

Right: A caboose brings up the rear of a long coal train on the Burlington Northern. Wagons used in modern American railroad service are huge and the caboose sports comforts scarcely dreamed of in the heyday of railroads.

Below: A Chicago Burlington & Quincy Railroad 4000 hp passenger locomotive.

homeland ahead of short-term money-making for himself – not that he was by any means poverty stricken when he died in 1909 leaving 53 million dollars.

The CB&Q – called for short 'the Burlington' or even 'the Q' – laid its rails over the flat wheatlands of the midwest – it is said nowadays to be never out of sight of a grain elevator. This country would have presented few problems in construction were it not for three rivers – the Mississippi, the Ohio and the Missouri – which crossed the Q's path. The bridge at Metropolis, Illinois over the Ohio includes the longest single girder span ever made – 720ft – in a total length of 7700ft. Subsidiary lines – like the famed narrow-gauge Denver, South Park and Pacific (later Colorado & Southern) – were built over less easy terrain.

The GN and the NP had to cross both the Rockies and the Cascades: GN's 7.75-mile Cascade Tunnel is the longest in the US. The 134-mile division in which it lay was electrified on the 25-cycle AC system, from 1912 until 1956 when diesel traction took over. The longest bridge on the system is the Young's Bay bridge at Astoria, Oregon, which is a 8184ft timber trestle of 592 spans. The highest is at Opal City, Oregon, which has a 340ft span arch 320ft high.

Burlington was notable as one of the handful of American railroads that constructed many of its own steam locomotives: excellent, sensible but not specially notable machines – many oilburning – emerged from the West Burlington shops. The railroad has its place forever as, after Germany, the pioneering path-finder of diesel-electric traction. The first of the famous streamline 'Zephyrs' went into service on 10 January 1934 between Chicago and St Paul-Minneapolis. Others followed including the overnight 'Denver Zephyr' with sleeping accommodation.

The other two partners reacted to the more severe nature of their terrain. When other roads were using 4-4-0s and 4-6-0s, both NP and GN were noted for using 4-8-0s or Mastodons – a type very rare elsewhere in North America, then or since. (One supplied to the GN in 1898 was noted as the heaviest locomotive in the world.) Both lines in the later years of steam had articulated power that was greater than Union Pacific's 'Big Boy' on particular counts. In fact, GN is reckoned to have had the first successful Mallet articulated in the USA, a 2-6-6-2 which came from Baldwins in 1906. In 1936, GN's own Hillyard shops turned out a 2-8-8-2 which had the largest heating surface ever successfully applied to any locomotive boiler. NP in 1938 obtained a 'Yellowstone' 2-8-8-4 from Baldwins which had the largest grate or fire area (182 sq ft) ever known. The reason for this was the local lignite coal used on NP. (It gave the British 4-6-2 *Flying Scotsman* [renowned for being unchoosy about the quality of its diet] severe indigestion and the indignity of diesel assistance when owner Alan Pegler went west – figuratively as well as literally – with it over NP in 1972.)

The same lignite put NP among the honourable handful of lines who have given their

name to a widely used locomotive type. The need for a big firebox meant a four-wheel instead of a two-wheel trailing truck under what would otherwise have been some 4-8-2s supplied by Baldwins in 1926; hence, the 4-8-4 or Northern which later became the standard passenger power on more than thirty US railroads. It was rightly felt that what was good for lignite burning would be even better for high quality coal. Later NP Northerns took the eighteen-car 'North Coast Limited' the first 1008 miles westward from St Paul without engine change, a world record for coal-firing locomotives.

As regards the new megalith, Burlington Northern, the welding of the parts into the whole was made easier by many years of close association, when most GN as well as most NP trains were handed over at St Paul to the Burlington for onward transit to Chicago and vice versa. One measure taken was the installation of Southern Pacific's computer-based railroad management system – called TOPS on SP but named COMPASS on BN. COMPASS was fully cut over in 1972.

As might be expected BN's combination of many a-few-cars-a-day branches in the farm belt with some prodigous transcontinental hauls has not made it terribly prosperous, but it has not yet fallen into a disaster situation either, although expenses of 1740 million dollars are 97 percent of receipts. Consolidation of duplicate lines and the like have permitted a reduction of BN route mileage from 31,725 in 1970 to 24,600 today. Currently, BN's 2500 locomotives annually haul 125 million tons of freight an average distance of 558 miles and, additionally, transport twelve million commuters in 119 passenger cars.

Left: Diesels-in-multiple head a climbing eastbound train towards the summit of Marias Pass on the Burlington Northern Railroad.

Below: A posed photograph of a Baltimore and Ohio train with 'President' class 4-6-2 in the 1930s.

CHESSIE SYSTEM INC
Terminal Tower,
Cleveland, Ohio 44101

Chessie's corporate history goes back to 1785 when the James River Company received its charter. As president of the Company we find no less a figure than George Washington and no railway in the world can claim a more distinguished father-figure than that. Chessie's oldest railway constituent was the fabled Baltimore & Ohio Railroad, incorporated in 1827, opened (with horse traction) in 1830. It thus became the first common-carrier railroad in the USA or, for that matter, on the American continent. Regular steam operation began the following year.

B&O remained in the forefront of progressive railroads – actually taking delivery in 1935 of the first production model diesel-electric locomotive units – until 1973, when financial problems allowed coal-hauler Chesapeake & Ohio to take over the company. B&O reached its declared objective, the Ohio River, in 1852. Other constituents (absorbed later) took trains to St Louis, Chicago and – via running rights over Central of New Jersey – to a passenger terminal on the west bank of the Hudson River opposite New York City.

At Baltimore in 1895, through the 1.5-mile Howard Street tunnel, B&O installed the first main-line electrification in the United States. Low-voltage DC was used; originally the conductors were overhead, but in 1901 the system was changed to third-rail. This was the longest tunnel on the line. The oldest railway viaduct in the world is also claimed: the Thomas Viaduct on the original line out of Baltimore. Other notable bridges include the

$1\frac{1}{4}$-mile bridge over the Susquehanna River at Havre de Grace, Maryland (the longest on the system) and a remarkable lifting bridge of 558ft span, which carries the connection to subsidiary Staten Island Rapid Transit across a stretch of water called Arthur Kill, in the New York area. This is thought to be the largest span of any moveable bridge in the world.

The 'Capitol Limited' was B&O's all-Pullman 'flag train' from Baltimore and Wash-ington to Chicago and in quality of service it rivalled its competitors' 'Broadway Limited' and 'Twentieth Century Limited'. Through cars were provided to and from New York.

Chesapeake & Ohio as a company did not appear until 1868, but *its* earliest railway con-stituent, the Louisa Railroad Company of Virginia, dated back to 1836. Expansion through amalgamation, purchase and new construction took C&O from its main base in the coal-fields of Virginia to the Atlantic Ocean at Newport News, as well as to Chicago, Washington, Detroit, Buffalo and into Canada along the northern shore of Lake Erie. Mil-waukee was served by car-ferry across Lake Michigan. The latest C&O take-overs before Baltimore & Ohio were the Pere Marquette RR (in Michigan) and the Western Maryland. Incidentally, the B&O absorption had been preceded by an 'affiliation' ten years earlier.

The peak of C&O steam power was a world peak in that some amazing 2-6-6-6 steam locomotives built in 1941 recorded the largest power output in service of any steam locomotive ever made. Their wheel arrangement was also unique and, like the rest of the fleet, two great air-pumps mounted on the smokebox front gave a ferocious appearance in keeping with their capabilities.

Inevitably, C&O's Number One train was called 'The George Washington'. It ran from Washington to Cincinnati with through cars serving New York, Chicago, St Louis and Detroit. In 1932 a re-equipment earned it the title of the first fully air-conditioned sleeping-car train in the world. Very little passenger traffic is now handled – there are only 25 passenger cars on the combined Chessie system – but one notes with pleasure that trains for steam lovers are included.

The longest bridge on the 11,190-mile combined system is 2.75 miles long at Richmond, Virginia, and the longest tunnel the 1.75-mile Big Bend tunnel, also in that State. A recorded 220 million tons of traffic each year are hauled an average distance of 250 miles, using a fleet of 2008 diesel locomotives and 205,000 cars. Expenses are currently 93 percent of receipts.

CHICAGO & ILLINOIS MIDLAND RAILWAY
See Other US Railroads

Top left: The Chesapeake & Ohio 'George Washington' express at Romulus, Michigan.

Extreme left: A Baltimore & Ohio M-1 class 2-8-8-4 on the Cranberry Grade, West Virginia, with coal for Terra Alta.

Left: A Chesapeake & Ohio coal train heads up the grade led by a 2-6-6-6 Mallet.

Right top: A Baltimore & Ohio train at Monroe, Michigan.

Right centre: A Chicago, Milwaukee, St Paul & Pacific double-deck push-pull train arrives at Chicago's Union Station.

Right bottom: A Chicago, Milwaukee, St Paul & Pacific road-switcher and local freight at Seattle.

CHICAGO, MILWAUKEE, ST PAUL & PACIFIC RAILROAD COMPANY –
The Milwaukee Road
Union Station,
Chicago, Illinois 60606.

The Chicago, Milwaukee, St Paul & Pacific is another railroad that remains as yet unaffected by the present merger mania.

The first section opened was the Milwaukee & Waukesha RR of 1851 and by 1863 the Milwaukee & St Paul Railway was operating 830 miles of road. It was extended to Chicago in 1873 (the next year saw Chicago added to the Railway's name) and by 1900, 6000 miles of line – tentacles went out as far afield as Kansas City – were operated. It became the anti-penultimate transcontinental when the Pacific was reached in 1909; the present title was adopted in 1913, making three (or four, if you count Union Pacific's sidelong approach) routes from Chicago to the Pacific northwest. Alas, it is now the exception that proves the rule that the big long-distance western railroads are financially viable. Its two main competitors – Great Northern and Northern Pacific – amalgamated in 1960 (see the Burlington Northern entry) and their combined strength has been too much for the Milwaukee RR. Bankruptcy could not be staved off, even by a reduction in expenditure that has involved 33 percent of the line's mileage being subject to slow orders. So many locomotives are laid up awaiting overhaul that others are having to be hired to cover day-to-day demands.

It is sad to see a once successful and inspiring concern in danger of losing its corporate identity. The Milwaukee is best known for two things: it was the only railroad in America where it was possible to make a journey of more than 400 miles entirely by electric traction and the only railroad in the world to run steam trains which needed to reach 100 mph to keep time. Begun in 1914, completed in 1920 and entirely justified by its economics, the electrification covered the mountain sections of the transcontinental route, where it crossed the Bitter Root and Cascade ranges respectively. The former covered the 440-mile section from Harlowtown, Montana, to Avery, Idaho, and the latter, the 207 miles from Othello to Tacoma, Washington. An extention to Seattle came in 1927. A 220-mile gap separated the two electric sections and this was never filled. Of the very powerful electric locomotives used, one might single out for mention the famous 'bi-polars' with 24 driving wheels or the triple-unit 'box cab' freight units of the 2-B-B + B-B + B-B-2 wheel arrangement. The line used 3000v DC current, generated by water power. It was the first of only two major main-line electrifications in the USA. In 1974 the wires were taken down after straight electric traction was abandoned and diesel-electric locomotives ran through over the previously electrified sections.

'Swift of foot was Hiawatha' – certainly the steam-hauled streamlined luxury expresses that were introduced by the Milwaukee Road in 1935 between Chicago, Milwaukee and St Paul-Minneapolis were appropriately named. Specially built oilburning 4-4-2s were used and handled up to nine cars on a $6\frac{1}{2}$ hour timing for the 425 miles, including eight stops. (The best Amtrak time today is $8\frac{3}{4}$ hours.) The trains were immensely successful and soon enough it was a question of 4-6-4s handling fourteen cars and it is thought that the run of 78.3 miles timetabled at 58 minutes between Sparta and Portage (81 mph) represented the fastest timing with steam power regularly scheduled anywhere in the world at any time. Other 'Hiawatha' trains served other Milwaukee Road destinations, including the 'Olympian Hiawatha', a luxury train from Chicago to Seattle, which was introduced after diesels had taken over from steam on the non-electrified sections.

CHICAGO & NORTH WESTERN TRANSPORTATION COMPANY – C&NW
400 West Madison Street,
Chicago, Illinois 60606.

A constituent of the Chicago & North Western Railway was the first railroad west of Chicago. This was the Galena & Chicago Union RR, on which the first train ran in October 1848. The C&NW was formed in 1859 and hence is one of the oldest surviving names in US railroading. By the turn of the century the system had extended to 8300 miles; currently it is almost 10,000. Unlike so many railways, it serves the exact area specified in its title, reaching Minneapolis, Duluth and connecting with the Union Pacific at Omaha.

For many years, although at least four other railroads provided a reasonable alternative, the C&NW carried the expresses of the Overland Route between Chicago and the interchange with Union Pacific at Omaha. This included the first transcontinental streamliner, 'City of Portland'. It also was well up in the three-way competition for the lucrative daytime passenger business between Chicago and St Paul-Minneapolis, although it is perhaps characteristic of the line that its '400' expresses (400 miles in 400 minutes) were good in a solid conventional way and had little of the flashiness associated

Extreme left: A Chesapeake & Ohio 4-6-2 pulls a local passenger train through Athens, Ohio. Baltimore & Ohio's 'Cincinnatian' takes water alongside.

Left: Milwaukee Road's No E4 is one of the famous 1-B-D+D-B-1 'bi-polar' electric locomotives of the early 1920s.

Below: A Chicago-Milwaukee train climbs through the Rocky Mountain forests during the snowy winter of 1935.

Top right and above: The Milwaukee Road's famous 'Hiawatha'. Pictured top right is the original high-speed train from Chicago to the twin cities of St Paul and Minneapolis, with oil-fired 4-4-2 locomotive in 1935. Above is a 1950 picture of the same train.

Left: An eight-coach elevated railway train crosses the Chicago River on the Lake Street two-tier opening bridge. The tower on the river bank is a lookout position for the bridge controller watching for river traffic.

with the 'Hiawatha' and 'Zephyr' creations of
its rivals.

History was made when, in 1965, in an
attempt to resolve a situation where no profits
could be made from railroad operations, the
company made over its railway interests to its
employees. The operation of the system has
continued in this way ever since.

Current statistics are:

locomotives	950
passenger cars	282
freight cars	34,000
passenger traffic	2.6 million
(in commuter service)	
freight carried	76 million tons
average length of haul	300 miles
expenses as % of receipts	96%

CHICAGO, ROCK ISLAND & PACIFIC RAILROAD COMPANY
See Southwestern US Railroads

*Right: Chicago & North Western Railway's
double-deck local train in the Chicago area, 1977.*

*Right below: The post-World War II inauguration
of diesel traction on the 'Twin Cities 400' trains of
Chicago and North Western Railway.*

*Right, bottom: The '400' express is a diesel-hauled
C&NW train which runs the '400' miles between
Chicago and the Twin Cities in '400' minutes.*

CHICAGO TRANSIT AUTHORITY
*Merchandise Mart Plaza,
Chicago, Illinois 60654.*

CHICAGO, SOUTH SHORE & SOUTH BEND RAILROAD
*North Carroll Avenue,
Michigan City, Indiana 46360.*

The Chicago Transit Authority operates one
of the only two 100+ mile (in fact the CTA
operates almost 200 miles) city transport railways in the world which are situated other than
in a national capital. Unlike other US cities,
where the unsightly 'L' or elevated railways
have now gone underground, the CTA has
still only ten miles of subway. The central loop
line down the centre of the streets in downtown
Chicago gives its name to the main business
district, the Loop, which it surrounds. The
system has been fully electrified (all except five
miles is equipped on the DC third-rail system)
since the turn of the century, after a few no
doubt rather traumatic years with Forney-
type steam bogie tank locomotives. These were
of a design suitable for traversing 90ft radius
curves at street junctions. Eleven hundred cars
provide service for ninety million passengers
carried each year.

What seems to be in process of becoming *de
facto* part of the Chicago Transit system is the
Chicago, South Shore & South Bend Railroad.
This concern operates – at a considerable loss –

the last seventy-mile remnant of the huge 25,000-mile network of electric inter-urban lines that, during the first quarter of the present century, briefly provided local passenger transport in the USA. Currently a fleet of sixty electric cars handles 1.8 million passengers annually at average speeds well over double that of the CTA.

Chicago also had a remarkable underground narrow-gauge (2ft) freight railway system which operated in 62 miles of tunnel under the principal areas of the city: the tunnels were shared with cables and pipes. There were 150 electric locomotives and 3500 freight cars. Many large warehouse, factories and, of course, depots of the main line railroads, were directly served by conveyors and elevators.

CONRAIL – CONSOLIDATED RAIL CORPORATION

Transportation Center, Six Penn Centre Plaza, Philadelphia, Pennsylvania 19104.

There is little doubt that the two greatest names there have ever been in railroading, financially, technically and operationally, were the New York Central and the Pennsylvania. Grand Central Station, New York and the 'Twentieth Century Limited', which left from it, were, respectively, the most famous station and the most famous train in the world. Penn's nickname 'Standard Railroad of the World' was no figure of speech. Even in 1955 it would have been unthinkable to suggest that twenty years later both would have been brought down into single ignominious bankruptcy, subjected to a thinly disguised form of government con-

Above: Forty-four new diesel locomotives were delivered to Conrail (Consolidated Rail Corporation) as a part of a 217-locomotive, 113 million dollar order received in 1978. With completion of this order, Conrail has more than 4500 diesel locomotives in its fleet, nearly 400 of which have been acquired (new) since Conrail began operations on 1 April 1976.

Left: Pennsylvania Railroad's 'Congressional' express hauled by a GG1 electric locomotive at Eddystone, Pennsylvania.

fiscation and finally swept up into what pessimists regard as a kind of old people's home for the last days of destitute and dying railroads. Optimists say that the conditions under which the Consolidated Rail Corporation will do business are such that there is a reasonable prospect of success, but only time will tell.

The oldest proper section of New York Central (and of Conrail) was the Mohawk and Hudson Railroad between Albany and Schenectady, incorporated in 1826 and opened in 1831. The name New York Central appeared first in 1853 as a consolidation of railroads connecting Albany with Buffalo. The NYC in its final form was created by a further amalgamation of lines in 1914, including the New York Central & Hudson River Railroad and

the Lake Shore & Michigan Southern Railway. The main line of the NYC – much of which was quadruple track until recent years – was the so-called Water Level Route between New York and Chicago; centres such as Montreal, Cincinnati, Columbus, Indianapolis and St Louis were also served. Through running between New York and Chicago was possible from 1866 onwards after completion of a bridge across the Hudson River at Albany.

The first section of what was to become the Pennsylvania Railroad also began operation in 1831, but later in the year. This was the Camden and Amboy Railroad in New Jersey; on 12 November that year, the locomotive *John Bull*, built in England, hauled its first passengers. The 'Pennsy' proper got its charter in

1846 for a line from Philadelphia to Pittsburgh; by 1874 it was a 10,000+ mile system, the largest in the country. The line's Keystone herald very fairly indicated the position it occupied in the economy of the eastern US. It served eight out of the ten largest cities in the USA.

The other lines which have been merged into Conrail had been in trouble longer. The Erie Railroad commenced operations from Pierpont, New York in 1841 and reached Lake Erie at Dunkirk in 1851. It was then the longest railroad in the country with 450 route miles laid to the widest gauge – 6ft – ever used in America. In 1878 conversion to standard gauge took place. There followed a period of wheeling and dealing in its shares which earned the Erie the title 'Scarlet Woman of Wall Street', the effects of which were still noticeable when the 2338-mile road amalgamated with the 968-mile Lackawanna in 1960.

Another lady, dressed in white this time, was Phoebe Snow of the Delaware, Lackawanna & Western Railroad, who made sales talk such as

'Phoebe says and Phoebe knows
   That smoke and cinders ruin clothes
So 'tis a pleasure and delight
   To take that road of anthracite'

to woo passengers to a line that used this clean-burning fuel. The Lackwanna also offered through cars to Chicago from the New Jersey shore; so did Lehigh Valley and Central of New Jersey, although in the last-named case it was just a matter of accommodating the Baltimore & Ohio service. All these lines and the Reading RR as well, served the area between the trunk routes of the New York Central and the Pennsy, providing – until Conrail took them all over – severe competition at any and all intermediate places.

The oldest constituent of the New York, New Haven & Hartford Railroad as well as the oldest of Conrail was the Granite Railway of Boston, built to bring in material for the Boston Bunker Hill monument in 1826. Of course, it was neither steam nor common-carrier. The New Haven was an amalgam of over 200 smaller lines; its trains were accommodated in the Pennsylvania Station in New York and served the New England area. They included the last all-parlour-car train to run in the USA, the 'Merchants Limited', between New York and Boston.

In respect of motive power, it almost suffices to say that New York Central was the owner of high-stepping 4-4-0 No 999, credited (rather dubiously) in 1893 with a world-speed record of 112 mph, while handling the crack 'Empire State Express', predecessor of the 'Twentieth Century Limited'. Right up until steam gave way to diesel, NYC remained in the forefront of locomotive development. Even then it did not give up without a fight, for the 'Niagara' 4-8-4s of 1946 went on and on, putting up figures for performance and overall economics that diesels could only match, not improve upon. Eventually, problems with coal supplies

gave diesel salesmen their chance.

There was a period in the early years of the century when scientific work at its famous Altoona test plant made Pennsy a much acclaimed world leader in steam design. By the 1940s, electrification of the main lines to Washington and Harrisburg had led to steam development taking second place. The picture then was of a fleet of modest-sized locomotives – the legendary K4 4-6-2s were a case in point. As with the diesels which replaced them, when more power was wanted one simply put two (or more) together. After World War II, Pennsy unwisely went away from the simple 'World Standard' concept of steam locomotive and

adopted the more complicated so-called 'Duplex' designs which were, in effect, two engines in the same set of frames. The 'Duplexes' were not successful and again General Motors' salesmen moved in.

Central of New Jersey, Lehigh Valley and Reading were famous for the steam locomotives known as 'camel-backs'. The driver's cab was mounted on top of the boiler half-way along; the fireman, of course, had to work in another cab in the conventional position, but the idea was to give better visibility in either direction. The identical principle has given rise to the 'hood-unit' layout of most modern diesels.

CNJ and LV were the only constituents of

Above: New York Central's New York to Chicago Train of Trains – the 'Twentieth Century Limited' at the peak of its luxury in 1938.

Left: Four GE diesel electric locomotives head a massive Erie Railroad freight train.

Extreme left, top: Conrail's famous Horseshoe Curve on the busy mainline west of Altoona, in central Pennsylvania's Allegheny Mountains.

Extreme left, centre: In the early 1950s even the coal-carrying Erie RR had gone diesel as shown by this posed picture of its then-most-modern three-unit locomotive.

Extreme left, bottom: The 'Empire State Express' near Albany on the New York Central main line.

Top centre: American railroads generally made little use of water troughs between the rails. However, New York Central's No 3130 makes a brave show at the head of a fast freight in July 1945.

Top right: New York, New Haven & Hartford Railroad's streamlined 4-6-4 No 1409 with standard heavyweight cars near Branford, Connecticut in 1938.

Conrail not to have some electrification. The Pennsylvania had by far the largest installation (670 miles at 11,000v AC, 25 cycles) still surviving in America, but much of this is now in Amtrak's hands as owners of the Boston–New York–Washington passenger corridor. Dieselization of all non-electric Conrail operations has, of course, been complete for many years; at present there are nearly 5000 units in service, the largest fleet in North America.

As regards passenger services, the erstwhile 'Twentieth Century Limited' still remains the standard by which other trains are judged, while Pennsy's 'Broadway Limited', still surviving in Amtrak hands, was as good. Conrail

still carries 112 million commuter passengers, annually using 893 cars, on services provided under contract to various state and local government authorities. Grand Central Station, New York, where a great deal of this traffic is handled, is the largest station in the world, with 44 platforms on a 48-acre site.

Conrail ranks first among US railroads on most other counts, including the amount of annual deficit, $626,133 in 1977. There are 145,000 freight cars, in which 269 million tons of freight are carried annually an average distance of 344 miles. Expenses are 120 percent of receipts. In 1979, 16,826 miles of track were controlled by Conrail.

CUMBRES & TOLTEC SCENIC RAILROAD – CATS
PO Box 789, Chama,
New Mexico 87520.

If one takes a view of railways as an art form, then one of the greatest masterpieces among recent survivors was the 200-mile narrow-gauge main line of the Denver & Rio Grande Western RR between Alamosa and Durango on the border between New Mexico and Colorado. It was definitely a railroad on which, when trouble comes, one would expect John Wayne to ride up to the rescue. Indeed he and his successors have done just that on many occasions when films were made using its evocative rolling stock and superb scenery. Such features as steam power driven wide open on four percent grades, rotary steam snow ploughs and whistles which scare the eagles off their nests for miles around, combined to make it something very special.

Carried away by the enthusiasm of the *aficionados*, the States of Colorado and New Mexico were inveigled into buying the 64-mile stretch between Antonito, Colorado and Chama, New Mexico including twelve 2-8-2 steam locomotives and a hundred or so cars. They thus obtained for themselves the dubious privilege of owning the longest museum railway in the world. Regular summer operation is supplemented by an occasional winter happening when the operable steam rotary plough puts on a show unparalleled in the steam-for-pleasure world.

DELAWARE & HUDSON RAILWAY D&H
D&H Building,
Albany, New York 12207.

The first US railroad to employ steam locomotives finds itself 150 years later with the same title – only having dropped the word 'canal' – but with a quite different transportation role. It is now a 'bridge route' connecting eastern Canada with the eastern USA rather than a local canal feeder and mine-run line. By managing to keep its identity although not its independence, D&H has illustrated that bridge routes are more viable propositions than many other types of railroads. (D&H is owned by, but has not merged with, conglomerate Norfolk and Western.)

D&H steam locomotive history is full of distinction. It was made notable for steam locomotives with smooth, almost English outlines, but of American dimensions, from 2-8-0s to 4-8-4s and 2-8-8-2s. Pipework and accessories were mounted chastely out of sight.

It was also notable for a sustained and technically successful effort to improve thermal efficiency by increasing the temperature and pressure of the steam. *Horatio Allen* was the appropriate name for the first 1924 attempt, which was a 2-8-0 with a special boiler permitting 350 lb/sq in pressure. There are great difficulties in designing locomotive boilers of normal pattern for pressures higher than 300 lb, but this one had a water-tube firebox of un-

orthodox type which could resist this modest increase of pressure. Three subsequent experiments in 1927, 1932 and 1935 respectively enabled D&H, who so sensibly decided to learn to walk before they could run, to take the steps up to a triple-expansion 600 lb/sq in 4-8-0 with tender booster. This was the only technically successful application of the triple-expansion principle (standard in marine practice) to a single-chassis locomotive. Alas this technical *tour de force* did not stand up to examination of its overall economics.

At present eleven million tons of traffic are carried annually an average distance of 340 miles, using a diesel locomotive fleet of 175 units and 6000 freight cars. About 1650 miles of railroad are operated for freight, but no passenger service is given.

Above: Two Delaware & Hudson Railway Baldwin diesels make fuel stops at Whitehall, NY in December 1950.

Top: A British-looking 4-8-4 of the Delaware & Hudson Railway in 1950.

Top right: Denver & Rio Grande Western Railroad runs this Durango to Silverton steam narrow-gauge tourist train, seen here in Lost Souls canyon.

Right bottom: Rio Grande freights head up the Wasatch Mountains out of Helper, Utah. The coal cars in the foreground are symbolic of the Carbon County coal fields of northern Utah which generate considerable railroad traffic.

DENVER & RIO GRANDE WESTERN RAILROAD – Rio Grande

No 1 Park Central, 1515 Arapahoe St, Denver, Colorado 80217.

To anyone who is ignorant of the topography and history of Colorado the 500-mile bridge route connecting Denver to Salt Lake City would seem unremarkable. Yet this outwardly rather conventional line is the result of one of the most exciting and romantic stories in the history of railroading – the truth being a good deal more spectacular than the plots of countless Western films which have located their train scenes on its metals. (An oft-used stage setting is the Canyon of the Lost Souls where one can look down a vertical rock face to the river 300ft below.)

In 1872 General William Jackson Palmer sent his construction crews south from Denver with the intention of reaching El Paso, Texas

via the Rio Grande Valley. However, the Santa Fe people got rails down first on the Raton Pass, the only practical route. Undaunted, Palmer then turned west and after a pitched battle with the rival road's gangs, won and held the Royal Gorge of the Arkansas for his railroad. The terrain to be served was as mountainous as any in the US and, moreover, was in the throes of a silver-mining boom. The economics of laying the rails close together seemed attractive and, accordingly, the narrow gauge of 3ft was chosen. The Rio Grande was the only *major* railroad in the USA to be laid in the narrow gauge.

By 1888 the Denver & Rio Grande and its companion the Denver and Rio Grande Western had covered Colorado, Utah and much of New Mexico with a network of 1670 miles of slim gauge lines reaching all the mining areas and extending as far west as Salt Lake City, Utah and south to Santa Fe, New Mexico. The devaluation of silver in 1892 led to bankruptcy and re-incorporation (the first of several) and the end of expansion. There was also complex financial juggling between the two companion roads before consolidation in 1908. The limited speed possible on the narrow gauge was a severe handicap to a long-distance carrier and, accordingly, the conversion of the main line

from Denver to Salt Lake City had been completed in 1890.

General Palmer's second thoughts on destination for his railroad had made its route a circuitous one. Some rerouting was done in connection with the regauging – to avoid the Marshall Pass with its four percent grades as well as the vulnerable trackage in the Black Canyon of the Gunnison River – but in 1934 a new line in the mountains, including the six-mile Moffatt Tunnel, gave the Rio Grande a direct route west from Denver, saving 175 miles on the journey to Salt lake City.

The same period saw the beginning of the end for the narrow gauge, although freight movement on the last section – the 250 miles from Alamosa to Farmington via Durango did not finally cease until 1967. This was the last 'normal' narrow gauge as well as the last steam freight common carrier operation in the USA. Passengers are, however, still carried (for pleasure) the 45 spectacular miles up the Lost Souls Canyon and back by steam. The 'Silverton Train' as it is called, is based in Durango and runs daily in summer; it has the highest earnings per mile of any passenger train in the US, has the status of a National Monument and is mentioned in many guide books alongside the Grand Canyon and Niagara Falls.

Book well ahead.

All the devices of the railway engineer were used to overcome the problems of the terrain at minimum cost. The narrow gauge permitted curves as sharp as 24° (243ft radius) while four percent (1 in 25) grades were normal and $4\frac{1}{2}$ percent ones existed. Zig-zag reverses, spirals and long return loops were used to gain altitude and many were the places where the trains crept along high up the walls of canyons on narrow ledges or teetered over high trestle bridges. Steam locomotive power also reflected the terrain. Air brakes were fitted long before they became compulsory, for example. In the early days, very few locomotives had less than eight coupled wheels because of the gradients and, later very few had more because of the curvature. A series of 2-8-0 'mountain ponies' supplied in their hundred became as much a classic for the narrow gauge as the American standard 4-4-0 was on standard gauge. Notable also in the early period were conversions of locomotives from narrow gauge to standard and, in the 1920s, the reverse operation. The latter produced some 2-8-2s that were very large for the narrow gauge; a weight of 27 tons, grate area 45 sq ft and 37,350 lb tractive effort was exceptional for 3ft between the rails. The later and bigger standard-gauge steam loco-

Extreme left: Rio Grande freight in Glenwood Canyon on the Colorado River.

Left: A Rio Grande 'rattler' (hobo slang for freight train) heads out of Salt Lake Valley, Utah.

Below: The only section of the Rio Grande's once great network of 3 ft 0in gauge track still to operate under its banner is the 45-mile Silverton branch out of Durango. Here one of the branch's Sports Models, 2-8-2 No 473 runs, decked out in fancy dress for a movie, alongside the Animas River.

Above: The other section of Rio Grande's narrow gauge still running is the now state-owned Cumbres & Toltec RR – a section of the one-time Alamoso-Durango main line over the Cumbres Pass. Never an easy line to work because of the steep gradients, it is today a spectacular tourist attraction during the summer season.

motives had additional linkage added to their Walschearts valve gear to give variable lead – very much akin to advancing and retarding the ignition on a motor car – as an aid to slogging up long mountain grades.

Standard-gauge steam came to an end in 1952 – the natural affinity of diesel locomotive characteristics to steep gradients has meant little in the way of specialities among the road's fleet of 260 modern diesel units.

When Amtrak was formed in 1970, the Rio Grande was one of the very few roads which opted out and it still runs its own 'Rio Grande Zephyr' three days a week on the spectacular run from Denver to Salt Lake City. This train is in fact a vestigial remnant of the remarkable 'California Zephyr' which, although now de-funct, brought new thinking to passenger operation (see Western Pacific). A fleet of 40 passenger cars protects the 'Zephyr' and 'Silverton' trains.

In respect of freight operation Rio Grande has tended towards short, fast and frequent trains rather than the immense drags typical of most US operations. Currently the Rio Grande handles 310,000 passengers and 30 million tons of freight annually, hauling the latter an average of 307 miles. Annual expenses are 92 percent of receipts.

DETROIT & MACKINAC RAILWAY
See Other US Railroads

DETROIT, TOLEDO & IRONTON RAILROAD
One Parklane Boulevard, Dearborn, Michigan 48126.

The Detroit, Toledo & Ironton Railroad was formed in the early years of the century from a collection of short lines in the neighbourhood of Detroit. In 1920, when it had become badly run down and was in dire financial straits, it was bought by car magnate, Henry Ford. (For some time he had been in the habit of going into print with articles such as 'If I Ran The Railroads'.) Strangely enough and unlike other amateur railwaymen, he was quite successful; in spite of a huge expenditure on reconstruc-tion, the line became profitable. Moreover, Ford electrified part of the line on the high-voltage AC system, but used locomotives which converted it to direct current for traction. In fact he did what the rest of the world (except Hungary) did not do until forty years later. A feature of the electrification was the use of reinforced concrete arched portals to hold up the overhead wires – some are still there today.

In the late 1920s Ford lost interest in playing

trains (it is said that he became fed up with the bureaucratic problems of running a public railway) and sold the DT&I, abandoning the electrification. The 480-mile railroad is still, however, in independent existence, carrying 13 million tons of traffic annually with a fleet of seventy diesel units and 4300 freight cars. Expenses are eighty percent of receipts. One feature is that its maximum permitted axle-load is as high as 38 tons.

DULUTH, MISSABE & IRON RANGE RAILWAY
See Other US Railroads

EDAVILLE RAILROAD
Box 7.
South Carver, Massachusetts 02566.

The present cult of preserving old-time steam railways is considered to have begun on 7 April 1947. On that day a little train, recovered and restored from abandoned 2ft-gauge railroads in the State of Maine, began a five-mile circuit of line which farmer Ellis D Attwood (hence the name EDAville) had laid down on his cranberry farm. Thirty years later, it is a major tourist attraction in an area which includes Cape Cod and Plymouth Rock.

ELGIN, JOLIET & EASTERN RAILWAY
See Other US Railroads

Above: Today steam has vanished from the regular American railroad scene and narrow-gauge tracks too are virtually extinct. Steam can, however, be seen on many preserved or tourist lines, the pioneer of which is the Edaville Railroad at South Carver, Massachusetts. This 2ft 0in gauge line is one of New England's premier tourist attractions and this Baldwin 2-4-4T from the Bridgton & Harrison Railroad is a wonderful working-museum-piece.

Bottom right: The 'Panama Limited' begins its 920-mile journey from Chicago to New Orleans circa 1960. This all-Pullman train was the Illinois Central Railroad's finest train.

Below: Florida East Coast Railway's General Motors diesel for the 'Florida Special'.

FLORIDA EAST COAST RAILWAY – FEC

St Augustine, Florida.

The story of the Florida East Coast Railway has all the qualities – and most of the ingredients – of a fairy tale. There is even a happy ending.

In 1883 a middle-aged oil millionaire called Henry Flagler, spent a holiday at a then-new beauty spot in Florida called St Augustine. To get there he had to cross the St Johns River by boat and trundle down the peninsula on a ramshackle narrow-gauge line called the Jacksonville, St Augustine & Halifax Railroad. Some might have shrugged off the inconvenience but not Flagler – he bought the railroad, bridged the river and, so that he could in future go all the way in his own train, brought the line up to main-line standard. He enjoyed railroad building so much that, with no prospect of financial return in what was then a wilderness, he extended the line right to the tip of the peninsula. An unknown place called Palm Beach was reached in 1894, another one called Miami in 1896. Even this did not satisfy his craving to play trains and, incredible to record, he took his line a further 57 miles, island-hopping across the sea to the very last fragment of Florida, an island called Key West. Of all the follies perpetrated in the history of railways, the Florida East Coast's extension to Key West, with its 17 miles of bridging across water stands alone. The only traffic objective was a modest speeding up of the journey by train and boat to Cuba, for which an expenditure of $20 million of the dollars of those days was hardly justified. Flagler was just able to enjoy the opening ceremony a few months before he died, aged 85, in 1912.

Although dividends were never paid, the FEC pursued a fairly lordly existence for a decade or so, until it was hit by the amazing Florida boom of the mid-1920s. Traffic multiplied several times over in three years and the railroad responded with a colossal re-equipment programme. Just as the up-dating was completed and needed to be paid for, came the 1929 crash. Inevitably, bankruptcy ensued; worse was to follow, for in 1935 the Key West extension was destroyed in a hurricane (it was later reconstructed as a highway).

Even though the road was bankrupt, trains such as the 'Florida Special' continued to run. This was an all-Pullman train from New York, the first train in America to be lit by electric light and to have enclosed vestibule connections between the cars. George M Pullman conducted the first run in person. During the 1930s' winters, in spite of the economic situation the train frequently ran in multiple; as many as seven parts were noted in one day in 1937. It shared with the 'Twentieth Century Limited' alone the *cachet* of regular red-carpet treatment – this at the Miami end.

The 'Florida Special' had just celebrated its 75th anniversary when the railroad brotherhoods declared a strike over a wage issue. Eleven days later – on 3 February 1962 – the little FEC, showing considerable courage, began running trains again, using supervisory staff in operating positions. Extreme measures, from the dynamiting of trains to political pressure from the White House, were used to force FEC to settle on the unions' terms; in the end, the FEC management won back its 'prerogative to operate the railroad', as they put it.

The position now is that, alone among the common-carrier railroads of the USA, the FEC does not have to abide by the steam-age work rules, those featherbeds of operations elsewhere. Before 1962, for example, there had to be five men on each FEC train and, because each crew could only work over one short designated division, three crews were needed for the run from Jacksonville to Miami. Now one two-man crew does the journey without change. Both ride on the locomotive; the caboose at the rear is eliminated having been replaced by a radio transmitting box fixed to the rear coupler, as a check that the train is complete and the brakes working. There were many other similar changes; in effect, one-half the employees now handle twice the workload of traffic. At present this amounts to nine million tons hauled an average distance of 210 miles, using a 1300-strong car fleet hauled by 59 diesel locomotive units.

The financial gains enabled a thorough rehabilitation of the physical plant to be put in hand. FEC's track, now welded rail on concrete sleepers, laid on a mountain of sharp stone ballast, comes closer to being truly a permanent track than most others. There were also funds to install the latest electronic systems of trackside safety surveillance.

The financial improvement (expenses have averaged sixty percent of receipts in recent years) of the 535-mile system has given employees job security, and the physical improvements have given them personal security and safety while on the job. The tragedy – for railroad employees as well as shareholders and the nation at large – is that the unofficial role of railroads elsewhere in the USA as sources of unemployment pay, precludes an FEC-type solution being applied nationally.

FRISCO
See Southwestern US Railroads

GEORGIA & FLORIDA RAILROAD
See Other US Railroads

GREEN BAY & WESTERN RAILROAD
See Other US Railroads

HAWAII
See Australasia, Oceania

ILLINOIS CENTRAL GULF RAILROAD
233 North Michigan Avenue, Chicago, Illinois 60601.

When the Illinois Central Railroad received its charter on 10 February 1851, it was the longest railroad which had been promoted up till then. It was also the first of many to receive a grant of lands as a subsidy on completion, in this case within seven years. In September 1856 the 705-mile line, which ran southwards from Chicago to the confluence of the Mississippi and Ohio Rivers at Cairo, was opened, thereby earning the land grant of 2,500,000 acres. Such non-railroad acquisitions have stood the company in good stead ever since and never more so than today, when railway operations are barely profitable.

Southwards from Cairo, freight and passengers could travel on by the famous Mississippi river steamers – such as the fabled *Robert E Lee* – to Memphis and New Orleans. Soon afterwards, the river part of the journey was confined to a ferry trip across the river and even this came to an end when the great four-mile bridge across the Mississippi at Cairo was inaugurated in 1889. Eight years before, 550 miles of the main line south of this point had been converted from 5ft gauge to 4ft 8½in in a single day, as preparation for through running.

While it was expanding, IC absorbed over one hundred smaller railroads, reaching out to Kansas City and Omaha to the west and Indianapolis and Louisville to the east. One of

those absorbed was the first railroad in the southern states, the 26-mile West Feliciana RR, on the border between Mississippi and Louisiana, which was completed in 1842.

In 1972 IC merged with Gulf, Mobile & Ohio, which since 1947 (when the Chicago & Alton was acquired), had also provided through service from Chicago to places on the Gulf of Mexico. Thus Illinois Central became the Illinois Central Gulf, a 9250-mile railroad, having 1060 diesel units, 47,000 freight cars and hauling 95 million tons an average distance of 315 miles each year.

IC's 'Panama Limited' from Chicago to New Orleans was one of two last all-Pullman luxury trains in the USA to run – it still operates less exclusively under Amtrak's banner. Such luxuries as the 'King's Dinner' of five courses were available to the end of IC working. Even today, IC is not out of the passenger business, since there is an electrified commuter service out of Chicago. Fourteen million passengers are carried annually, using a fleet of 162 cars.

IC's steam operations are rather overshadowed by the immortal song and tale of Casey Jones, 'Who mounted to the cabin with his orders in his hand, On his farewell trip to the promised land' ... because of course, J L Jones was an actual Illinois Central engineer, who came to grief after a particularly flagrant disregard for regulations. His 4-6-0 was very

typical of its day and this remark perhaps can be applied to virtually all IC motive power. It was a little unusual in that the few new locomotives built in the latter years of steam were homemade in the line's own Paducah shops; furthermore, rather than purchase new power during the lean years of the 1930s, these new shops undertook the major surgery involved in such operations as rebuilding old 2-8-2s into 2-10-2s.

ILLINOIS TERMINAL RAILROAD
See Other US Railroads

KANSAS CITY SOUTHERN RAILWAY COMPANY – KCS
See Southwestern US Railroads

KATY
See Southwestern US Railroads

LONG ISLAND RAIL ROAD
Jamaica Station,
Jamaica, New York 11435.

The Long Island Railroad received its charter in 1834 and is therefore among that select fraction of the world's railways who have carried on under one name since the 1830s. It is definitely not, however, among the four or five in the world who have remained in the same

ownership. In its early days the LIRR was the main line to Boston; travellers went from Brooklyn terminus to Greenport, thence by ferry across Long Island Sound and then took the Old Colony Line. An all land route was opened in 1850 and the LIRR then settled down to a peaceful country branch-line existence for half a century. In 1900 it was purchased by the Pennsylvania Railroad and started a new phase of existence as a New York commuter line. Electrification (third rail DC) was begun in 1904 and in 1910 LI trains began using the then-new Pennsylvania Station.

Political interference in the form of a thirty-year fare freeze, from 1918 to 1948, led to bankruptcy in 1949 in spite of financial aid from Pennsy. Eventually the line, by then a byword for all that was disreputable in the industry, was bought in 1964 by the New York State Metropolitan Transit Authority. Modernization and renewal was then put in hand, but political pressure to speed the work led to a hurried design. Following some tedious modification, the new trains, consisting of 620 cars and capable of 100 mph began running and in the end greatly improved the service. Currently some 250,000 'daily bread' riders are carried into and out of New York each working day. Some freight is also handled.

line climbs the mountain at a maximum inclination of one in 2⅔.

NATIONAL RAIL PASSENGER CORPORATION
See Amtrak

NEVADA NORTHERN RAILROAD
See Other US Railroads

NEW YORK CITY TRANSIT AUTHORITY – NYCTA
370 Jay Street,
Brooklyn 1, New York.

With 137 miles of route in tunnel, the New York City Transit Authority is by far the largest underground railway system in the world. It began as a famous elevated railway back in the 1870s using steam traction, but from 1904 on, the 'L' has been gradually replaced by an underground system; the only

MAINE CENTRAL RAILROAD COMPANY
242 St John Street,
Portland, Maine 04102.

Once upon a time the little Maine Central ran all-Pullman trains whose passenger lists rivalled the 'Twentieth Century Limited' in including the best-known names in America. All summer the 'Bar Harbor Express' and other trains rolled east to the Atlantic coast via Portland from Boston, New York and Washington. Another unexpected extravagance in the history of what is now a small down-to-earth freight-only road was the ownership – unique among Class I railroads – of a large 2ft gauge system. This was the fabled Sandy River & Rangely Lakes Railroad, relics of which survive at Edaville including a tiny parlour car.

It is said that Maine has two seasons, July and winter; no doubt the advantage which flanged wheels and steel rails possess over unploughed roads and slippery snow are one reason for the MEC's independent survival.

The line currently operates 900 miles of route with 65 locomotives (all diesel) and 4000 freight cars. Eight million tons of freight are hauled by the Maine Central Railroad an average distance of 110 miles. Expenses are ninety percent of receipts.

MILWAUKEE ROAD
See Chicago, Milwaukee, St Paul & Pacific

MISSOURI – KANSAS – TEXAS RAILROAD COMPANY
See Southwestern US Railroads

MISSOURI PACIFIC RAILROAD COMPANY
See Southwestern US Railroads

MONONGAHELA RAILWAY
See Other US Railroads

MoPAC
See Southwestern US Railroads

MOUNT WASHINGTON COG RAILWAY
See also Norfolk & Western Railway Company
Mount Washington,
New York.

The very first cog railway in the world was built up New Hampshire's 6290ft Mount Washington and opened in 1869. It still runs, using eight steam locomotives of the same original 1875 design, plus one repeat order delivered in 1975, thereby having both the oldest and the newest standard-gauge steam locomotives running in the USA. The 3.5-mile

Constructed in 1869 the Mount Washington Cog Railway is the world's oldest cog railway. Today the railway is still a great tourist attraction and its ancient engines battle their way to the cloudy summit crewed during peak periods by students on vacation.

Aside from the Union Pacific's position as a pioneer of luxury streamlined trains, its passenger trains were always of good standard. It is however a sign of the times that the 'Overland Mail', once the 'flag' passenger train of the route, is now a fast freight with a timing of fifty hours between Chicago and Oakland, barely slower than Amtrak's passenger train between the same two points.

Now as always, the lifeblood of the system is the immense flow of ordinary freight tonnage – currently amounting to ninety million tons annually, which UP hauls an average distance of 660 miles, earning $1.3 million gross and $150,000 net in the process, the largest net revenue in the industry.

WESTERN PACIFIC RAILROAD – WP
Western Pacific Building, 526 Mission Street, San Francisco, California 94105.

Around the turn of the century, railroad tycoon George J Gould, son of empire builder Jay Gould, planned the first true US transcontinental, that is, one road connecting the Atlantic to the Pacific. Towards this end, as a result of his famous father's efforts he already controlled the Wabash, Missouri Pacific and Denver & Rio Grande roads, but control of an existing line from Salt Lake City to the Pacific was denied him. Accordingly he set out to build his own, a duplicate of the original Overland Route across Utah, Nevada and California to San Francisco Bay. The final spike was driven without ceremony on 1 November 1909, the last one to be driven on a line crossing the American West.

Gould never achieved an ocean-to-ocean

railway, in fact the financial burdens of building WP were such that he and his family lost control of his railway empire. His line, however, soldiered on through various financial vicissitudes, wheeling and dealing. There was a dubious bankruptcy in 1915 and a more genuine one in 1935. Today the 1340-mile railroad is in reasonable financial health with expenses running at 86 percent of receipts.

The route chosen took the main line south of the Great Salt Lake, at that time fairly close to rivals Southern Pacific (then still Central Pacific) across the Nevada Desert. Since 1924 the usage of the two tracks over a 180-mile stretch have been pooled. Instead of the SP's notorious climb over the Sierras, WP crosses the range at 2000ft less elevation, through the Feather River Canyon to the north. It offers a one percent grade instead of SP's 2.2 percent, at the cost of an additional 150 miles distance. The easier line was and is a great advantage in moving freight economically, which WP (the 'Wobbly') does nowadays to the tune of 9.5 million tons a year, with an average 525-mile haul, using a fleet of 140 diesel units and 6500 cars.

WP is now out of the passenger business completely; it does not run passenger trains and does not allow passenger trains to run on it except occasionally when the SP route is blocked by a wreck or landslide. However, from 1949 to 1970, WP was a partner in one of the most remarkable and well-liked trains ever to cross the continent. This was the brand-new 'California Zephyr', run in conjunction with the Rio Grande and Burlington lines. With its 53-hour Chicago-Oakland timing, the train hardly competed with rival railways, let alone

aircraft. What it did offer, though, was an unexcelled scenic ride, with ample vista-dome viewing space as well as an observation car, excellent food, and timings so that the best scenery was seen in daylight. For night-time, excellent beds were not only offered, but taken; there were capacity loads run after run, with a clientele who came for the pleasure of the journey rather than for whatever lay at its end. Five train sets provided daily service. Even so, the end for the 'California Zephyr' came after twenty years when its equipment was beginning to age, and when rising losses began to overtake reason.

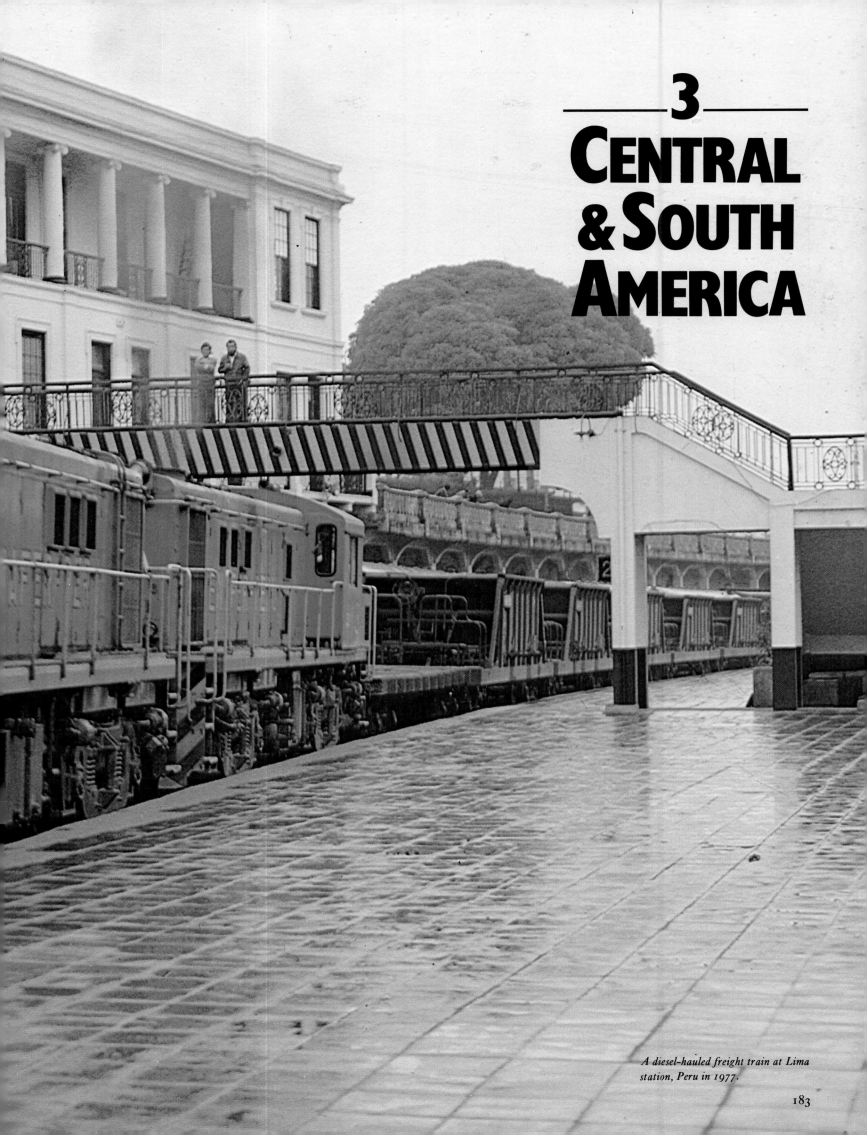

3
CENTRAL
& SOUTH
AMERICA

A diesel-hauled freight train at Lima station, Peru in 1977.

Argentina Argentine Railways Rio callegos – Rio Turbio Industrial Railway	**Cuba** Cuban National Railways	**Paraguay** President Carlos Antonio Lopez Railway
Belize	**Ecuador** Ecuador State Railways	**Peru** Peruvian National Railways
Bermuda	**Falkland Islands**	**Salvador, El** National Railways of El Salvador
Bolivia Bolivian National Railways	**Guatemala** Guatemala Railway	**Surinam** Surinam Government Railway
Brazil Brazilian Federal Railways Vitória a Minas Railway	**Guyana**	**Uruguay** Uruguayan State Railways
Chile Chilean State Railways	**Honduras**	**Venezuela** Venezuela National Railways
Colombia National Railways of Colombia	**Jamaica** Jamaica Railway Corporation	**West Indies: The Smaller Islands**
Costa Rica National Atlantic Railroad Pacific Electric Railroad	**Nicaragua** Pacific Railway of Nicaragua	
	Panama Panama Railroad	

ANTIGUA
See West Indies: the Smaller Islands

ARGENTINA

See map on pages 186-187.

ARGENTINE RAILWAYS – FA
Ferrocarriles Argentinos,
Avenida Ramos Mejia 1302,
1104 Buenos Aires.

It is a happy quirk of nomenclature that the South American country with by far the largest and most highly developed railway system is the first to be described.

Railways first came to this vast food-producing country in 1857, when a short 5ft-6in-gauge line from Buenos Aires to Flores was opened. (The reason for the gauge chosen is understood to be that some equipment ordered for India was acquired by Argentina.) This signalled the start of an explosion of railway construction which in its turn led to a great increase in prosperity. The Flores line was the start of what became the 7400-mile Buenos Aires Western. The 4000-mile Central Argentine Railway's first component was opened in 1862 and in 1865 the first section of the largest South American privately financed railroad, the 5300-mile Buenos Aires Great Southern, was opened. The 3200-mile Buenos Aires & Pacific (which in good American tradition, never got there) began operations in 1888. These four systems still preserve a measure of independence as separate divisions of the national network. They use names of four past national heroes – respectively, Domingo F Sarmiento, General Mitre, General Roca and General Martin.

A disconnected 2000-mile standard-gauge

system grew up in the north-eastern corner of the country, between the River Parana and the river Uruguay, (the latter forms the frontier). Neither river has yet been bridged, so inconvenience of break of gauge is not yet a problem. The two associated companies were called, appropriately enough, the Entre Rios ('between rivers'), and the Argentine North Eastern; they are now called the General Urquiza Railway.

There were also a number of metre-gauge railways, totalling over 8000 miles in extent, in outlying areas. The biggest concentration of these railways is in the mountainous but sparsely populated north-western area of the country. The rewards to be gleaned from this area were sparse also, so British-owned companies were less eager, allowing the state, a provincial government and a French company opportunities for railway ownership. These lines are now known as the General Belgrano Railway.

The honeymoon stage of this marriage to foreign capital really lasted a surprisingly long time. British investors made money for themselves, it is true, but the companies were good employers and the services they offered brought prosperity to the country. At the same time they invested heavily in up-to-date equipment and took a long-term and responsible view of their future. But, like other marriages on not too solid a foundation, bliss did not survive hard times. These came in full measure during the 1930s when for a number of years none of

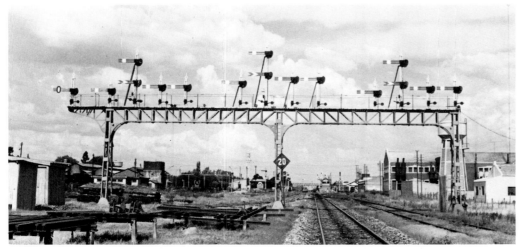

Left: Buenos Aires' suburban Escalada station, looking towards Plaza Constitucion Terminus.

Extreme left: A British-built 4-8-0 and local train at Tandil, Argentina. Note the semaphore signals.

Centre left: A vintage San Martin Railway 4-6-0 pulls a mixed train at Rufino, a small pampas town 270 miles west of Buenos Aires.

Bottom left: An essentially British signal gantry at the west end of Rufino station.

Bottom right: The magnificent overall station roof at La Plata, Argentina.

the British companies could pay any sort of dividend. Of course, similar problems applied to railways everywhere, due to road competition and the worldwide slump. The result was that in 1948 the state, using sterling balances accumulated during the war, was able to enforce the purchase of the foreign-owned railways. It is no pleasure to write that politicians' control has not yet led to a railway system of which Argentina can be proud, although better-advised efforts are now at last being made.

The majority of Argentina's 25,000 miles of railway are laid in easy farming country – a stretch of dead straight and dead level track 205 miles long on the BA & Pacific line tells its own tale. However, the lines approaching the crossings of the Andes are a very different story.

The first and most famous of these, the Trans-Andean Railway, made a direct route between Buenos Aires and Valparaiso in Chile. It was built with British capital and opened just before World War I. The mechanical solution to mountain climbing, that is, rack-and-pinion working, was adopted, together

The so-called Atlantic line to Limon on the Caribbean coast is diesel-operated with no signalling apart from primitive semaphore arms at some of the principal stations and junctions. The principal traffic on this line and its three lengthy branches is bananas and spurs of considerable length extend through the banana plantations to each of the packing stations. There are no roads through much of the banana growing area and in only a few cases is it feasible to bring produce to the larger railheads by motorized road vehicle.

With this type of traffic the volume loaded at each station varies considerably from day to day, and the urgency of getting the bananas down the line to Limon and loaded into the ships in the shortest possible time to avoid deterioration of quality calls for a very flexible operating pattern with a different train schedule from day to day.

The daily passenger train from Limon to San José passes through spectacular scenery and despite its leisurely schedule is a remarkable experience for the tourist. Nevertheless it is a journey not without its risks for where else in the world would a passenger have his watch stolen from his wrist by an urchin running alongside the moving train.

CUBA

See map on pages 190–191.

CUBAN NATIONAL RAILWAYS
Ferrocarriles Nacionales de Cuba,
Havana.

Cuba is an island of substantial size, being almost 800 miles long. Railways came to it early; a line from Havana, the capital, to

Bejucal was opened on 19 November 1837. Development of the system was entirely in private hands. Havana and Santiago were joined in 1902 and twenty years later there were 3000 miles of public railway, divided mainly between two companies. There was the British-owned United Railways of Havana in the west (including that Bejucal line) and the US-owned Consolidated Railroads of Cuba in the east. The systems were nationalized in the 1950s and now operate under the title of National Railways of Cuba. The lines are and were almost entirely built to the standard gauge and North American style equipment was used, including – in the 1920s – cars supplied and operated by Pullman.

In addition, and highlighting one of the staple traffics of the system, there are 6200 miles of non-public railways, about half of which are narrow gauge, serving (mainly) the sugar industry.

Like all Communist countries, Cuba is shy on some railway statistics, although it is noted that eleven million tons of freight and eighteen million passengers are carried annually on the public system. Before the Castro regime took over there were 300 steam and 172 diesel locomotives, sixty railcars, 330 carriages and 8000 wagons; since then it is noted that forty Russian, twenty Canadian, thirty French and ten British diesels have arrived. Twenty electric locomotives were shown as operating on the ninety-mile erstwhile Hershey Cuban Railway, electrified at 1200v DC.

DOMINICAN REPUBLIC
See West Indies

DUTCH GUIANA
See Surinam

ECUADOR

See map on pages 186–187.

ECUADOR STATE RAILWAYS
Empresa de Nacional Ferrocarriles del Estado.
Carrera Bolivar No 443,
Quito.

Work began in 1871 on a 3ft 6in gauge line to link Quito, the capital of Ecuador (at 9375ft altitude) with the Pacific port of Guayaquil. It was to be 288 miles long, with a summit at 11,840ft. Various financial and engineering problems delayed construction and Quito was not finally reached until 1908.

Past a place called Devil's Nose there is a steep section 22 miles long, much of which is at the extremely severe gradient of one in eighteen, made worse by being combined with curvature down to 200ft radius. There are four zig-zags as well.

US and British staff were hired to work this problem road, but they must have enjoyed it, for the Guayaquil & Quito Railway was known in those days as the 'Good & Quick'.

When the railways were nationalized in 1960, the G&Q was the largest constituent of what is now a 700-mile system (it included an isolated 100-mile section of 2ft 5½in gauge), with 29 steam (nominally) and seventeen diesel locomotives on the books plus 35 carriages and 500 freight cars. A reported 1.7 million passengers and 600,000 tons of freight are carried annually.

EL SALVADOR
See Salvador

FALKLAND ISLANDS

See map on pages 186–187.

It is not known exactly when the Falkland Islands opened its 2ft gauge railroad which ran three miles from Port Stanley to the radio signal station. There was one small steam locomotive, which monopolized the provision of motive power in one direction. In the other, which coincided with the prevailing winds, an informal but more frequent service was provided by sail-driven rail cars. The railroad has since been abandoned.

GUATEMALA

See map on pages 190–191.

GUATEMALA RAILWAY – FEGUA
Ferrocarril de Guatemala,
Guatemala City.

Virtually all the railways in Guatemala originally belonged to a company called Interna-

Right: The crew of 4-6-0 No 57 gets a good view of Guatemala's 12,000ft volcano Agua in October 1961. Escuintla was the helper terminal for the loaded banana trains which have to work through a series of loops before reaching the high coastal plateau at Palin, near Guatemala City.

Extreme right, top: The 4-6-4T Sir Graeme on Guyana's Georgetown-Rosignol train.

Extreme right, below: Steam runs no more on Jamaica's standard-gauge railway system and Britain has stepped in with some modern Rolls-Royce engined railcars. This picture was taken at Spanish Town where the Port Antonio and Montego Bay lines divide.

Below right: Built in 1948, 2-8-2 No 199 is seen on the International Railways of Central America at Ipala Hill. The climb from here ascends the escarpment by means of six loops. This is the La Cuesta loop where, once the train emerges from the tunnel it immediately jumps across the steel trestle bridge on the upper left of the picture. There is a helper engine in the middle of the train.

tional Railways of Central America of Jersey City, USA (who, apparently, still dispute their ownership), which was incorporated in 1904. By 1970, when the state took them over, the IRCA had constructed over 500 miles of operational 3ft-gauge railroad plus other mileage in neighbouring Salvador. At that time there were ninety steam locomotives (many of modern construction) and seventeen diesels; 3.4 million passengers were carried each year using 150 carriages and 1.2 million tons of freight was hauled an average distance of 150 miles. It is understood that dieselization is now virtually complete although, in the disturbed state of the country, reliable information is not easy to come by. North American practice is followed.

GUIANA, BRITISH
See Guyana

GUIANA, DUTCH
See Surinam

——GUYANA——

See map on pages 186–187.

The first railroad to have been built in South America was constructed in what is now Guyana. On 3 November 1848, in the recent and tiny British colony of British Guiana, the Demerara Railway opened the first section of a 21-mile 4ft 8½in-gauge coastal line linking Georgetown with Mahiba. By 1900 the line had been extended to Rosignol (sixty miles), near the frontier with Dutch Guiana (now Surinam)

and there was also a short 3ft 6in-gauge coastal line west of the River Demerara. In 1922 the colonial government took over the working.

It is noted that the first locomotives to arrive were Sharp-Stewart 2-2-2Ts, named, significantly, *Mosquito*, *Sandfly* and *Scorpion*, and that the last (in 1946) were Hunslet 4-6-4Ts *Sir Gordon* and *Sir John*, a repeat order of two supplied in 1923. In 1972 six years after independence, the Guyana government closed both lines, which in 1962 had been carrying three million passengers a year, plus a small amount of freight.

A bauxite mining firm, the Demerara Bauxite Company operates a 3ft gauge fifty-mile line at Linden, which carries passengers as well as the firm's products.

HAITI
See West Indies

——HONDURAS——

See map on pages 190–191.

The railways of Honduras which began operation in 1869, are divided into three systems. First, there is a small system, the Ferrocarril Naçional, owned by the state; then there are two other railroads, the Vaccaro Railway and the Tela Railroad, owned by the Standard Fruit Company of San Francisco and the United Fruit Company of Boston respectively.

The scale of each's operation is indicated by
the following:

Railways of Honduras	Nacional	Vaccaro	Tela
Length of route	128	270	210
Gauge	3ft 6in	3ft oin	3ft 6in
Locomotives, steam	12	—	—
Locomotives, diesel	8	24	25
Passenger cars	150	25	90
Freight cars	600	700	1400
Passengers carried annually, millions	3.9	?	1.4
Freight carried annually, millions of tons	0.5	0.7	1.6

JAMAICA

See map on page 190.

JAMAICA RAILWAY CORPORATION
PO Box 489, 142 Barry Street,
Kingston.

The 205-mile Jamaica Railway is remarkable
in two particular ways. First, it was the first
railway in the British Colonial Empire when
it opened on 21 November 1845 over the twelve
miles between Kingston and Spanish Town.
Second, that while nationalization is the common fate of railways the world over, one that has
been nationalized twice is rare indeed. The
government bought the 4ft 8½in gauge line in
1870 and did some extending; they found running a railway an expensive business (it was a
time when tax-payers had a say in how their
money was being spent) and sold out nineteen
years later to American interests, by which time
there were 108 miles of line.

Railroading on a small island did not suit the
new owners either and the state had to take it
over again in 1900.

Diesel railcars were introduced before World
War II but current operations (one million
passengers and four million tons of freight –
mostly bauxite – annually) are handled by 25
diesel locomotives, 25 carriages and 380
wagons. After steam was phased out, one 4-8-0
was set aside for a tourist operation (Jamaica is
a famous holiday isle) but boiler problems
occurred and the scheme had to be abandoned.

MEXICO
See North America, Mexico

NICARAGUA

See map on pages 190-191.

PACIFIC RAILWAY OF NICARAGUA
Ferrocarril del Pacifico de Nicaragua,
Aparado Postal No 5,
Managua.

The 200-mile state-owned Pacific Railway was opened in 1886. It was intended to connect the capital, Managua, with the Pacific port of Corino. Until 1903 the journey down to the coast began with a long steamer trip on Lake Managua, but in that year the line was completed through to the capital. About 500,000 passengers ride annually in four diesel trains while nine steam and ten diesel locomotives look after the small amount of freight (60,000 tons) that is carried in the 100-strong wagon fleet.

PANAMA

See map on pages 190-191.

PANAMA RAILROAD
Box 5067,
Christobal, Canal Zone.

In spite of assertions to the contrary, the US does have a railroad that connects the Atlantic and the Pacific Oceans. Moreover, it is state-owned and it opened fourteen years before Union Pacific. The Panama Railroad is 5ft gauge, 47 miles long and was built, with heavy loss of life, between 1850 and 1855. The line provided, across the Isthmus of Panama, a land link in a route from the east to the west of the USA, which avoided the perils of the covered-wagon trail and the hazards of Cape Horn. The fare was $25.00 single, a month's pay in those days, perhaps.

It was used, re-aligned and finally doubled in connection with, first, de Lesseps and second, the US government's attempts to build the Panama Canal. Currently the now single-line road, which runs from Colon to Panama, has six diesel locomotives, 24 passenger and 274 freight cars, and handles one million passengers and 180,000 tons of freight annually.

The other railway in Panama, the 3ft-gauge 100-mile Chiriqui National Railroad, was intended to be part of a Pan-American railway link between North and South America. However, this was not to be and the line is now of local interest only; its operations are on a very small scale.

Right: A locomotive refuelling point at Asunción, Paraguay.

PARAGUAY

See map on pages 186–187.

PRESIDENT CARLOS ANTONIO LOPEZ RAILWAY

*Ferrocarril Presidente Carlos Antonio Lopez,
PO Box 453, Calle Mexico 145,
Ascunión.*

The first section of railway in Paraguay was put in hand as early as 1854 by Dictator Lopez; two British engineers were engaged for the purpose. The army provided labour and the first forty miles southwards from Asunción, the capital of Paraguay, was completed in 1861. War stopped further progress and in 1866 a British company, the Paraguay Central, took over. By 1911 the main objectives, the Parana River and the river port of Encarnación, were reached, 144 miles from Asunción, providing an outlet for Paraguay's farming products. After 1913 there was a connection by train ferry to Argentina's railways, here fortunately laid to the same standard gauge. Through sleeping cars were run to Buenos Aires until a few years ago, hauled over PC metals by handsome woodburning 2-6-os of archetypical British appearance and design.

Equally archetypical political South American events then intervened and 65 years later the whole system is still there, almost as if it had been chemically preserved. It does demonstrate the extraordinary powers of survival of an old-fashioned steam railway. Since 1961, it has belonged to the state but funds for modernization have not been forthcoming. At the same time, the government is reluctant to close the line. It provides 500 jobs as well as a convenient way of regulating truckers and busmen on the parallel highway.

Meantime, Paraguay is the only all-steam country in the world; its 21 locomotives, thirteen carriages and 200 wagons handle 207,000 passengers and 144,000 tons of freight. Surprisingly, with expenses at only 84 percent of receipts, the financial results are in the top league among state-run railways.

PERU

See map on pages 186–187.

PERUVIAN NATIONAL RAILWAYS – ENAFER

*Empresa Nacional de Ferrocarriles del Peru
PO Box 1379, Ancash 207,
Lima.*

Railways came to Peru on 17 May 1851, when the nine-mile line from the Port of Callao to the capital city of Lima was opened. It was inspired by Richard Trevithick, the builder of the first steam locomotive, who had spent some time a few years earlier installing steam pumps to drain the silver mines in the high altitude area known as Cerro de Pasco in the Andes. The two factors which have dominated railway construction in Peru are the Andes mountains and their mineral deposits. No mountain range except the Himalayas matches them and the Himalayas have yet to be crossed by rail.

The second line essayed the foothills of the Andes, connecting 7500ft-high Arequipa, the second city of Peru, with the ocean at Mollendo. A man from San Francisco called Henry Meiggs (he had left there in a hurry fifteen years before) built the seventy-mile route, between 1868 and 1870. There was a £4000 per month bonus for completion in under three years, with a penalty of the same amount for time over, so he did reasonably well.

Already the Peruvian government had decided to carry the line on up into the mountains. Puno on Lake Titicaca (altitude: 12,500ft) was reached in 1874 and finally Cuzco in 1907. This line was later known as the Southern Railway. Via its steamers on Lake Titicaca, a connection into Bolivia was provided.

In the meantime Meiggs was occupied

further north on what was to be his greatest feat of railway construction. This was the Oroya Railroad, later the Central Line, which Brian Fawcett, its chronicler and one-time locomotive chief called 'the highest and hardest railway in the world'. The Southern rose to great altitudes, but approached the mountains gradually, while the Central went straight at them. All these railways were built to standard gauge.

Revolution, war, Meiggs death in 1877 and bad financial problems held up construction. In fact, the line was not completed through to Oroya until 1895. Peru had pledged its accumulation of bird droppings to get these railways built but there was a limit even to the guano. Now the country had to rely on direct foreign investment.

The concession to complete the Central fell to British investors, who also acquired the Southern; they took the name of the Peruvian Corporation. The mining concession for the Cerro de Pasco mines as well as a 75-mile railway feeder line to Oroya, remarkable in that its lowest point was above 12,000ft altitude, went to US interests.

By Andean standards, the grades on the first 25 miles from Lima to Chosica in the foothills are virtually flat, only 1 in 37: but over the next 75 miles the train has to climb 12,875ft to the summit in the three-quarter-mile Galera Tunnel at 15,693ft, just 155ft short of the world's highest. (This also is nearby, on a mine spur at La Cima.) On the climb there are eleven reversals at V-switches and a further two on the descent into Oroya. The ruling grade is a hideous and nearly continuous 1 in 22 and, combined with curvature as sharp as 330ft radius, it governs every move Andean railwaymen make; one careless moment and a runaway train is plunging to destruction down an unbelievable precipice. The wreckage of some of them can be seen today.

One must salute the bridges on the Central, not so much because of their span or length but because of the amazing locations in which they were erected. The Carrion Bridge over the

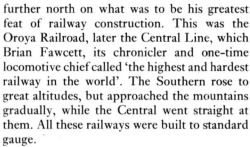

Above: An interior view of Uruguay's Montevideo Central Station.

Top extreme left: The summit station at Galera, Peru is 15,681ft above sea level.

Top centre: A Lima-bound train stops at Galera Station.

Centre, second from top: A switchback at Viso, Peru. The train will back up from the line in the foreground until it reaches the upper level from which it will proceed normally.

Centre, second from bottom: From the end of the 'most wonderful railway in the world' at Huancayo a 3ft 0in gauge line runs 92 miles to Huancavelica, dropping from 10,000ft to 8000ft and then climbing to 12,000ft. It was once intended to connect to Cuzco but this never materialized – the 150 miles, as the crow flies, which would link it with the terminus of the line out of Cuzco is too steep, hazardous and uneconomic. The line is worked by modern railcars together with steam locomotives.

Extreme left bottom: A daily train, forty miles out of Cuzco, awaits help.

Left: Uruguay's new Hungarian-built diesel train at Punta del Este station.

Verrugas Gorge, 572ft span and 252ft high, is named after Dr Daniel Carrion, who died after experimenting on himself in an attempt to find a cure for Verrugas fever which had carried away hundreds of workers. The great bridge called Chaupichaca (the name is onomatopoetic for steam locomotive) higher up, is notorious for having collapsed when, in 1909, a runaway hit a work train on the bridge.

Among operating features peculiar to these mountain lines should be mentioned the supplies of oxygen carried on the trains, to be administered to passengers suffering from mountain sickness. Another one, this time peculiar to the Central, which has a flow of copper downhill and a flow of oil uphill, is a combined gondola-tanker car. It can be loaded with copper or with oil, but not both without exceeding the permitted axle-load of 17.5 tons. Much empty-car movement is avoided by using this two-way system.

One objection to a zig-zag railway is that the length of the trains is governed by the length of the stalk of the reversing spur at each zig-zag and, by definition, there is almost always some major obstacle to extending them. If not, the extra distance available would already have been used in the first place to gain extra height. Hence, length of trains on the Central remained sensibly constant and, accordingly, the 2-8-0 served from first to last. The famous oil-fired 'Andes' 2-8-0, developed in 1935, was the result of forty years of traumatic operational experience. It combined the ruggedest North American design features with the best Beyer-Peacock English workmanship. BP went on getting repeat orders for 'Andes' locomotives from both the Central and Southern lines until the firm went out of the locomotive-building business. In fact, their very last steam locomotive order in 1957 was for a batch of 'Andes' engines for the Cerro de Pasco Railway.

The natural affinity of diesel locomotives to mountain railroading has been mentioned but, in contemplating dieselization, the Andean roads had a problem for some time. Like people, diesels cannot breathe properly at very great heights and the standard US products needed some refinements; on their home ground, they never got above 10,000ft. At the same time, the efficiency of steam locomotives gets better as they go higher. This has to do with the lower temperature at which water boils. These factors delayed dieselization until the mid-1960s. A loan from the World Bank was obtained for this and it proved the Peruvian Corporation's undoing. Under Andean conditions, the increase in productivity which is necessary to finance dieselization could not be obtained. For example, train lengths could not be increased. So, in the financial turmoil of 1973-74, a position was reached in which there was no money to pay the interest on the loans. The liability thus fell on the Peruvian government who, in return, confiscated the railways, adding them to a few short state lines that already existed.

There are now six separate and unconnected lines; of these, two include breaks of gauge. The last figures available show 1725 miles of route (1490 is standard, 210 is 3ft and 125 is 2ft) on which 29 steam and 146 diesel locomotives run, hauling 4050 freight and 200 passenger cars.

PUERTO RICO

See North America: United States of America: Ponce & Guyana Railway

SALVADOR

See map on pages 190-191.

NATIONAL RAILWAYS OF EL SALVADOR – FENADESAL

Ferrocarriles Nacional el Salvador,
Palacio Nacional,
San Salvador.

Two foreign-owned railway companies operated in El Salvador; the biggest was the 280-mile British Salvador Railway Company, dating from 1896. There was also 100 miles of the US-owned International Railways of Central America, whose main operations were centred in neighbouring Guatemala. The El Salvador Railway was taken over by the government in 1962, and the IRCA lines were taken over in 1973. In 1975 the present administration was formed, with 385 miles of route. The port of Cutuco is the southern end of continuous tracks which extend (with break of gauge at the Mexico-Guatemala frontier) to points in Northern Canada. Passenger trains are not, however, worked beyond the customs stations at any border except the US-Canada one, so a through-traveller faces three short taxi or bus rides, assuming his visas are in order.

FENADESAL has some twelve diesel and fifty steam locomotives, 85 passenger and 730 freight cars. Currently expenses are 120 percent of receipts; 400,000 tons of freight and 1.6 million passengers are moved annually.

SURINAM

See map on pages 186-187.

SURINAM GOVERNMENT RAILWAY

Oneverwacht, Paramaribo.

This small 83-mile metre-gauge railway operates out of Paramaribo, the capital of what was once called Dutch Guiana. There were eleven steam locomotives and a few diesel railcars, but the scale of its operations may be judged from the fact that fifteen passenger and fifty freight cars sufficed for the traffic. Recent information indicates that truncation to around fifty miles has taken place and it is not certain whether operation continues at all.

In compensation, some distance to the west at Apoera on the Guyana border, a 45-mile standard-gauge line is planned, in order to serve a bauxite mining area.

TRINIDAD
See West Indies

URUGUAY

See map on pages 186-187.

URUGUAYAN STATE RAILWAYS

Administracion de Ferrocarriles del Estado,
Calle La Paz 1095, Casilla de Correo 419,
Montevideo.

The Uruguayan State Railways was formed in 1952 from the British-owned 980-mile Central Uruguay and 505-mile, Midland Uruguay railways together with other previously state-owned lines; today's system is 1865 miles long, all on the 4ft 8½in gauge. The actual purchase was made by the government in 1948, using sterling funds earned by Uruguay during the war.

Work started on the Central in 1867; it was a line 127 miles long, running north from Montevideo, the capital and main port, to Durazno, in easy but pleasantly undulating country. Steady development over the next 45 years led to the present system of seven lines radiating out from Montevideo. Four go as far as the Brazilian frontier, to connect (with break-of-gauge) with the Brazilian Railways.

The frontier with Uruguay's other neighbour, Argentina, is the wide River Plate to the south and the Uruguay River to the west. The latter river is not at present bridged, although the Argentine railways on the other side have the same gauge.

Essentially, British 2-6-0s and 2-8-0s were the mainstay of the Uruguayan Railways for many years and even now provide a useful backup to diesel traction; in fact, they have out-

Left: Train ready to depart from Montevideo Station.

Below: View of buffer stops and circulating area at the main terminus at Montevideo.

Bottom: The Island of Haiti still collects its sugar together by rail though today little, if any, steam runs. Back in 1960 the Compagnie de la Plaine du Cul-de-Sac had a 2ft 6in gauge line which used some fascinating steam engines.

lasted not only postwar steam locomotives from other sources but many of the first batch of diesels acquired by Uruguay. It was in fact a sad example of how useless big new shiny diesels are on an old-fashioned railway, if no other steps are taken to provide for them, such as new workshops, permanent way and so on. When diesels first came, it was frequently the case that only one in five were serviceable. Currently there are twenty steam and (nominally) 110 diesel locomotives, 45 railcars (in fifteen modern three-car sets), ninety passenger coaches and 3000 wagons in service. Records show 6.4 million passengers and 1.6 million tons of freight are carried each year, the latter an average distance of 190 miles. British practices still prevail, other than in new motive power and rolling stock.

VENEZUELA

See map on pages 186-187.

VENEZUELA NATIONAL RAILWAYS
Ferrocarriles Naçionales de Venezuela, Estacion Camo Amarillo, Apartado 140, Caracas.

Venezuela, having divested itself of one railway system is presently going to market to buy another. During the last quarter of the nineteenth century fourteen narrow-gauge lines were opened, the longest – the 138-mile Ferrocarril Bolivar – had the narrowest gauge, of 2ft. However, 2ft 6in, 3ft, metre and 3ft 6in lines existed as well; two lines, the La Guira & Caracas and the Venezuela Central were partly electrified. The former had a rack section. The overall total length was 600 miles.

During the 1930s and 1940s many systems

closed; others survived to be nationalized in 1961 and then closed. The current mileage – in a country measuring 800 miles by 600 with twelve million inhabitants – is 170 miles of standard gauge plus a nine-mile 2ft gauge steam historical railway. This is the Empressa del Ferrocarril Historico del Encanto, Caracas.

Recently the Government asked for tenders for the first 700-mile stage in providing Venezuela with a 2100 mile national railway system; one strange omission – a line to Caracas, the capital, in which a thirty-mile rapid transit system is being built.

WEST INDIES

See map on pages 190-191.

Unless the rules are distorted by some random factors like state subsidies or a railway enthusiast in the royal house, the survival and, indeed, the original existence of a railway is

governed by its arithmetic. Railways are economic because many loads can be hauled by one locomotive; it is normally forgotten that it costs money to accumulate loads into trains. It follows that it is only worth forming up a train if it is to run a reasonable distance. By definition, on a small island this cannot be so and, hence, the small islands are the ones that lose their railways to the motorcar and lorry. Very small ones, of course, never got railways, even in horse transport days. Where the traffic can be accumulated into train loads at very small cost at, say, a coal mine, then short railways can survive.

All this is well illustrated by the railways of the West Indies; hence, the disappearance of railways from Antigua, Barbados, Haiti and Trinidad, as well as their degradation from a common-carrier role in Dominican Republic. Other and smaller islands, such as Grenada, Tobago and the Bahamas appear never to have had significant public railways; Cuba and Jamaica have systems of significance which merit their own entry.

4
AFRICA

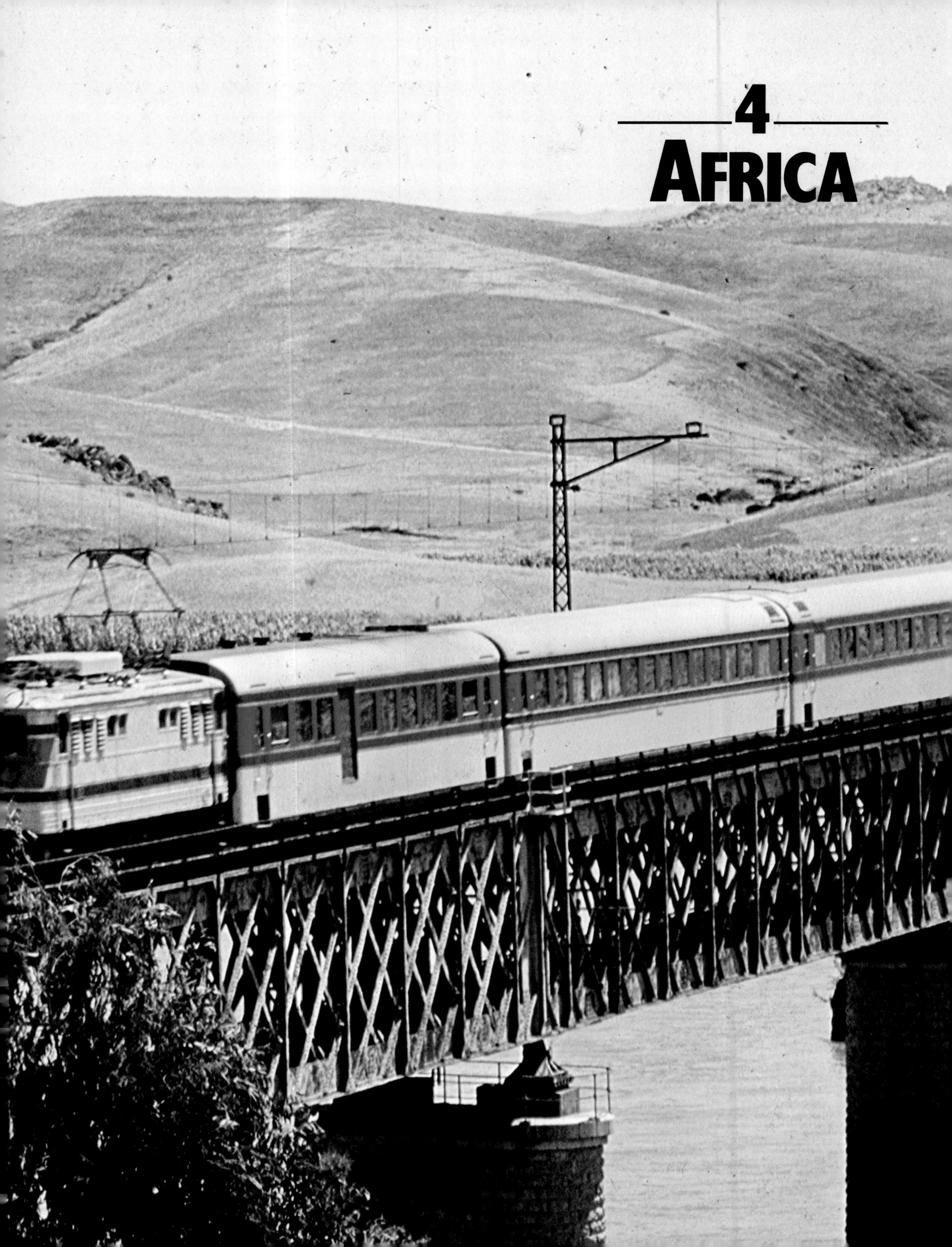

The Cape to Cairo Railway

African Offshore Islands
Azores
Canaries
Madeira
Mauritius
Réunion

Algeria
Algerian Railways

Angola
Benguela Railway Company

Benin, People's Republic of
Benin Railways

Botswana

Cameroon
Cameroon National Railways Authority

Congo, People's Republic of the
Congo – Ocean Railway

Egypt
Egyptian Railways

Ethiopia
Northern Ethiopia Railways Share Company
Djibouti to Addis-Ababa Railway

Gabon
Gabon State Railway

Ghana
Ghana Railway and Ports

Kenya
Kenya Railways

Lesotho

Liberia
Bong Mining Company
Lamco J V Operating Company

Libya

Madagascar (Malagasy Republic)
Malagasy Railways

Malawi
Malawi Railways Limited

Mauritania, Islamic Republic of

Morocco
Moroccan Railways

Mozambique, People's Republic of
Mozambique State Railways

Namibia

Niger

Nigeria
Nigerian Railway Corporation

Rhodesia/Zimbabwe
Rhodesia Railways Board

Senegal, Mali, Guinea, Ivory Coast, Upper Volta
Senegal Railways
Mali Railway
Guinea Railways
Ivory Coast Railway (also serving Upper Volta)

Sierra Leone

South Africa
South African Railways

Sudan
Sudan Railways

Swaziland
Swaziland Railway

Tanzania
Tanzanian Railways Corporation
Tanzania Zambia Railway Authority – Tan-Zam Railway

Togo
Togo Railways

Tunisia
Tunisian National Railways

Zaïre
Zaïre National Railways

Zambia
Zambia Railways

THE CAPE TO CAIRO RAILWAY

There was a time when railways were regarded as a main influence in 'civilizing' and, it was implied, bringing 'peace and order' to 'savage' communities. Regarded years ago as the Dark Continent, Africa seemed to cry out for such a 'civilizing' railroad. A Cape to Cairo Railway was suggested by an English clergyman's son called Cecil Rhodes. He was born in 1853 and reached South Africa in 1870.

Rhodes, with the aid of a fortune acquired from diamond mining, got some way with his project. In fact, his railroad progressed as far as the Congo (Zaïre) town of Bukama, 2600 miles from Cape Town but still 3500 miles from his objective. He did it partly by financing the project himself and partly by bullying the government. When he died in 1902, much of the impetus was lost.

After World War I, when the whole distance was spanned by lands under British control and frontier problems were at a minimum, economic difficulties precluded construction. Since World War II, economic conditions have been better and new construction in Zambia, Tanzania and Uganda has filled in some of the missing sections. Alas, political problems have never been worse and border barriers have

Left : A typical South African steam-hauled train is headed by the customary 15E class 4-8-2. It is a fast train from Kroonstad to Harrismith and Durban.

Right : The Johannesburg main line out of Cape Town is now electrified. A coal train hauls its load through the Hex River Valley, Cape Province.

Below : Railway building in Uganda during quieter times (1964). The north-western extension reaches beyond Gulu towards the Nile not far from the Sudan border.

Below right : A diesel-hauled passenger train enters Ingumbi tunnel on the Tan-Zam Railway.

appeared at several points on the route.

Nowadays, a Cape to Cairo traveller who had sufficient political clout to break down these barriers, could travel by Rhodes' route from Cape Town via Kimberley and Mafeking as far as Bulawayo. Then across political barrier No 1, the Zambesi, at the Victoria Falls, the 'carriages washed by the spray' as Rhodes wished. One is diverted from Rhodes' originally proposed route at Kapiri Mposhi where one takes the new Chinese-built Tan-Zam line to Dar-es-Salaam. Every line so far has been laid to a uniform 3ft 6in gauge, but a change to metre gauge now ensues, although provision has been made for many years on East African railways for eventual conversion to 3ft 6in.

Kenya is entered close to Mount Kilimanjaro (or would be if Kenya and Tanzania were on speaking terms) whence the original Uganda Railway is taken via Nairobi and Tororo to East African Railways' furthest point north at Gulu, close to the Sudan border. The same line continues a little further west to Pakwach on the River Nile, but regular steamer services north from there no longer run.

A journey of a mere 100 miles by road brings one into the hands of the Sudan Railways at Juba. However, one must take one of its steamers not one of its trains, and after nine

days and 900 miles one would arrive at Kosti, 200 miles south of Khartoum. The SR is 3ft 6in gauge in anticipation of the first through express. Yet another Nile steamer is necessary before the last lap by Egyptian 4ft $8\frac{1}{2}$in-gauge train to Cairo.

Other information on the Cape to Cairo route appears under South Africa, Botswana, Rhodesia, Zaïre, Zambia, Tanzania, Kenya, Uganda, Sudan and Egypt.

Apart from a rail link-up between Tunisia, Algeria and Morocco, the rest of Africa's nations are, with almost no exceptions, the possessors of isolated and fragmented systems. Most of them were constructed by their colonial owners to open up the hinterland and connect with the port and capital of the original European settlements. There are in fact 22 of these separate 'standard' colonial systems and one or two others which by-pass unnavigable reaches near the mouths of big rivers.

Page 210/211 : The Casablanca to Marrakech express en route in typical country.

AFRICAN OFFSHORE ISLANDS

Some appear on map on pages 218–219.

AZORES, CANARIES, MADEIRA, MAURITIUS, REUNION

Of the smaller islands off the coasts of Africa, none currently offer public rail service, but in the past quite interesting systems existed. For example, the widest gauge used on any railway in the world was Isambard Brunel's 7ft $0\frac{1}{4}$in used by the Great Western Railway of England until 1892, after which it became extinct. Or so one thought, but it does appear that there is (or was until recently) a line of that gauge, complete with steam locomotive, used for repairing the harbour wall at Punta Delgada in the Azores, a group of islands in the Atlantic Ocean.

From 1890 to 1937, a 4.5-mile tramway of metre gauge ran between the port and the town of Las Palmas in the Canary Islands. It would not be mentioned but for the fact that when during the war, gasoline was in short supply, a steam locomotive was sent over from Spain to

haul trains of dead electric tramcars over the line, the electric equipment having been dismantled on closure. Other tracks (but not of public railways, it is understood) have been observed at Santa Cruz on the island of Tenerife.

Funchal on the main island of Madeira had a steam rack railway known as the Monte Railway. It was built in 1892 (and extended in 1912) was 2.5 miles long, worked on the Riggenbach system and possessed five steam locomotives. It closed following an accident in 1939.

A 4ft 8½in gauge railway system, 111 miles in extent and based on Port Louis, existed on the island of Mauritius. In its heyday a fleet of 52 steam locomotives (including six Beyer-Garratts) nearly 200 carriages and 750 wagons handled the traffic. Passenger services ceased in 1956 and all traffic in 1967. British equipment and practice prevailed.

The island of Réunion of similar size to Mauritius, had a rail system of French origin smaller in gauge (one metre) and also proportionately smaller in extent and amount of equipment. This also has been closed recently.

ALGERIA

See map on pages 218-219.

ALGERIAN RAILWAYS – SNFT
Société Nationale des Transports Ferroviaires,
21 Boulevard Mohamed V,
Algiers.

The first railway in Algeria was a thirty-mile standard gauge line, running south-west from Algiers, which opened on 8 July 1862. Problems in working soon led to a take-over by the Paris-Lyons-Mediterranée Company; Algeria was then not just a colony but a department of France. The PLM completed the 260-mile route from Algiers to Oran in 1871. Another company, the Algerian Eastern, served the east, linking Algiers with Constantine by 1870. The eastern lines had to be taken over by the state in 1904.

Other lines, some 3ft 5½in gauge, led to the interior. By 1910 the town of Bechar, 500 miles from the sea and well out into the desert, had been reached. Leading south from this point, the proposed 1300-mile Trans-Saharan or, to give it its correct title, the Mediterranée-Niger Railway, almost put Tombouctou on the railway map. But tracklaying ceased in 1942 and has not been resumed.

In 1933 the railways in Algeria were unified

Extreme left, top: The famous steel-arched bridge at Victoria Falls on the Cape to Cairo Railway.

Extreme left, below: An 'open air' train on Monte Rack Railway at Funchal, Madeira.

Left: One of the powerful narrow-gauge Garratt locomotives in use on Algeria Railways during French rule. The locomotive is a 4-8-2+2-8-4 with a PLM number.

Below left: Benguela Railway woodburning Beyer Garratt 4-8-2+2-8-4 at Huambo (Nova Lisboa) in 1974.

Below: A diesel-hauled train on the Benguela Railway at Canocha in Angola.

and in 1939 their operation was finally nationalized. World War II and Independence in 1962 had only temporary effects on the rail network. Since then some narrow-gauge mileage has been converted to standard, but 750 miles still remain out of a total of 2400.

Locomotive Landmarks

The steam locomotive fleet was all based on and many were actual examples of current French designs, particularly the distinctive machinery of the PLM. A notable but somewhat brief episode was the introduction in 1934 of high-speed Garratts to work the Oran–Algiers–Constantine expresses. The Garratt type of articulated steam locomotive was generally built as a low-speed mountain climbing big puller, but its geometry, unlike that of other articulated types such as the Mallet, was eminently suited to high speed. The 29 4-6-2+2-6-4s could unassisted handle huge trains on the one-in-fifty grades as well as travel at up to 75mph on the level sections. Alas, the designers could not resist adding complications, such as an electrically worked reversing gear. This and a few other novel but unnecessary features proved to be the Achilles heel of these remarkable locomotives when, under wartime conditions, maintenance left a good deal to be desired.

Desert conditions in Algeria made the railways there a natural case for dieselization.

Before reliable French designs had been achieved, standard US diesels were imported. Steam was eliminated as early as 1955.

Electrification of iron-ore hauling lines in the east, based at the port of Annaba, began in 1932 and now extends 180 miles.

At the present time, on the standard gauge, forty electric and 137 diesel locomotives haul 400 passenger carriages and 10,000 wagons. The corresponding figures for the 3ft 5½in gauge are 0, 24, 33 and 1000 respectively. About 3.5 million passengers travel annually and 4.2 million tons of freight are hauled an average distance of 120 miles. Expenses are 99 percent of receipts.

ANGOLA

See map on pages 226–227.

Angola was a Portuguese colony dating from the sixteenth century, which achieved independence in 1976. Civil war broke out immediately afterwards and in 1977 the Communist side achieved control, although there is thought to be still some opposition outside main centres. There are three significant railway systems of which the principal was called the Benguela Railway.

BENGUELA RAILWAY COMPANY
Cia do Caminho de Ferro de Benguela,
PO Box 32,
Lobito, Angola.

The Benguela Railway was opened on 28 August 1928. Its principal *raison d'être* was to provide a direct outlet to the sea for copper, mined in what is now Zaïre and Zambia. For passengers from Europe to such places as Bulawayo or Salisbury, in Rhodesia/Zimbabwe, it saved three days in travel time compared to the route via Cape Town. Through trains were run – the gauge was the normal Southern African one of 3ft 6in. An Englishman called Robert Williams had obtained a 99-year concession from the Portuguese government in 1902 (a station on the railway is named after him) and accordingly the line was built with British capital. In theory at least, it still belongs to a British company.

Like most long-distance mineral hauling railways it has been financially successful – in some recent years expenses have been as low as 56 percent of receipts and the system has been maintained in top condition. This was, of course, before the recent war put it out of action.

The line runs inland due east from the port of Lobito, a distance of 840 miles to join the Zaïre railways at Dilolo. The principal operating problem was the climb from the coast to the 5000 + ft altitude of the inland plateau. The original alignment involved 1.5 miles of 1 in 16 grade and rack and pinion (Riggenbach) traction. A second, completed in 1948, involved a main climb at 1 in 33 and a much longer distance at 1 in 50. Yet a further one, completed in 1974, in spite of the uncertain future – kept the grade down to 1 in 80. The new line has 90 lb/yd rail but much 60 lb still exists elsewhere.

Like so many African Railways, especially those laid with lightish rails, the Benguela was faithful to the Beyer-Garratt articulated steam locomotives for hauling its principal traffic. Most of them in Angola are remarkable in one special way in that they use wood for fuel, the only case in the world in which a modern railway adopted *as deliberate policy* a primitive source of energy that in most other places did not out-last the first few puffs of steam.

The company planted eucalyptus forests at appropriate intervals along the line and they provide clean self-replacing and sweet-smelling fuel for its trains. The problem is that, while eucalyptus is little inferior to oil or coal in heat produced per *ton*, in terms of heat produced per *cubic yard* it is four or five times less effective. Although the locomotives carry huge cages in which the logs are stacked, not only are two firemen needed but wooding stops are required perhaps twice as often as coaling or oiling ones would be. Almost all the steam locomotives ever supplied to the railway – 107 in all – are still in service including some of the last ever to be built in England.

Near the coast where the heaviest grades are, eucalyptus does not grow and coal and oil burning power was used here even before the arrival of US standard diesels, 22 of which had been received by 1976.

In the early 1970s, problems between Zambia, Rhodesia and Mozambique had meant extra copper traffic on the Benguela, but since the Angolan troubles began, the railway has been closed to through traffic. At the same time the Tan Zam line provides another outlet for Zambian copper. A big question mark hangs over a line which four years ago was handling 2.5 million tons of traffic annually over its single line of metals.

Through passenger boat trains from Lobito to Elizabethville (now Lubumbashi) ceased several decades ago, but the daily passenger train which ran as far as the Congo border continued in service until 1975. There are 1830 freight cars, all equipped with the vacuum brake.

In Angola there are also three other separate smaller coast-to-inland systems, based on Luanda, Porto Amboin and Mossâmedes respectively. Prior to independence, these were separate entities, but it is likely that they are now administered as one. There are altogether 930 miles of 3ft 6in gauge and about 100 miles of 1ft 11½in with a fleet of 75 diesel and 35 steam locomotives (the latter mostly stored), sixty passenger cars and 2000 goods wagons.

AZORES
See African Offshore Islands

BASUTOLAND
See Lesotho

BECHUANALAND
See Botswana

BELGIAN CONGO
See Zaïre

BENIN

See map on pages 218–219.

BENIN RAILWAYS – OCBN
Organisation Commune Benin-Niger des Chemins de Fer et des Transports,
PO Box 16,
Cotonou.

The Benin Railways were begun in 1900 by a company which enjoyed a concession from the French government for a railway into the interior from the port of Cotonou. Its present terminus at Parakou, 275 miles from Cotonou, was achieved on 1 January 1935. There is talk of an extention to Gaya on the River Niger, which would double the length of the line. Currently eleven diesel locomotives and eight railcars haul 24 carriages and 350 wagons carrying 1.5 million passengers and 0.3 tons of freight. Receipts are 98 percent of expenses.

BOTSWANA

See map on pages 226–227.

A 400-mile stretch of the Cape to Cairo Railway has run through this sparsely populated country on its way from Mafeking to Bulawayo ever since 1897. Since independence in 1966 (Botswana was formerly the British Protectorate of Bechuanaland), Rhodesia Railways have operated the line. It is understood that the Botswana government has now taken over the line.

CAMEROON

See map on pages 226-227.

CAMEROON NATIONAL RAILWAYS AUTHORITY – REGIFERCAM
PO Box 304,
Douala.

In 1905, when Cameroon was a German colony, the Kamerun Eisenbahn Gesellschaft set out to build lines into the interior from Bonaberi and Douala, settlements on either side of the mouth of the River Wouri. The 100-mile western line was completed in 1911, but construction of the eastern one soldiered on into the days of the French mandate and then independence. The line was not opened to Ngaoundere, 585 miles from Douala, until 14 February 1974. There are presently 733 miles of metre-gauge route, 48 diesel locomotives, 94 carriages and 11,500 wagons in service. Expenses are 122 percent of receipts.

CANARIES
See African Offshore Islands

CONGO

See map on pages 226-227.

CONGO – OCEAN RAILWAY – CFCO
Chemin de Fer Congo – Ocean,
PO Box 651,
Pointe Noire.

This 3ft 6in gauge line, 320 miles long, was opened on 29 May 1934. It connected the port of Pointe Noire, on the Atlantic with Brazzaville on the Congo River, situated opposite Leopoldville (now Kinshasha, capital of Zaïre). The CFCO by-passed the barely navigable reaches of the river near its mouth. At one time the Wagons-Lits company provided sleeping and dining cars on the journey.

The CFCO provides common-carrier services on a 177-mile branch from Mont Belo to M'Bindo, built in 1962 by a mineral consortium known as COMILOG, who in turn operate their own ore trains through to Pointe Noire.

Statistics for the combined systems show 77 diesel locomotives with 58 passenger and 1540 freight cars, carrying 5.1 million tons of freight an average distance of 235 miles, in addition to 1.2 million passengers. The vacuum brake is used and the speed limit is 50 mph.

DAHOMEY
See Benin

Left, above: Mixed trains meet at Pobé, Benin.

Left: A Benguela Railway train on Angola's inland plateau. East of Huambo (Nova Lisboa) and Silva Porto most passenger trains were hauled by 4-6-0, 4-8-0 and 4-8-2 locomotives, the major hill-climbing having been accomplished.

Above: Multiple-unit railcars of French origin at Eséka, Cameroon.

Above centre, left: Construction work in the Congo.

Above centre, right: In days of steam, passengers await a steam train amid the banana plantations.

Top: A Rhodesian Railways 12th class 4-8-2 pulls a through Johannesburg–Bulawayo train.

─NORTH AFRICA─

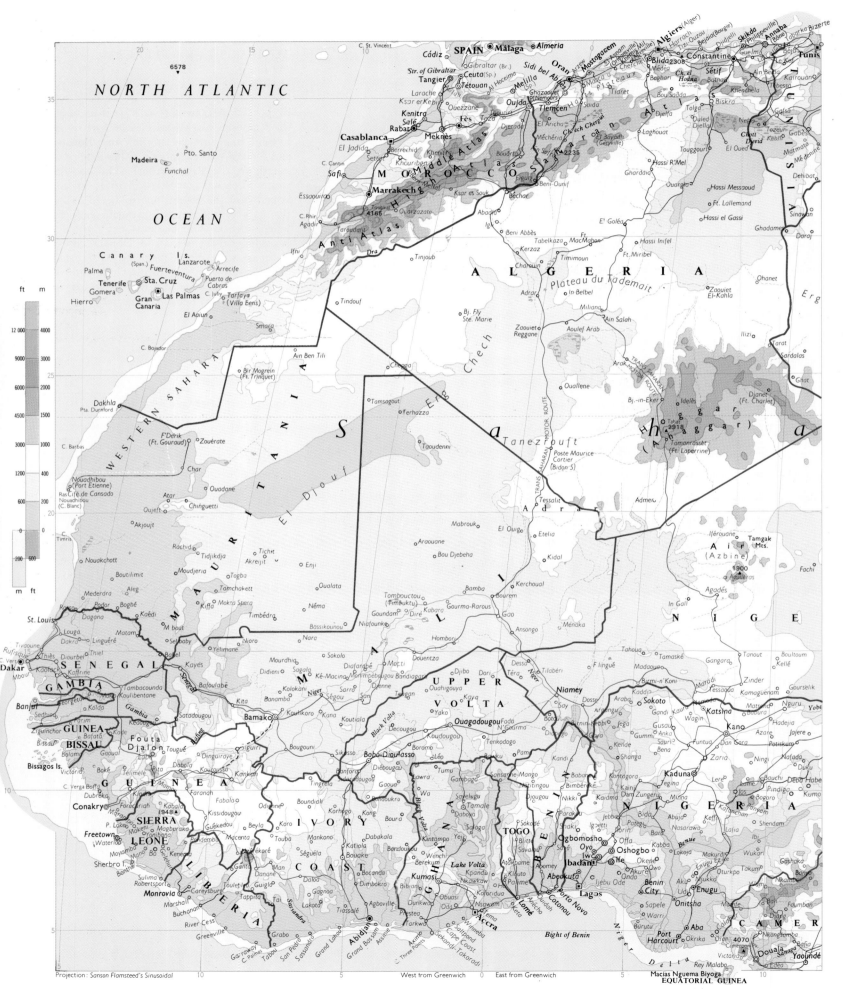

NORTH ATLANTIC

OCEAN

C. St. Vincent
SPAIN • Málaga • Almería
Cádiz
Str. of Gibraltar Gibraltar (Br.)
Tangier Ceuta (Sp.)
Larache Tétouan Al Hoceima
Melilla

Algiers (Alger)
Harrach
Blida 2308
Médéa
Mostaganem
Oran Sidi bel Abbès
Tiaret
Tlemcen

Constantine
Sétif
Skikda
Philippeville (Bône)
Annaba
Bizerte
TUNISIA
Tunis

6578

MOROCCO

Kenitra
Salé
Rabat
Casablanca
El Jadida
Berrechid
Safi
C. Cantin
Settat
Essaouira
Marrakech
High Atlas 4165
Anti Atlas
Agadir
Taroudant
Ifni
Dra

Fès Meknès
Middle Atlas
Khouribga
Khenifra
Ksar es Souk
Ouarzazate

Oujda
Taza
Figuig
Beni-Ounif
Béchar
Abadla
Igli
Beni Abbès

Saharan Atlas
El Aricha
Méchéria
Aïn Sefra 2235
El Bayadh (Geryville)
El Goléa

Laghouat
Ghardaïa

Touggourt
El Oued

ALGERIA

Canary Is. (Span.)
Palma Lanzarote
Tenerife Fuerteventura Arrecife
Gomera Sta. Cruz Puerto de Cabras
Gran Canaria Las Palmas
Hierro C. Juby Tarfaya (Villa Eens)

Madeira
Pto. Santo
Funchal

Plateau du Tademaït

WESTERN SAHARA

El Aaiún
Smara

C. Bojador
Dakhla
Pta. Durnford

MAURITANIA

C. Barbas
Nouadhibou (Port Etienne)
Ras Cap de Cansado
Nouadhibou (C. Blanc)

Bir Mogrein (Ft. Trinquet)
Aïn Ben Tili

Chegga

Tindouf

Bj. Fly
Ste. Marie
Zaouïet Reggane
Reggane

In Belbel
Adrar
Miliana
Aïn Salah
Aoulef Arab

Ouallene

Arak (MOTOR ROUTE)

TRANS SAHARAN

Zaouïet
El-Kahla

Ohanet

Erg

Ilizi

Tarat

Sardalas

Ghadamès
Daraj

Hassi R'Mel
Ouargla
Hassi Messaoud
Ft. Lallemand
Hassi el Gassi
Sinaoun
Dehibat

Chott Djerid
Gafsa
Tozeur
Kébili
Matmata
Médenine

Ain Ben Tili
Zouérate
F'Dérik (Ft. Gouraud)
Char
Atar
Chinguetti
Ouadane
Akjoujt
Oujeft

Tamsagout
Terhazza

Taoudenni

El Djouf

Tanezrouft
Poste Maurice
Cortier (Bidon 5)

Tessalit
Adrar

Bidj-in-Eker
Idelès
Tamanrasset (Ft. Laperrine)

Hoggar
(Ahaggar)
2918
Tahat

Djanet (Ft. Charlet)

Ghat

Mabrouk
El Ouig
Etelia

Iférouane
Tamgak
Mts.
1900
Assamakka

Aïr (Azbine)

Agadès

In Gall

Fachi

Nouakchott
Boutilimit
Mederdra
Aleg
Moudjéria
Tidjikja
Akreïjit
Tichit
Togba

Enji
Oualata

Néma
Bou Djebeha

Araouane

Tombouctou (Timbuktu)
Kabara
Bamba
Gourma-Rharous
Gao

Kerchoual
Kidal

Ménaka

Tanout

Gangara
Boultoum

C. Timris
Rosso
Podor
Boghé
Kaédi
Kiffa
Timbédra
Bassikounou
Niafounké
Goundam Diré
Ansongo
Hombori

MALI

Tahoua
Tamaské
Madaoua

NIGER

Kellé
Nguru
Yobe

St. Louis
Louga
Dagana
Matam
Linguère
M'bout
Selobaby
Yélimane
Nioro
Nara

Bamba
Douentza
Dessa
Tilabéri

Birni-n'Koni

Tchin Tabaraden
Maradi
Tessaoua
Kamagueua
Gourselik

C. Vert
Dakar
Thiès
Tivaouane
Diourbel
Kaolack
Mbour
Kaffrine
SENEGAL

Bakel
Kayes

Sokoto
Kita

Sokolo
Ségou
Mopti
Diafarabé
Ké-Macina
Djenné
San

Djibo Dori
Ouahigouya
Téra
Niamey
Say Dosso

Araba
Gandi Kaura
Sokoto
Gummi
Funtua
Dan Gora

Zinder

Matameye
Magaria
Daura

Kano
Azare
Jajere

Hadejia
Potiskum
Nafada Duku
Deba Habe

GAMBIA
Banjul
Georgetown
Kolda
Sédhiou
Ziguinchor
GUINEA
BISSAU
Bissau
Bolama
Bissagos Is.

Tambacounda
Koulibentane
Satadougou
Kédougou

Bafoulabé
Bamako
Koulikoro Kana
Banamba
Koutiala
Sikasso

Bobo-Dioulasso
Léo
Boromo
Koudougou
Tenkodogo
Pama
Kandi

UPPER
VOLTA
Yako
Ouagadougou
Fada N'Gourma

Kontagora
Kaduna
Lere
Bauchi
Pindiga
Kumo

GUINEA
Conakry
Dubréka
Forécariah
Kindia
Kankan
Kérouané
Beyla
Macenta
N'Zérékoré

Kissidougou
Faranah
Dabola
Dinguiraye
Siguiri

Bougouni
Banfora
Gaoua
Batié

Tougan
Dédougou

SIERRA
LEONE
Freetown
Waterloo
Makeni
Magburaka
Bo
Kenema

Odienné
Boundiali
Korhogo
Ferkessédougou

Gambaga
Wa
Navrongo

Tamale
Salaga
Yendi

Benin
BENIN
Natitingou
Bembéréké
Parakou
Nikki

Kaltungo
Numan
Yola
4070

CAMER

LIBERIA
Monrovia
Robertsport
Careysburg
Marshall
Buchanan
River Cess
Greenville
Tappita
Ganta

Man
Danané
Touba
Séguéla

IVORY
COAST
Bouaké
Katiola
Dabakala
Bondoukou
Bouna

Kumasi
GHANA
Bibiani
Obuasi
Dunkwa
Prestea
Tarkwa

Black Volta
Bole
Kintampo
Lake Volta
Kpandu
Ho

TOGO
Sokodé
Blitta
Atakpamé
Kpalimé
Lomé

Abeokuta
Ibadan
Oyo
Ife
Ilesha
Ondo
Ekiti
Ado
Oshogbo
Kabba
Lokoja
Okene
Benin
City
Sapele
Warri

NIGERIA
Abuja
Kontagora
Minna
Bida
Zungeru
Keffi
Nasarawa
Lafia
Makurdi
Wukari
Gashaka

Enugu
Nsukka
Onitsha
Abakaliki
Aba
Umuahia
Port
Harcourt

Gagnoa
Daloa
Dimbokro
Agboville
Abidjan
Grand Bassam
Assinie
C. Palmas
San Pedro
Sassandra
Tabou
Grabo
Three Points

Accra
Winneba
Cape Coast
Sekondi-Takoradi

Keta
Cotonou
Porto Novo
Lagos
Lomé
Ouidah

Bight of Benin

Niger
Delta
Bonny
Okrika
Oron
Calabar
Ikom

Rey Malabo
Macías Nguema Biyoga
EQUATORIAL GUINEA

Doula
Bafia
Sanaga
Yaoundé
Edéa

Victoria

ft m

12 000 4000
9000 3000
6000 2000
4500 1500
3000 1000
1200 400
600 200
0 0
200 600

m ft

West from Greenwich 0 East from Greenwich

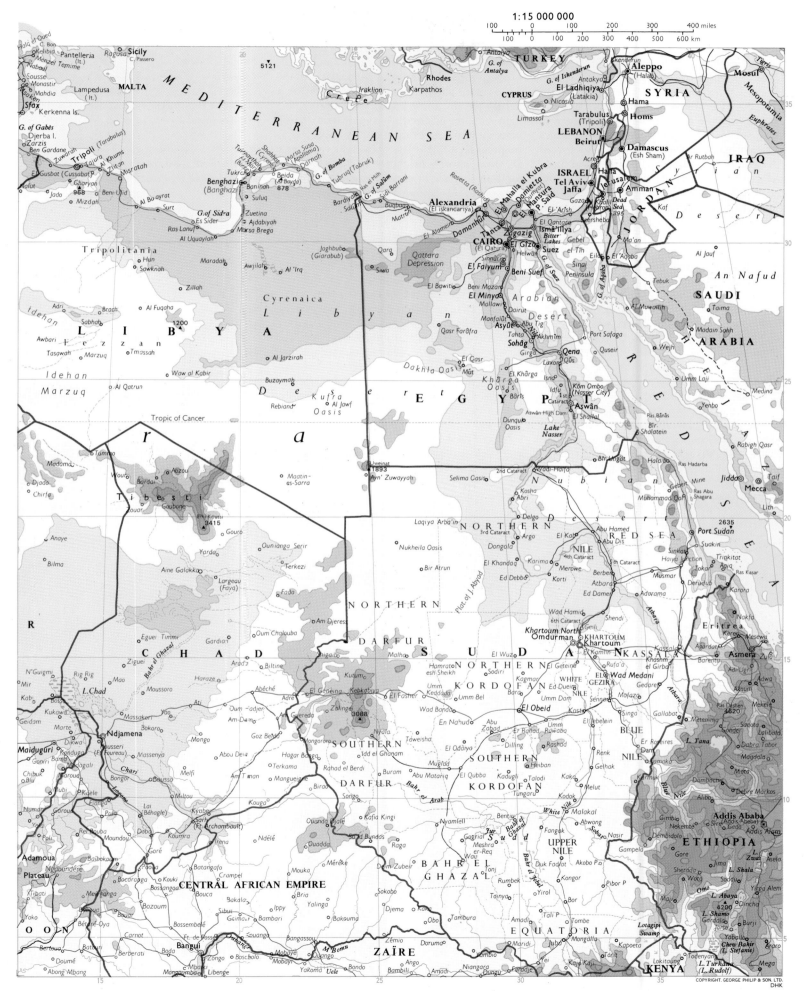

1:15 000 000

100   0   100   200   300   400 miles
100   0   100   200   300   400   500   600 km

EGYPT

See map on pages 218-219.

EGYPTIAN RAILWAYS
Rameses Square,
Cairo.

The idea of a railway to connect the Mediterranean with the Red Sea was first mooted in 1834 but in fact it was not until 1858 that a standard-gauge railway was opened between Alexandria, Cairo (reached in 1856) and Suez. Before that time animal transport was relied on, the Peninsular Oriental Steam Navigation Company owning 3000 camels for this purpose. The railway, on the other hand, was state-owned.

Robert Stephenson, no less, was chief engineer and, when the first section out of Alexandria opened in 1854, railways had come not only to Egypt but also to Africa. After the Suez Canal was opened in 1869, the Cairo-Suez section across the desert was found to attract little traffic and accordingly closed. Extensions followed to cover all the fertile parts of the country (which is another way of saying that railway development was confined to the River Nile and its delta).

Asyût, 230 miles south of Cairo, was reached in 1874, Luxor (340 miles) in 1878. El Shellal, a point quite close to the present terminus at Sadd-el-Ali (561 miles from Cairo) was at that time accessible from Luxor on a 3ft 6in gauge military line; this was converted to standard gauge in 1926.

World Wars I and II, in both of which Egypt was a main base, brought temporary extensions into Palestine and Libya of what was effectively the Egyptian railway system.

Steam power was partly of British and partly of French design and construction for some reason, exceptionally handsome and well-proportioned. This applied particularly to the 4-4-2s and 4-6-0s, types very suitable for a flattish terrain. Little known were thirty noble high-stepping oil-fired 4-6-2s with 81in driving wheels, built in France during 1955; it is tragic to record that less than eight years later all these superb machines had gone to the torch in the face of diesel onslaught. By 1963 the system was entirely dieselized, except for a fifteen-mile suburban electrification in the Cairo area.

The Egyptians learned the art of comfort in rail travel from that master of the craft, the Compagnie Internationale des Wagons-Lits, who ran the sleepers, diners and Pullman saloons in the country for many years.

For both main-line and branch-line services, self-propelled diesel trains had been a feature for many years; currently these consist of 430 vehicles. There are 620 diesel locomotives, 1350 carriages and 17,500 wagons. Approximately 230 million passengers and 13.6 million tons of freight are transported annually. Expenses in the year 1978 are 103 percent of receipts.

There used to be a large system of 2ft 6in gauge light railways in the Nile Delta, developed by a British Company but state-owned after 1955. It extended at one time to 600 miles, but is now reported to be closing.

Right: One of the British LMS-designed 2-8-0s imported to Egypt by the War Department during World War II.

Centre right: An Egyptian electric train built by Siemens of Germany.

Bottom right: A scene at Djibouti in 1910.

Bottom: A British-built 2-6-0 at Geneifa in the Egyptian Canal Zone in 1950.

Below: With Cairo main station in the background, a British-built 4-4-0 heads a train of mixed six-wheeled and bogie coaches past the locomotive shed in 1946.

ETHIOPIA

See map on pages 218–219, 226–227, 250–251.

NORTHERN ETHIOPIA RAILWAYS SHARE COMPANY
PO Box 218,
Asmara.

DJIBOUTI TO ADDIS-ABABA RAILWAY
Compagnie du Chemin de Fer Franco-Ethiopien de Djibouti a Addis-Ababa,
PO Box 1051,
Addis Ababa.

The Ethiopians are a race whose military prowess has never led to easy colonial exploitation – the Italians paid dearly for their brief occupation from 1936 to 1941 – but both the railways that exist there are of the classic colonial port-to-interior pattern.

The oldest ran inland from the port of Mesewa, then in Eritrea, which was Italian territory at that time. It had not got far when the Italian defeat at Adowa held things up for twenty years. Work began again in 1907, Asmera was reached in 1911 and Agordat in 1922. At present, most of the railway is out of use due to terrorist activity, but there are nominally eighteen steam and three diesel locomotives, five railcars, nineteen passenger coaches and 600 wagons running on the 190-mile line.

The Eritrean Railway (later administered by the Northern Ethiopia Railways Share Company) was not absolutely the first line; in 1867 a British military railway was laid briefly in 1867 inland for eleven miles from Zula, a short distance south of Mesewa. Its purpose was to aid General Napier's expedition to rescue British prisoners held at Magdala and has gone down in history as an almost perfect example of how *not* to build a military railway. Although a tremendous effort had gone into the planning, much useless and incompatible equipment was supplied, with the result that four months work in easy territory produced only eleven miles of line.

The second permanent line in Ethiopia was a French enterprise, commenced in 1897, to connect the port of Djibouti in French territory (then called French Somaliland but recently independent Afars & Issas) with the Ethiopian capital. Bankruptcy intervened in 1902, when the line had reached Dire Dawa (296 miles). Work started again in 1909 and Addis Ababa (485 miles) was reached on 7 June 1917. The locomotive fleet came largely from Switzerland (a 2-8-0 is noted as being named *Tcher-Tcher* – presumably Abyssinian for puff-puff). Dieselization was complete by 1956; most unusually, some of the 26 diesel-electrics came from Switzerland. There are 42 passenger cars and 640 wagons; 600,000 passengers and 0.5 million tons of freight are handled in a typical year, although recently Somali insurgents have interrupted traffic.

Top: A train from Pointe Noire arrives at Brazzaville in the Congo.

Above: A modern Ethiopian diesel-electric locomotive takes a freight towards the hills.

FRENCH WEST AFRICA (SENEGAL, MALI, GUINEA, IVORY COAST AND UPPER VOLTA)

See Senegal *et al*

GABON

See map on pages 226–227.

GABON STATE RAILWAYS – OCTRA
Office du Chemin de Fer Transgabonais
BP 2198,
Libreville.

The August 1978 and 1979 issues of *Thomas Cook's International Timetable* offers, under the entry for Gabon, a blank table with the encouraging words 'Service to commence shortly'.

Output from manganese and uranium mines at Franceville in the southeast of the country had always been sent out by a 48-mile ropeway across the border to a railroad in the Congo Republic. The ropeway had limited capacity and was, of course, no use for the transport of anything other than minerals. The alternative of a 438 mile all-purpose railway to the Gabonese port of Libreville was naturally preferred by the government. Work began in March 1975.

Diesel power is supplied from the USA and France; many other countries have contributed materials. A very large loading gauge is provided; 20ft 4in high by 13ft wide – this eclipses the Soviet gauge, which had been the largest in the world. Fortunately the terrain is not exacting.

GERMAN EAST AFRICA
See Tanzania

GERMAN SOUTH WEST AFRICA
See Namibia

GHANA

See map on pages 218-219.

GHANA RAILWAY & PORTS – GRP
PO Box 251,
Takoradi.

Before independence in 1957, Ghana was known as the Gold Coast; it is thus not surprising that the first section of railway there was built to serve the gold mines at Tarkwa forty miles inland from what is now the port of Takoradi. Makeshift port facilities were provided at Sekondi nearby and work began in March 1898. The mines were reached in 1901.

It had been decided to continue the line a further 128 miles inland to the trading centre of Kumasi; and this was put in hand. The Gold Coast was the original 'White Man's Grave' and it is on record that ten chief railway engineers had been expended before Kumasi was reached on 1 October 1903.

A line connecting Kumasi with Accra, the capital, situated further along the coast, but then only a 'surf port', was begun in 1909, delayed by the war and completed in 1923. The great deep-water port at Takoradi was opened in 1928. Other connecting lines and branches followed, making up the 600-mile 3ft 6in gauge system of today.

A series of handsome 4-8-2s were the mainstay of the line in steam days. The GCR was not able to avoid Garratts entirely; some were supplied in World War II on a new branch financed by the British Ministry of Aircraft Production to serve bauxite mines. Sixty-four steam locomotives are still on the books.

Eighty-eight diesels haul the majority of the six million passengers and one million tons of freight (average length of haul – 180 miles) now carried. This traffic is, alas, insufficient for solvency, expenses being 180 percent of receipts. There are 230 coaches and 4000 freight cars.

Above: A steam locomotive in Ghana at the turn of the century.

Top: A US-built 2-8-2 sits on the turntable outside the shed at Kumasi, Ghana.

Above: A class 29 2-8-2 pulls a freight train bound for Nakuru, Kenya.

Right: Trainloads of hardwood from Ghana destined for Europe.

Centre top: A Kenyan 59 class 4-8-2 + 2-8-4 Garratt at Nairobi East signal gantry. Inherited from Britain is the practice of the signalman's waiting to take the electric token (for single line working) from the fireman.

Centre below: Henschel diesel-hydraulic 660 hp B-Bs stand in Nairobi station yard in their new blue livery, May 1978.

Extreme right, top: Masai warriors take a look at a North British Company 84 class diesel shunter.

Below: A 60 class 4-8-2 + 2-8-4 Garratt with roller bearings on all axles – a truly modern machine. These engines were in regular use until the late 1970s.

GOLD COAST
See Ghana

GUINEA
See Senegal *et al*

IVORY COAST
See Senegal *et al*

KENYA

See map on pages 226–227.

KENYA RAILWAYS
PO Box 30121,
Nairobi.

On 11 December 1895 George Whitehouse (later, Sir George Whitehouse, KCB) stepped ashore at Mombasa to commence construction of the British government's 580-mile Uganda Railway. It was a curiously reluctant piece of empire building, violently opposed at home, yet, in the end, one of the most successful. Against all reason the project soon became viable: the Arab slave-trade, the suppression of which was one of the objectives, came to an end; Nairobi, then just a survey peg in the scrub, became, seventy short years later, the capital of a great and respected independent nation.

The site of Nairobi was reached in 1899 and the objective, a landing place on Lake Victoria called Port Florence, later Kisumu, in 1901. Entebbe in Uganda was reached by a 150-mile steamer trip across one corner of the immense lake which is effectively a source of the River Nile. In 1931 the railway was extended across the Nile to Kampala, Kisumu then becoming the terminus of a 130-mile branch; it was finally extended to a point close to the Zaïre border and the Mountains of the Moon at Kasese (near Kilembe), 1080 miles from Mombasa, was reached in 1956. The 315-mile Tororo-Gulu-Pakwach branch reaches to within 100 miles of the Sudan border.

In 1926 the system became the Kenya-Uganda Railway and in 1948 the East African Railways & Harbours Administration, when the lines in what is now Tanzania became included. The system finally reached 3700 miles, the second largest in Africa, but in 1975 friction between what had in 1960 become three separate nations had reached a point where the administration of a single joint railway system became impossible. The railways in Tanzania had always been, in any case, a separate operating entity but, so far as Kenya and Uganda were concerned, any separation must be more *de jure* than *de facto* to start with.

Construction problems included marauding lions, hostile natives, disease and terrible supply difficulties. The now-regrettable decision to adopt a gauge other than the British Africa standard of 3ft 6in was taken at the last minute by the home government in order to permit the use of Indian equipment, conveniently to hand 'across the bay'; 32,000 Indians were brought over to do the construction work and 2500 died.

The traction problem in Kenya was a severe one. From sea level at Mombasa, the original railway climbed to over 6000ft. When the main line was extended into Uganda, more than 9000ft of altitude had to be surmounted. In fact Timboroa station, 9136ft, was the highest

railway location in the British Empire. Much easing of gradients was done – there are four spirals on the system – but the problems remained acute until the coming of the Beyer-Garratt locomotive, which in 1957 accounted for 129 out of a total stock of 450.

The first Garratts were supplied in 1926 and were basically two of the line's standard 4-8-0s joined together, inner pony trucks added, making them 4-8-2 + 2-8-4s. They shared the ten-ton axle-load of the 4-8-0s, enabling operation on 50 lb/yd rail. The Garratts marked the beginning of the end of eucalyptus wood-firing, although on some of the remoter lines it continued until after coal was superseded by oilburning at the end of World War II. The last Garratts supplied were the magnificent '59' class 4-8-2 + 2-8-4s of 1955, 104ft long, with 21-ton axle-load, now the most powerful steam locomotives running in the world and able to take full advantage of the heavier 95 lb/yd rail which by this time had been laid on the main line. They handle, in 1978, 1200-ton trains with ease between Mombasa and Nairobi. The overall cost of operation was then, less than would be involved in changing over to diesel traction. Their successors, were to have been the '61' class, the largest Garratts ever designed, 125ft long with 25-ton axle-load, but in the

end it was decided to dieselize instead. This process was to be completed by 1980 except for some minor operations.

An interesting feature of operation is the so-called 'caboose' system, whereby on long runs one train crew can rest while a second one takes over. In 1977 the East African administration was broken up and the three countries, Kenya, Uganda and Tanzania, resumed responsibility for their own systems. Kenya Railways Corporation began official operations on 20 January 1978. Kenya Railways operates a fleet of 103 steam and 130 diesel locomotives, 513 coaching stock vehicles and 6637 freight wagons. The last statistics available (1976) for the *whole* East African system show a fleet of 235 steam and 192 diesel locomotives, 16,000 freight and 530 passenger cars. The system carried six million tons of freight an average distance of 420 miles as well as 5.7 million passengers. Token working is used, with semaphore signalling. The air brake is used in Kenya and Uganda; both air and vacuum brakes are used in Tanzania.

SOUTHERN AFRICA

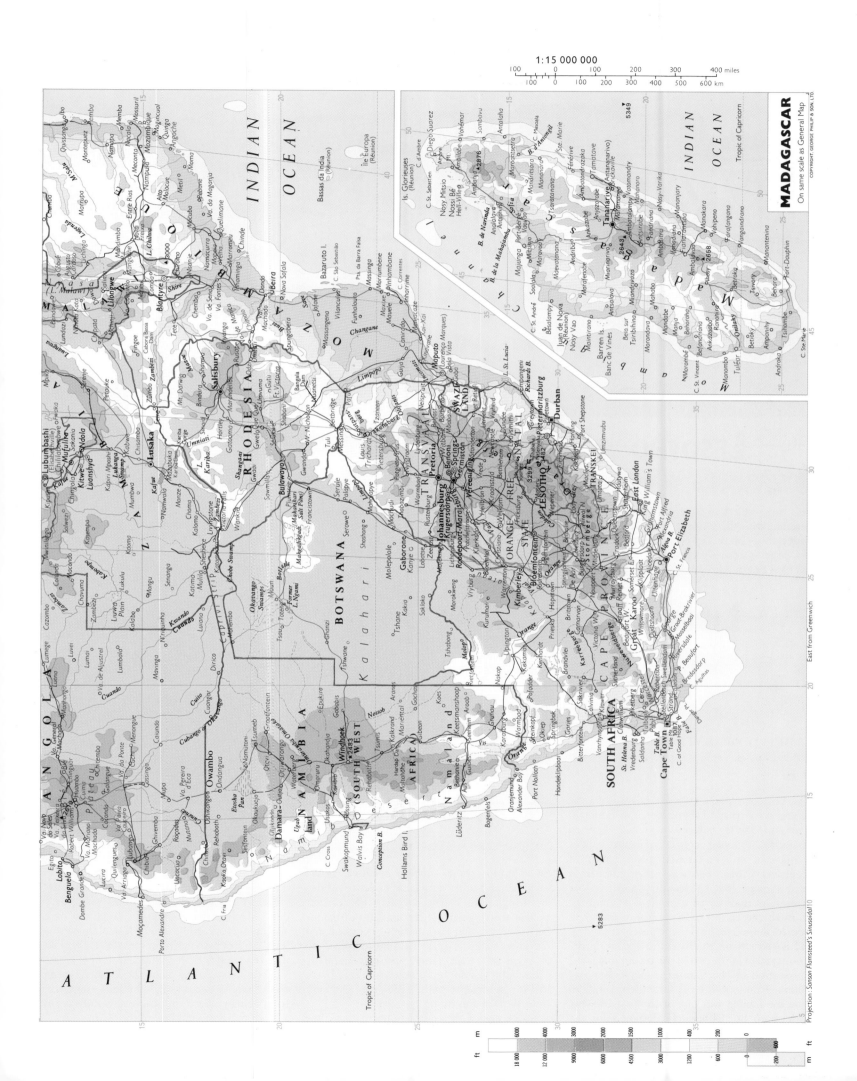

1:15 000 000

MADAGASCAR
On same scale as General Map

LESOTHO

See map on pages 226–227.

One thing the Kingdom of Lesotho has in common with the Vatican City is an absurdly short railway (in this case 1.25 miles) belonging to a large and totally enclosing neighbour, in this case South Africa.

LIBERIA

See map on pages 218–219.

BONG MINING CO.
PO Box 538,
Monrovia.

LAMCO JV OPERATING CO.
PO Box 69,
Monrovia.

Not being anyone's colonial possession, the natural resources of Liberia were not exploited at all until shortly before World War II, when Firestone obtained concessions for rubber plantations on the coastal plain south of Monrovia. After that war other companies were allowed into the country and iron-ore deposits were discovered in the north and the south of the country. One railway was built from Monrovia to the Bong Mines in the north, and another from Buchanan to a mine in the Nimba range in the east of the country near the intersection of the Guinea, Ivory Coast and Liberia frontiers. The latter railway built in 1962 for Lamco was one of the first iron-ore railways to be deliberately designed for the

operation of long trains and to be fully equipped with centrally controlled signalling and other modern aids to efficient operation.

The line is standard gauge with 130 lb/yd rail to American standards and the normal train size is ninety wagons each carrying about 94 tons of ore giving each a total gross load of 10,530 tons, hauled by three 2000hp locomotives. The 160-mile route is single track, and has eight intermediate stations with passing loops. The maximum tonnage of ore transported has been thirteen million tons/year. Since the total fleet is 510 ore cars and fourteen locomotives this calls for a very high standard of operations and maintenance.

Plans have been drawn up for increasing production at the mine to 16 million tons/year and for opening a new mine in Guinea with a production of 15.0 million tons/year. This will involve a 12-mile extension of the existing railway, lengthening of the train to 125 wagons, partial doubling of the main line and new terminal facilities at each end of the line.

LIBYA

See map on pages 218–219.

So far as railways are concerned, Libya has had a chequered history with independent ventures in various parts of the country. The earliest railway was constructed at 75cm (2ft 5½in) gauge between 1911 and 1916 to serve Benghazi and the surrounding area. In 1918 it was converted to 95cm (3ft 1.4in) gauge and was gradually extended to a total of 69 miles reaching Barce in 1927; a separate 35-mile line was also built from Benghazi to Sulug.

In the west of the country a 95cm gauge line

was built from Tripoli to Zuwarah between 1912 and 1915 with some branches inland and eastwards from Tripoli. Initially this group of lines was used for military purposes. Later it carried general freight and passenger traffic and in 1938 a diesel railcar service was introduced for the journey between Tripoli and Gharyan. During World War II these western lines were again taken over for military purposes and for a short period between 1943 and 1944 were converted to metre gauge to overcome a shortage of 95cm gauge stock. The lines out of Tripoli were closed in 1960 and much of the formation was used for the location of a new coastal highway. Several of the two-storey station buildings with their shady balconies and verandahs can still be seen beside the road.

The eastern lines radiating out of Benghazi were closed in 1965. The only other railway in Libya was a 60-mile standard-gauge wartime extension from Egypt to Tobruk. This line was cut short at Salûm in 1946 and the Libyan portion of the track was lifted.

More recently plans have been made for a standard-gauge line linking Tripoli with Sfax in southern Tunisia. This line will run slightly inland of the coastal highway and pass to the south of each of the principal towns; short branches to ports and other industrial developments are included in the proposals. The layout of the passenger and freight terminals in Tripoli will permit the line to be extended eastwards to Misratah at a later date. Preliminary designs have also been made for a 300 mile standard-gauge route from Misratah southwards to Brach to permit the exploitation of an iron-ore deposit there. The aspiration to create a continuous rail link along the Mediterranean coast from Morocco to Egypt is still a long way from being realized, but these new railways in Libya provide a vital link in the chain.

MADAGASCAR

(MALAGASY REPUBLIC)

See map on page 227.

MALAGASY RAILWAYS
PO Box 259,
Avenue de l'Independence,
Tananarive.

Madagascar is the only off-shore island around Africa to retain a public railway system, no doubt because of its great size.

A metre-gauge line runs from Tamatave, a port on the east coast of the island, to the capital Tananarive in the central highlands and then southwards along the mountain chain to Antsirabe. Since the line climbs to an altitude of 5500ft in the 100 miles from Brickaville on the coast to Tananarive it is not surprising that gradients as steep as 1 in 29 and curves as sharp as 164ft radius are involved, or that operating speeds are very low. However, the location of the capital city in the comparatively temperate climate of the mountain range in the centre of the island makes this inevitable. The main station in Tananarive has an ideal location across the end of the principal boulevard in the shopping district which indicates the greater importance the railway enjoyed in the days before domestic flights took over the bulk of inter-city passenger travel.

A separate railway on the island of Nossi Bé off the northwest coast of Madagascar provides a complete constrast to the national system. This serves a sugar estate and was constructed almost entirely of secondhand materials from other countries. Originally worked by steam locomotives designed to use bagasse, the waste-product from the sugar mills as fuel, the only recent acquisitions are two small diesel locomotives which now work the twelve-mile main line leaving the remaining octogenarian 0-6-0 tender engine to shunt to and from the cane yard and to make short trips to nearby stations. The cane wagons were adapted from ammunition carriers from the trenches of World War I and the rails generally date from the same period. The line includes a number of steep gradients where, despite the high axle-load of the locomotives, sanding is required to assist adhesion. The notorious unreliability of mechanical sanding devices is avoided by placing a sack of sand on the buffer beam and getting a member of the train crew to squat on the sideplates sprinkling handfuls of sand onto the rail whenever he hears the wheels begin to slip. This description may suggest a decrepit and rundown system unworthy of appearing in the same book as the sophisticated national networks, but the extreme enthusiasm of the train crews, the amazingly high utilization of its antiquated stock, and above all its picturesque setting make it a railway to remember.

MALAWI

See map on pages 226–227.

MALAWI RAILWAYS LTD.
PO Box 5144,
Limbe, Malawi.

The building of the railway in Nyasaland, as Malawi was then known, involved three stages. The Shire Highlands Railway, completed in 1908, ran up-country to Blantyre, the capital, from Nsanje on the Shire River, a tributary of the great Zambesi. A desire for more reliable movement when the river was low led to an extension, completed in 1914, and located

partly in Portuguese territory, to Vila Fontes on the Zambesi. This section was known as the Central Africa Railway. A further desire to avoid transhipment from ocean-going ships into river barges led to a further project to extend the line across the Zambesi (hence the name Trans-Zambesi Railway) to the port of Beira. This was put in hand after World War I and completed in 1935, in which year the up-country line (by now called the Nyasaland Railways) was extended to Salima on Lake Nyasa. The Zambesi was crossed by the famous bridge at Sena, the longest in Africa, 12,064ft in length, with 33 spans. This structure is now in independent Mozambique but was effectively an integral part of the Nyasaland system.

The colonial settlers established their political and commercial centres on the southern highlands to avoid the risk of diseases then prevalent in the low-lying areas in the Shire River valley and around Lake Nyasa. As a result the railway had to climb very steeply to reach Blantyre and nearby Limbe, the headquarters. This section includes gradients of one in forty and curves as tight as $5\frac{1}{2}$ chains (363ft) radius, creating considerable operating and maintenance problems. The continuation of the line northwards from Blantyre to cross the Shire River near Matope and to approach the shore of Lake Nyasa involved similarly steep gradients and sharp curves which severely limit the operating capacity of the line. The new connection from Nkaya eastwards to cross the border into Mozambique at Nayuci has gentler gradients (one in 115 against exports) and has provided an opportunity for opening up the agricultural potential of the central part of the country. The system has recently been extended westwards to the new capital, Lilongwe, and a connection from there to Chipata in Zambia is planned.

In 1976 a Zambia Railways diesel locomotive and a number of Rhodesia Railway coaches were working in Malawi. Their return home was rendered virtually impossible by the political situation between neighbouring countries.

MALI
See Senegal *et al*

MAURITANIA

See map on pages 218–219.

MAURITANIA RAILWAY – SNIM-COMINOR
Chemin de Fer F'Derik a Nouadhibou,
PO Box 42,
Nouadhibou.

The Mauritania Railway is a newish iron-ore railway, 400 miles long, skirting the Western Sahara border. It was completed in 1963 and is owned by a mining organization, but passenger trains also operate. There are 37 diesel locomotives, fifteen passenger and over one thousand freight cars. Eighteen million tons, mostly minerals, are carried annually.

MAURITIUS
See African Offshore Islands

MOROCCO

See map on pages 218–219.

MOROCCAN RAILWAYS – ONCFM
Office National des Chemins de Fer du Maroc,
19 Avenue Allal ben Abdallah,
Rabat.

An extensive system of 1100 miles of 1ft 11½in gauge military railways was built in Morocco during the period (1912 onwards) when it was being brought under the control of the French Army. In 1915 the principal links were opened for public service, including a 580-mile 'main line' on more or less the present route, from Oujda on the Algerian border via Fes, Rabat

and Casablanca to what is now the famous desert resort of Marrakech in the far southwest. A maximum speed of 15 mph made for rather tedious travel.

In 1914 an 85-year concession was given to a joint French and Spanish concern, for a standard-gauge railway joining Tangier to Fes. After delays due to World War I, this 200-mile line was completed in 1927. It still retains a nominal independence, although working is

Top left: New diesel-electric locomotives in Malawi in 1973.

Top centre: Diesel railcar No 198 UP rounds the bend to Chipoka station on its way to Salima from Blantyre. This trip of 160 miles was run twice weekly in 1962.

Left: A 1964-built diesel-electric set waits in the modern station at Casablanca with a train for Tangier in 1971.

Below centre: An electric train set nears Sule on the electrified route from Casablanca to Fez.

Below: The Fez-Rabat-Casablanca express. The route was electrified well before World War II.

in the hands of the Moroccan Railways. Further standard-gauge lines were by then also under construction, most superseding narrow-gauge ex-military ones and by 1934 there was a through route from Marrakech via Casablanca, Rabat and Fes to the Algerian border; it was part of a line running under French control all the way to Tunis, 1500 miles in all. A further line in the east running due south to Bouârfa, in an area where coal is mined, was constructed between 1927 and 1931 by a private company, the Morocco Eastern Railway. This was taken over by the state in 1963. The proposal to extend this line across the Sahara to Tombouctou was referred to in the Algerian section.

Electrification was envisaged from the start and the first contact wires were energized (at 3000v DC) as early as 1927 in the Casablanca area. At present all the main lines from Marrakech and Tangier to Fes are worked electrically, together with certain branches serving mining areas. Water power from the Atlas Mountains is used to generate current. About 440 miles (out of a total of 1090) of route are now electrified, with 61 locomotives; 81 diesels operate the remainder of the system and there are altogether 300 passenger and 8700 freight cars. Twenty-two million tons of freight and 4.3 million passengers are carried annually. Expenses are currently 104 percent of receipts.

MOZAMBIQUE

See map on pages 226–227.

MOZAMBIQUE STATE RAILWAYS
Caminhos de Ferro do Estado de Moçambique, Maputo.

A number of independent 3ft 6in gauge lines and one 2ft 5½in gauge line, were built at various times in the last eighty years to foster development of the country by providing connections to suitable port locations, at Maputo (formerly Lourenço Marques), Inhambane, Beira, Quelimane and Lumbo (near the town of Mozambique).

From Maputo there are connections to Swaziland (via Mlawula), the Republic of South Africa (via Komatipoort) and Rhodesia/Zimbabwe (via Malvernia). The latter line follows the river Limpopo. (Its construction crossed the routes taken by wild animals to their watering places. The animals were afraid to cross the new track formation and had to be herded across by game wardens to prevent them dying of thirst.) The line from Inhambane is narrow gauge and steam operated. Locomotives and rolling stock are shipped to Maputo for maintenance and the depot and workshops there incorporate mixed-gauge tracks for this purpose.

From Beira, there are connections to Rhodesia/Zimbabwe (via Umtali) – the sanction-breaking route closed by the Mozambique government early in 1976. At Dondo, some fifty miles from Beira is the junction with the Trans-Zambesi Railway which runs northwards to cross the River Zambesi between Sena and Dona Ana and continues northwards into Malawi. This was built and operated by a British Company but is now virtually nationalized. At Dona Ana, immediately north of the Zambesi bridge, is the junction with the Tete division of the Mozambique Railways which relies on the TZR for its connection with the rest of the system and which serves the coal mines at Moatize, Mozambique's only mineral resource to have been developed at the present time. Moatize is deep in the Zambesi valley near the regional capital of Tete whereas the main line is high on the north side of the valley on an alignment suitable for future extension into the northern plateau and across into Zambia. The gradients from Moatize to the highest point of the line at Caldas Xavier are very severe and present a considerable problem for expansion of production at the coal mine.

The railway bridge at Sena provides the only way of crossing the Zambesi for some considerable distance upstream and downstream. The TZR used to operate a form of motorail service across the bridge with end-loading docks in the stations at each end and a special flat wagon kept for the purpose. Cars could be carried on any train by application to the station-master at either end of the bridge but this was less convenient than it sounds because the flat-car had to be conveyed to a station some distance north of the bridge where it could be

shunted and brought back to be placed on the loading dock.

From Quelimane, there are no other connections and the line only serves agricultural areas in the coastal plain.

In the north a new port is being developed at Nacala and a branch line has been built from Rio Monapo to this port which has virtually replaced the service through Lumbo.

The working timetable for this branch includes a footnote that trains are not to cross at one particular station during the hours of darkness. The line is worked by telegraph and ticket with no signals and no staff at intermediate stations so that the guard has to change the switches for crossing movements. One night a guard getting down from the train to perform these duties was attacked and killed by a lion; this unfortunate event gives a macabre explanation for the timetable footnote.

The maintenance facilities for this route are

located at Nampula, the regional capital; steam on this line is being superceded by diesel traction and a new servicing shed has recently been built. Major repairs would require locomotives to be shipped from Nacala or to be taken through Malawi and down the TZR to Beira and then via Rhodesia/Zimbabwe to Maputo, a total distance of over 2000 miles!

In its original form the northern line terminated at Nova Freixo some 300 miles from the coast and its purpose appears to have been to carry imported goods for the colonial settlers as much as exported products from the region since the track gradients are equally steep (1 in 52) against both imports and exports. Now that the line has been extended northwards to Vila Cabral and westwards via Entre Lagos into Malawi and is carrying copper from Zambia to replace the route through Rhodesia/Zimbabwe these severe gradients against exports are something of an embarrassment.

NAMIBIA

See map on pages 226–227.

As these words are written, Namibia (until recently Southwest Africa and before that German Southwest Africa) is undergoing a painful birth. Its railways are now a close-knit part of South African Railways but once upon a time they were remarkable enough to stand by themselves in any general book on railways. The reason is that most very narrow narrow gauge railways – in this case 1ft 11½in-gauge – are proportionately short; however, the Otavi Railway was 360 miles long. It was built in 1905–06 to serve a copper-mining area inland at Tsumeb; a sleeping car (thought to be the only one ever to operate on such a slim gauge as this) was provided to ease a two-day journey. Conversion to 3ft 6in took place in 1956, but locomotives and equipment from the Otavi can still be found running on the 2ft gauge lines in other parts of South Africa.

NIGER

See map on pages 218–219.

This land-locked state in the centre of the bulge of Africa has no railways as yet. However, its government has caught the railway disease sufficiently badly for study to be made of the feasibility of providing a railway system. It could connect with any or all of the systems of four neighbours: Benin, Ivory Coast (see Senegal), Togo or Nigeria.

Left, top: Mozambique has a fascinating 2ft 5½in gauge line powered by American Locomotive Company 2-6-0s and Baldwin 2-8-0s. The coastal terminus is at João Bela (Xai-Xai), a small town near the north side of the mouth of the Limpopo.

NIGERIA

See map on pages 218–219.

NIGERIAN RAILWAY CORPORATION
Ebute Metta.

When the railway came to Nigeria, the country had been part of the British Empire for thirty years. In 1893 work began on the 3ft 6in gauge Lagos Railway, intended to run up-country for 700 miles to Kano. The first section to Ibadan (120 miles) was opened in 1901. This relatively slow progress did not satisfy the inlanders who stirred matters up by starting off on their own. Therefore work was also started from Baro on the north bank of the Niger River, which is navigable for shallow craft (as described in Edgar Wallace's famous *Sanders of the River* books) for hundreds of miles from its mouth. Kano was reached in 1911, but before this the southern section had reached the great river at Jebba. A new branch (shortly to become the main line) was built from a point opposite Jebba to Minna on the Baro-to-Kano line. A train ferry provided the connection.

In 1916 the Niger bridges were opened, crossing the two channels of the river with steel structures 660ft and 1525ft long respectively. This opened a through rail connection between Lagos and Kano via Kaduna. The Lagos Railway and the Baro-Kano railway were amalgamated to form the Nigerian Railway in 1912, becoming a typical colonial railway used for bringing raw materials from up-country down to the port of Lagos. Ground nuts and tin were two of the principal commodities.

In the meantime (1913) an eastern line was begun out of Port Harcourt, originally to serve coal fields 150 miles inland, but later it was extended. By 1934, when the 2625ft Benue River bridge was opened, there was through-communication between Port Harcourt and Kaduna. The present terminus, Nguru (850

miles from Lagos) was reached in 1930 and there have been other extensions since, one of which made redundant a 2ft 6in gauge line which, between 1914 and 1957, ran from Zaria to serve regional tin mines. Mileage presently stands at 2200.

In steam days 4-8-2s and 2-8-2s were the main types in use; the 'River' class 2-8-2s supplied from 1948 onwards was the standard in the latter days. Beyer-Garratts (also named and painted red) were supplied to haul on 45lb rails the same trains which had been brought up from the coast by 'straight' locomotives on 80 lb or 60 lb iron. Recently diesels have taken over more and more of the working; currently there are 180 such units on the books, against 133 steam. Since the main lines are shortly to be replaced by a 4ft 8½in gauge railway on new high-speed alignments, further diesel purchases will no doubt be for that system.

Currently around four million tons of freight and nine million passengers are carried at a cost which is two and a half times the receipts, but this position is expected to be transformed when the competitiveness and economy of the new standard-gauge railway comes into play.

NYASALAND
See Malawi

REUNION
See African Offshore Islands

Top centre: A new English-Electric diesel locomotive heading the Royal train prepares to depart from Lagos, Nigeria before independence.

Top right: A coal train arrives at Kaduna Junction in the heart of Nigeria behind the locomotive River Belwa *in May 1959.*

Left, centre: An ex-Rhodesian Railways 2-8-2 + 2-8-2 Beyer-Garratt – now a CFM locomotive – acts as station pilot at the frontier station with Rhodesia/Zimbabwe near Umtali.

RHODESIA/ ZIMBABWE

See map on pages 226–227.

RHODESIA RAILWAYS BOARD
PO Box 782,
Metcalfe Square,
Bulawayo.

At the time the city of Bulawayo was founded in 1893, it was a four month journey by ox-cart to travel there from the coast. When the dreaded rinderpest struck down the oxen even that was not possible. Accordingly the Cape to Cairo line, here known as the Bechuanaland Railway Company, was pressed forward over easy country to reach Bulawayo from the south on 19 October 1897.

Long before this line had reached the Rhodesian border, agreement had been reached with the Portuguese government for a line to the port of Beira in Mozambique. Construction began in 1892; a decisive reason for the slow progress was the heavy death rate, particularly among the white employees, imposed by indigenous fevers and disease. In both 1892 and 1893, over sixty percent of them died.

The 216-mile section in Portuguese territory was laid very lightly, using 2ft gauge and 20 lb/yd rail; that in Rhodesia was built to the normal African standard of 3ft 6in. Through communication from Beira – with break of gauge at Umtali – was possible from 22 May 1899; within the year, the Portuguese section was converted to 3ft 6in also, when operation (but not ownership) was taken over by the then Mashonaland Railway Company. Salisbury and Bulawayo were connected by rail in 1902, uniting the two lines in Rhodesia/Zimbabwe.

Towards the north, the railway reached the Victoria Falls in 1904 and then, by one of the world's most spectacular and spectacularly sited bridges, crossed into what is now Zambia. The Victoria Falls bridge built in a short eighteen months, is a steel arch of 500ft span, 400ft above the boiling waters of the Zambesi River at the foot of the great falls. It was opened on 12 September 1905.

The Bechuanaland (Bechuanaland is now Botswana) and Mashonaland Railways became in due time the privately owned 2436-mile Rhodesian Railways; the shares were bought by the government after World War II. Since then some contraction has taken place: Mozambique took over ownership and operation of the line to Beira in 1948; Zambia and the RR lines therein became independent in 1964. Additional connections with the outside world have been made, including the Rhodesian section of a route to the Mozambique port of Lourenço Marques (now Maputo) in 1951 and a line, independent of Botswana territory, completed in 1972 to connect with South African Railways at Beit Bridge in the extreme south. The current mileage is 2100.

As a country rich in coal but lacking oil, Rhodesia was naturally inclined to hold on to

Extreme left, top: A Beyer-Garratt locomotive takes on water at Victoria Falls, Rhodesia/Zimbabwe.

Left: A waiting room for third- and fourth-class passengers on the West Nicholson branch of Rhodesia Railways.

Below: A Rhodesian freight train double-headed with Beyer-Garratt locomotives.

steam. This tendency was increased by the United Nations' sanctions which have been applied to the country since its Unilateral Declaration of Independence (UDI) in 1965. The RR was also the extreme example of the use of Beyer-Garratt locomotives; these double-hinged monsters have formed three-quarters and more of the steam fleet in recent years. In Rhodesia/Zimbabwe, steam loco-motives are Garratts unless described specific-ally as being 'straight'. The articulated fleet covered the whole spectrum of duties in a particularly well-arranged way. As a tribute to one of the most modern and logically designed collections of steam power, their significant dimensions are – quite exceptionally for this

book – given below.

In spite of sanctions the Rhodesia RR has succeeded in supplementing a few pre-UDI English Electric diesels with a substantial eighty-strong fleet which currently covers the operation of over one-half of the trains.

Unlike the situation in South Africa, there was no colour bar against coloured members of the population aspiring to responsible positions on Rhodesian Railways, such as locomotive drivers.

Rhodesian passenger trains are unusual in providing four classes of accommodation; again, there is no *apartheid* in respect of their use by various ethnically divided sections of the population. Approximately 500 brown-

and-cream cars cater for three million passen-gers each year, while 12,000 freight wagons are involved in carrying 12.8 million tons of freight an average distance of 300 miles; however, one should note that some of these figures are a little suspect because the division of rolling stock and other matters between Zambia and Rhodesia/Zimbabwe has yet to be agreed, even after fifteen years of separation.

Extreme left, bottom: This photograph, taken during the days of the Federation of Rhodesia and Nyasaland, shows a cross-border train on the then-new Bannockburn to Lourenço Marques (now Maputo) rail link.

Rhodesian Steam Power

Class	Type	Number Built	Cylinders (Bore × Stroke)	Coupled Wheel Diameter	Traction Effort lb	Grate Area sq ft	Maximum Axle-load in tons	Comments
14/14A	2-6-2 + 2-6-2	38	16in × 24in	48in	39,560	39	$13\frac{1}{2}$	Lightly built locomotives for lightly built branch lines
15/15A	4-6-4 + 4-6-4	74	$17\frac{1}{2}$in × 26in	57in	41,908	50	$15\frac{1}{4}$	Large-wheeled locomotives for passenger trains.
16/16A	2-8-2 + 2-8-2	50	$18\frac{1}{2}$in × 24in	48in	51,338	50	$14\frac{3}{4}$	General purpose
20/20A	4-8-2 + 2-8-4	61	20in × 26in	51in	61,176	63	$17\frac{1}{4}$	RR's heavy artillery

SENEGAL & NEIGHBOURS

See map on pages 218-219.

SENEGAL, MALI, GUINEA, IVORY COAST, UPPER VOLTA

SENEGAL RAILWAYS
BP 265, Dakar.

MALI RAILWAY
PO Box 260, Bamako.

GUINEA RAILWAYS
PO Box 581, Conakry.

IVORY COAST RAILWAY
PO Box 1394, Abidjan

UPPER VOLTA – served by the Ivory Coast Railway

Senegal, Mali, Guinea, Ivory Coast and Upper Volta are five adjoining countries that were formerly united and called French West Africa. Transport in the area is dominated by the River Niger, the source of which is not too far from the coast in the neighbourhood of Sierra Leone. The river then makes a vast loop into the interior of the bight of Africa before reaching the sea in distant Nigeria. For most of its length the river is navigable and runs through the vast area of what is now the Mali Republic.

One problem which faced the French was that the mouth of this river was in another power's hands, *viz* Britain. This occurred before the days of *entente cordiale,* so steps were taken in 1881 to connect the Senegal River with the Niger River by rail, thereby

providing – via another railway along the coast, which had been started the previous year – an all-steam route to the port of Dakar in what is now Senegal.

Navigation on the Senegal River was seasonal and in 1924 a direct connection to Dakar was completed, giving a 775-mile route from the coast to Bamako, now the capital of independent Mali.

During 1900 to 1913, another line was completed in what is now Guinea, connecting Conakry (the capital) with Kouroussa, (390 miles) the upper limit of navigation on the great river. Between 1903 and 1955, the third of these railways to be built runs inland 711 miles from Abidjan (the capital of what is now the Ivory Coast) eventually reaching not the River Niger but a place in the republic of Upper Volta called Ouagadougou. A connection is proposed between Bobo-Diouasso (the capital of Upper Volta) and Bamako in Mali, and another one as a link between Bamako and the Conakry line in Guinea.

At present there are three separate systems in four independent countries; statistically they stand up as follows:

All these lines are metre gauge. In Guinea some heavy-duty standard-gauge lines are being projected and built in order to exploit mineral resources, iron ore and bauxite. On these North American (Canadian) standards will prevail, replacing the French practices which have heretofore been the rule in all these countries.

Both the Senegal-Mali and Ivory Coast systems offer sleeping cars (first class only) and dining cars on their best train. In addition, the latter offers the very rare facility of a railcar train with sleeping accommodation; railcars in fact provide virtually all the ordinary train services on all three systems.

SIERRA LEONE

See map on pages 218-219.

Sierra Leone has the sad position of being the largest and most populous country in the world to have lost its railway system. Construction began out of Freetown in 1895. Kissy was

Statistics	Senegal	Mali	Guinea	Ivory Coast Upper Volta
Length of route, miles	642	400	540	730
Number of diesel locomotives	60	22	30	65
Railcars	10	3	16	20
Carriages	90	50	20	105
Wagons	930	330	500	1240
Annual Passenger traffic millions	3.6	c.6	*	2.8
Annual freight traffic, millions of tons	1.5	0.3	*	0.9
Length of haul	*	50	*	150
Expenses as % of receipts	*	115	*	*

* not available

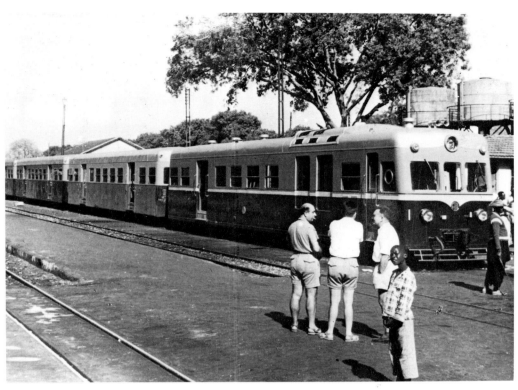

Extreme left: A re-enaction of the first train at Dakar, Senegal.

Centre left: The Ocean-Niger Express from Dakar to Bamako in Mali – a long hot haul.

Left: Modern autorails in service on the main line out of Dakar show the French influence.

Bottom left: The 2ft 6in line out of Freetown in Sierra Leone was still pulled by steam in 1954. Here a train crosses the bridge at Hastings.

Bottom right: Cape Town's Table Mountain guards the city's modern station. Only clean electric trains frequent this station; steam does not begin until the shed at Parden Eiland.

reached the following year, Bo (135 miles) in 1903 and Pendembu, the terminus (226 miles), in 1905. Branches brought the system eventually up to 320 miles. There were no serious engineering problems.

As recently as 1955, new Beyer-Garratt 4-8-2+2-8-4 locomotives were supplied, providing 22,500 lb of tractive effort in spite of the five-ton axle-load limit imposed by 30lb/yd rails. Subsequently, a series of diesel hydraulic locomotives were provided.

After independence from Britain, the government lost enthusiasm and the railway closed in 1976. Since then a fifty-mile 3ft-6in-gauge private mineral-hauling line has all but closed; the Marampa Mineral Railway is still used occasionally to transport supplies to and from the port and the mine.

So, what school-children in the town of Kissy used to sing has finally come to pass . . .

> 'The train to Bo
> She no agree to go
> The engine she done tire
> For lack of plenty fire. . . .'

SOUTH AFRICA

See map on pages 226-227.

SOUTH AFRICAN RAILWAYS – SAS/SAR

Suid-Afrikaans Spoorweg,
Paul Kruger Building, Wolmanans Street,
12001, Johannesburg.

The South African railway system came into being on 26 June 1860, when a two-mile standard-gauge line from Durban to Point was opened. Another standard-gauge railway out of Cape Town to Wellington (45 miles) was the first line to be started (1859) but it was not to be completed until 1863. At this time what is now South Africa was divided into four political entities; British Cape Colony and Natal, as well as the Transvaal and the Orange Free State.

Diamonds were discovered at Kimberley in 1870 and this was an objective indeed. The government produced the money and, from Wellington, after a slow start, Worcester was reached in 1876, Beaufort West (339 miles) in 1880 and De Aar in 1884, coinciding there with the completion of another line from Port Elizabeth, which had been started in 1874. Kimberley (653 miles) was reached in 1885. In the meantime, distant Westminster (London) felt that two colonies, so far away, did not quite rate standard gauge and suggested a slightly lesser one – not the indignity of two-foot-something narrow-gauge nor the foreign nonsense of metre gauge but 3ft 6in; a dimension which was to become standard in South Africa and many other countries. All these government railways were laid to the new gauge, a third rail being laid from Wellington into Cape Town, where 4ft 8½in held out until 1880.

The discovery of gold in the Johannesburg area led to a race between the various ports – Cape Town, Port Elizabeth and Durban – to be the first one connected. Furthermore, President Kruger of the Transvaal, wishing for

an outlet independent of the British, promoted a line Lourenço Marques, now Maputo, in Portuguese territory. All these lines were completed by 1895. The mileage on the outbreak of the Boer War in 1899 was 7577 (Cape Province 3834; Natal 1043; Transvaal 1706; Orange Free State 994.)

All these railways were unified in 1910, when South African Railways were formed, then as now, the largest network in Africa. After 1918 the railways in German South West Africa (now Namibia) were included. They had been hurriedly joined to the SAR in connection with General Botha's campaign to occupy the territory. Completion of the Republic's network had led to the present day 14,600-mile system, all 3ft 6in gauge, except for 440 miles of feeder lines built to 2ft gauge.

South Africa joins India, China and Poland as the four nations who still operate steam locomotive fleets of 1000 plus. As if challenged by those distant politicians who specified a lesser gauge, straight steam locomotives are running in South Africa heavier, bigger and more powerful than ever ran on standard gauge in Britain. The '25' class 4-8-4 has tractive effort of 45,600 lb, a grate area of 70 sq ft and an overall weight of 208 tons. The condensing version of this locomotive, for use in bad water areas, is the world's only successful large-scale application of this advanced feature, producing puffers that do not puff.

In 1910 came the class 3A 4-8-2 'final form' steam locomotive, that is, with two piston-valve cylinders, outside Walschearts valve gear, wide firebox and superheater; successive versions, each more American looking than the

last, form the bulk of SAR steam power today.

Following trials in 1924 with Mallet and Garratt articulated locomotives, SAR went on to have both the largest number of Garratts as well as the largest Garratt design ever to see regular service. This was the GL class 4-8-2 + 2-8-4, tractive effort 89,140 lb, grate area 75 sq ft and weight 211 tons. On the 2ft gauge Natal lines, the sixteen NGG class 2-6-2 +

2-6-2s have a dainty six-ton axle-loading for 30 lb/yd rail, but can produce 17,000 lb tractive effort. A batch of these were the last steam locomotives supplied (1968). The total steam fleet currently numbers 1800 (including sixty 2ft gauge) and is maintained in first-rate order.

In a country which has cheap and ample coal, but is without indigenous oil, electrification is more attractive than dieselization. In

operation, including twenty for the narrow gauge.

The original railways were built as single lines, largely following the contours of the land. More engineering work has been necessary to turn them into double-track arteries of commerce with reasonable curves and gradients than was necessary to build them in the first place. The five longest tunnels in the Republic of South Africa are all on these latter-day re-alignments. The actual longest is the 3.5-mile Cedara tunnel, completed in 1960. The longest bridge (3514ft) is at Upington, leading across the Orange River to Namibia. The highest is the Van Staaden's Gorge Bridge on the Avon-tuur 2ft-gauge line, 250ft high.

Apartheid, the segregation of the public according to skin colour, causes problems in station design. Small country stations need two foot-bridges, and the great stations of Cape Town, Durban and Johannesburg have to have duplicate concourses, with all that that entails. Trains are, of course, always marshalled so that the 'black' carriages (first, second and third class) are at the front and 'white' ones (first and second class) are at the rear.

The famous Blue Train, which runs twice a week on a 27-hour timing each way between Cape Town and Pretoria is, in sharp contrast with its namesake in Europe, one of the very few trains in the world that is *De Luxe* in the old-fashioned sense of the word. Comfort, food and service are impeccable and the train is fully booked ('whites' only, of course) weeks ahead.

Since the maximum permitted speed is 62.5 mph, passenger trains in South Africa are not fast; for example, the trip between Cape Town and Port Elizabeth, only 400 miles apart as the crow flies, means two nights in the train; not luxury, but wonderful scenery, clean accommodation and good food. SAR also provide worldwide and internal passenger air services – harbours and lighthouses too – so there is no incentive to run fast trains which interfere with freight-train operation.

South African Railways carry 140 million tons of freight an average distance of 325 miles as well as 635 million passengers annually, using a fleet of 10,300 passenger and 186,000 freight cars. Buck-eye type couplers are used and the vacuum brake; signalling is based on British practice, with much modernization. Expenses are eighty percent of receipts.

Extreme left, top: The 'Baby Garratt' in Natal.

Extreme left, below: South Africa's most powerful and perhaps most famous tender engines are the class 25 4-8-4s. Built for use in dry country, these huge water-saving machines are now almost all converted to non-condensing class 25NC.

Top left: A Beyer-Garratt with freight near Bethesdaweg on the Graaff-Reinet to Rosmead line.

Centre left: A South African Railways triple-headed electric freight train leaves Newcastle.

Left, bottom: An SAR 4-8-2 locomotive on the coaling stage at Burgersdorp in central Cape Province.

South Africa a beginning was made on the Natal main line in 1926, using the 3000v DC system. Since then steady progress has been made, including much suburban electrification in the Johannesburg and Cape Town areas. Since 1970, certain lines with lesser traffic have been electrified on the 25,000v fifty-cycle AC system. The electrified mileage now stands at 3440, on which 1691 electric locomotives run.

A start on dieselization was made with the lines in South West Africa (now Namibia), where traffic density was much too low for electrification and, moreover, absence of water plus remoteness from coal supplies made steam operation a problem. Accordingly 115 'World' diesel locomotives were ordered from General Electric (USA) in 1958, to be followed by many others. Currently 1200 diesel units are in

SOUTH WEST AFRICA
See Namibia

SUDAN

See map on pages 218-219.

SUDAN RAILWAYS
Atbara.

> So 'ere's to you, Fuzzy Wuzzy, at your
>   home in the Soudan;
> You're a poor benighted 'eathen but a
>   first class fighting man;
> An' 'ere's to you, Fuzzy Wuzzy, with
>   your 'ayrick head of hair;
> You big black boundin' beggar – for you
>   broke a British square!
>
> Rudyard Kipling

The fighting qualities enshrined in Kipling's famous words gave birth to the first section of the Sudan Railways. Two short military lines had in fact been constructed in connection with the events described above, in 1881 and 1884, but after the British withdrawal, the Mahdi (the Dervish Leader) had the rails of the first one flung into the River Nile, alongside which it was built. The second, which ran inland from Suakin on the Red Sea, was also destroyed.

The problem along this stretch of the river, which connects Egypt with the Sudan, is that the flow over the so-called cataracts is much too fast for steamers to make headway against the current. In 1895 General Kitchener was put in charge of an expedition sent out to avenge the death of General Gordon in Khartoum ten years earlier. He had the utmost respect for his adversaries' fighting ability and, accordingly, determined that he would not offer battle until an adequately equipped army could be put into the field. The solution was a 3ft 6in gauge railway, 385 miles long, starting at a place called Wadi Halfa, just below the first cataract. It ran for 200 miles across the desert, by-passing a great loop of the river, then running alongside a further bad stretch to reach a place

Extreme left, top: The line from Cape Town to Port Elizabeth has always been known as the Garden Route because of the magnificent scenery and the wonderful climb up over the Montague Pass. The station at George is the last stop before the climb really starts and the Beyer-Garratts took water here.

Extreme left, centre: The longest 2ft gauge line in South Africa takes a westerly line out of Port Elizabeth to the hills of Avontuur. New diesels now work the intensive service of stone trains to and from Loerie, but the NG15 class 2-8-2s take the through-train from Assegaabos to the upper terminal.

Left: A Sudanese Co Co diesel-electric locomotive leaves Atbara heading a Wadi Halfa to Khartoum express. Note the British style semaphore signals.

Below: An English Electric Co-Co locomotive of Sudan Railways.

Extreme left, bottom: Double-headed Beyer-Garratts pull a train on the southbound climb out of Rosmead on the Graaff-Reinet to Rosmead (via Middelburg) line in 1978. The mountains are crossed using the Lootsberg Pass.

Left: A Sudan Railways oilburning Pacific No 270 leaves Atbara with a train for Wadi Halfa.

called Atbara. The whole line was constructed in 1896–97 and is a classic of military engineering. It is interesting that some of the locomotives supplied for the run across the waterless Nubian Desert were equipped with condensing units to recover feed water from steam exhaust.

Well-equipped and fresh after a rail journey, the British defeated the Dervish army (a young soldier called Winston Churchill was there) at a place called Omdurman. The Sudan then became *de jure* an Anglo-Egyptian condominium, but *de facto* part of the British Empire, and so, of course, had to be provided with a well-run railway system.

Kitchener's railway – now extended to Khartoum – made a good starting point and, during the next sixty years, tentacles were sent out to such far corners of an enormous country as were fertile (by local standards) and inhabited. A new harbour – Port Sudan – on the Red Sea was set up and given rail access in 1906. The present system extends 2950 miles; Sudan Railway steamers on the Nile connect with the Egyptian Railways and – almost – with the Uganda Railways. The Sudan became peacefully independent in 1955, although malcontent groups caused trouble for a number of years after this, particularly in the west and south; the railways were not seriously affected. After independence in 1961, the network was extended into lion country to Wau in the far southwest, 873 miles from Khartoum and 1450 miles from Wadi Halfa.

In steam days, standard British colonial locomotives were supplied; now all that remain are some of the 42 oil-fired 4-8-2s supplied by North British Locomotive Works in 1956, that respected firm's last big steam order – also, of course, the last steam order placed by Sudan Railways. Water had always been a problem in the country, so it is not surprising that all principal trains are now in the charge of the 162-strong diesel fleet, the first of which was supplied in 1959.

Passenger traffic amounts to 2.6 million annually, freight to 2.5 million tons, hauled an average distance of 560 miles. There are 385 coaches, including excellent dining and first-class sleeping cars and 6600 freight wagons. Expenses are 108 percent of receipts.

South of Khartoum is the Gezira, an irrigated cotton-growing area whose crops are handled by a 1ft 11½in gauge railway system 500 miles in extent. There are seventy locomotives (all diesel) and trains of bagged cotton up to 400 tons are worked over the level terrain.

SWAZILAND

See map on pages 226–227.

SWAZILAND RAILWAY
PO Box 58, Mbabane.

A 3ft 6in gauge line was built in the early 1960s primarily to carry iron ore from Kadake in the northwest of the country through

Above: A Swaziland Railway double-headed iron-ore train near Mantenga Falls.

Right: Dar-es-Salaam on the Tan-Zam Railway.

Bottom extreme right: A Tunisian National Railway's diesel-hauled train at Bir Bou Regba.

Below: A class 30 2-8-4 of the then-East Africa Railways at Tabora, Tanzania.

Mlawula in the northeast to the port of Maputo (formerly Lourenço Marques) in Mozambique. The mountainous terrain in northern Swaziland necessitated a circuitous route passing well to the south of the two principal towns at Mbabane and Manzini. This means that there is no demand for passenger services, and none are provided. The western section of the line from Kadake to Sidvokodvo, the main depot and railway township, is steeply graded (1 in 50) and steam traction is used. At Sidvokodvo trains are re-marshalled and diesel traction is used over the gentler gradients to Maputo.

The iron ore at Kadake is virtually exhausted but new traffics have been established to ensure a future for the railway. These include wood pulp from the Usutu forests, said to be the largest manmade forests in the world, sugar products from Phuzumoya and Mlawula, and coal from Mpaka. Newly discovered coal deposits in the southeast of the country have prompted detailed investigation for a branch from Phuzumoya to the frontier at Gollel where it would join the South African Railway network and provide an alternative route in the event of political difficulties between Swaziland and Mozambique.

The line is controlled by a CTC system with coloured light signals but the tracks at intermediate passing stations are staggered so that trains always enter by the straight route and depart by the curved route through the switches. By spring-loading the switches in the straight position the need for point motors has been avoided, saving power generators.

TANGANYIKA
See Tanzania

TANZANIA

See map on pages 226-227.
**TANZANIAN RAILWAYS
CORPORATION**
Dar-es-Salaam.

**TANZANIA ZAMBIA RAILWAY
AUTHORITY – TAZARA – TAN-ZAM
RAILWAY**
Dar-es-Salaam.

In what was then called German East Africa, a company known as the Deutsch-Ostafrika Usambara-Eisenbahn began constructing a metre-gauge line out of the port of Tanga, 120 miles north of Dar-es-Salaam, in 1893. The objective was Lake Victoria, but the company went bankrupt in 1899, was taken over by the German government with a purely local objective. Moshi, 220 miles inland from Tanga, from where a connecting line now runs into Kenya, was reached in 1912.

In 1905 the present main line out of Dar-es-Salaam was begun. Lake Tanganyika was reached at Kigoma, 782 miles, in the fateful year of 1914. Surrounded by enemies, the meagre German forces did well to hold out until the Armistice, but the railway suffered.

After the war (1919), the country was granted a British League of Nations mandate and was called Tanganyika. In 1946 it became a United Nations territory under British administration. The railways were repaired and a new 245-mile line was laid, mostly on formation constructed by the Germans, north from Tabora to reach Lake Victoria at Mwanza.

Amalgamation with the Kenya-Uganda Railway took place in 1948 and the resulting East African Railways administration lasted until 1976. The ownership of the railways has now reverted to the individual governments. Tanzania's metre-gauge railroads are controlled by the Tanzanian Railways Corporation.

(In 1961 Tanganyika became self-governing and in 1964 became a people's republic and changed its name from the United Republic of Tanganyika and Zanzibar to the United Republic of Tanzania.)

Up until 1976 all railways had been built to the metre gauge. However in 1976 one of the most remarkable railway projects ever mounted in Africa was completed; this was the 3ft 6in gauge Tan-Zam Railway which connects Dar-es-Salaam with the main southern African rail systems. Primarily, of course, it is an alternative outlet for Zambian copper. The line was financed and constructed by China on the basis of an interest-free loan repayable over thirty years from 1983 onwards. Any doubts felt about the ability of the Chinese to build such a railway were unfounded; in fact, there are more engineers with large-scale railway-building experience in China than in any other country. Six hundred miles of the 1160-mile line are in Tanzania.

Motive power in Tanzania before 1914 was the typical German of the period; after 1919 it was British. Dieselization began under East African auspices in 1958, but one notes a surprising order to India for a batch of six standard steam YG 2-8-2s, rather secretively placed as late as 1974. The Tan-Zam line is reported to be worked by 102 Chinese diesel-hydraulic locomotives and to have 100 passenger and 2100 freight cars. Air brakes are used, but the freight stock also has vacuum brakes for working in Zambia and Zaïre. Apart from the locomotives, equipment is very simple; for example, most of the stations have oil-lit semaphore signals and working between stations is by train order. At Dar-es-Salaam a magnificent modern station is provided for but six passenger trains a week.

TOGO

See map on pages 218-219.

TOGO RAILWAYS – RCFT
*Régie des Chemins de Fer de Togo,
PO Box 340,
Lomé.*

Togoland – then a German Colony – entered the railway age early in the twentieth century when three typically colonial railways were constructed leading from the port of Lomé. The first one, running 28 miles eastward to Anécho was opened on 18 July 1905, originally to 2ft 5½in gauge. Northward and northeastward lines (102 and 72 miles long respectively) followed quickly. The system was extended even further north to its present terminus at Blitta in 1934, during the period of the French mandate. Steam came to an end in 1960, coinciding with independence.

Current returns show twenty diesel locomotives, ten railcars, sixty passenger cars and 375 wagons. About 1.5 million passengers are carried annually and 112,000 tons of freight. Unusually passenger accommodation is designated first and third class.

TUNISIA

See map on pages 218-219.

**TUNISIAN NATIONAL RAILWAYS –
SNCFT**
*Société Nationale des Chemins de Fer Tunisiens,
67 Ave Farhat Hached,
Tunis.*

The earliest railways in Tunisia were built to serve the capital city and comprised a 2.5-mile line from Tunis to Bardo and a twelve-mile route from Tunis to La Marsa. These were built to standard gauge in 1874. The route to

La Marsa passed along the north side of Tunis Bay and a branch line served the industrial area at La Goulette. In 1905 a causeway was constructed across the bay and a new railway was laid along it to give direct access to La Goulette from a new terminus on the east side of the city. This route was electrified at about the same period, while the Bardo line was replaced by trams. The new line to La Goulette was later extended through Carthage and over the hill past Sidi Bou Said to provide an end-on connection with the earlier line at La Marsa. Subsequently the old route along the north side of the bay was abandoned, and the section through La Marsa itself was converted into a road by-passing the town centre. The electric trains working between Tunis and La Marsa have only recently been replaced by new stock and large portions of the track have been re-laid. A third-rail is used for current collection but in the depot area simple overhead catenary is provided. The old trains had a considerable variety of trolley booms, pantographs and bow collectors to enable them to move in and out of the depot.

Outside the capital and its immediate vicinity, standard gauge was adopted for the route westwards to Algeria, on which construction began in 1877, and for a local line to Hammam-Lif built in 1882. The latter was closed in 1897 and subsequently re-opened as a metre-gauge line. This was later doubled and now carries such a considerable volume of commuters, that there have been proposals for its electrification and extension of the commuter services to Bordj Cedria. A metre-gauge line was built southwards from Tunis to Sousse in 1896 and in 1912 this was extended to link up with other routes built slightly earlier to carry phosphate from deposits in the southwest of the country to the port at Sfax. The proposed standard-gauge line between Sfax and Tripoli in Libya will have an interchange station for passengers and freight at Sfax but provision is being made for the metre-gauge line to Tunis to become standard gauge at a later date.

The main terminus in Tunis, currently being replaced with a more extensive passenger concourse, already has two gauges with platforms for standard gauge on the west side of the station and platforms for metre gauge to the east. The routes diverge immediately south of the station but the maintenance depots and workshops southeast of the station cater for both gauges, and this necessitates some unusual 'diamond' crossings where the standard gauge crosses the metre-gauge track to gain access to the depot area. A similar series of hybrid gauge crossings is provided at Djebel Djelloud a few miles further south where the standard-gauge line crosses the metre-gauge main line again to enter a major freight depot and warehousing area.

UGANDA
See Kenya

UPPER VOLTA
See Senegal *et al*

ZAIRE

See map on pages 226–227.

ZAÏRE NATIONAL RAILWAYS – SNCZ
Société Nationale des Chemins de Fer Zairois, PO Box 297, Place de la Gare, Lubumbashi.

The first railway in what is now Zaïre – but was then the Belgian Congo – was completed in 1892. It started at the port of Matadi, near (by African standards) the mouth of the great river after which the country was and is named, and ran inland 250 miles to the capital, then called Leopoldville, but now Kinshasa. The object was to avoid the rapids in the lower reaches. This role of a railway being handmaiden to noble woodburning stern-wheel steamers on one of the greatest rivers in the world was repeated twice (each time the gauge was different) over other un-navigable stretches, first past the Stanley Falls and then past the Hell's Gate Rapids. The limit of navigation is Bukama, 3050 steamer and 550 train miles from the river's mouth. From 1918 Bukama was connected by rail to the copper-belt area in the southeastern corner of the country (and also, of course, by Cecil Rhodes' route to Cape Town, as described earlier).

In the 1920s it was decided to build a line running diagonally across the country and connecting Bukama with the capital. It reached its present terminus at Ilebo (then called Port Francqui) in 1928; from here it was a mere week – instead of a month or so by the original route – by river steamer to Leopoldville (Kinshasa). Already in the 1930s the line from Port Francqui to Leopoldville (Kinshasa) was specified as 'surveyed and projected' a situation that appertains today.

In 1931 the Benguela Railway arrived at the Angola border at Dilolo and this, the shortest possible outlet to the Atlantic Ocean, was met by new construction in the then Belgian Congo.

A further international connection ran from the river at Kabalo to Albertville (now Kalemie) on Lake Tanganika; cross-lake steamers led to Kigoma and hence by rail to Dar-es-Salaam on the Indian Ocean. Since then isolated lines in the southwest have been connected to the main system, based at Bukama and Lubumbashi (previously Elisabethville), making it up to its present size of just over 2400 miles.

In this area in 1952 a very early example of what is now the world's standard system of electrification was inaugurated – high voltage AC at ordinary industrial frequency. The scheme covered the 64 miles between Jadotville (now Likasi) and Tenke; it has since been extended 400 miles into the copper-belt area. There are over seventy electric locomotives in use. Elsewhere in Zaïre a fleet of 250 diesels, supplemented by a small remnant of steam together with 260 carriages and 8400 wagons carry 3.2 million passengers and eleven million tons of freight annually.

Finally, in the remote northeast of Zaïre, appropriately situated right in the geographical centre of the 'Dark Continent', is an extraordinary mystery system comprising no less than 750 miles of 1ft 11½in gauge. This is the Vicicongo Railway or, in full, Chemin de Fer Vicinal de Zaïre (CVZ), whose nearest rail neighbour is in Uganda. It runs from Aketi and Bondo to Mungbere. Returns show it to have 29 steam and fifteen diesel locomotives, nineteen carriages and 350 wagons and to handle 300,000 tons of freight and 100,000 passengers each year; but otherwise, nothing seems to be known about it except that it not only appears on the map but also still functions.

ZAMBIA

See map on pages 226–227.

ZAMBIA RAILWAYS
PO Box RW65,
Ridgeway, Lusaka.

Until the breakdown of friendly relations with Rhodesia/Zimbabwe, the principal connection between Zambia and the outside world was the railway southwards through Rhodesia/Zimbabwe and South Africa. Now that the traffic working across the Victoria Bridge at Livingstone Falls is so restricted, the route southwards from Kabwe, the railway head-quarters, through Lusaka is comparatively little used. Passenger traffic has also been lost with the creation of a good standard main road parallel to the railway providing a faster and more frequent express bus service.

The recently built Chinese-financed Tan-Zam railway, also known as the Tazara, from north of Kabwe, via Serenje, Mpika and Kasama to Dar-es-Salaam in Tanzania has provided a new outlet for Zambian copper and a route for essential imports of fuel and other commodities, but its capacity is limited and much traffic continues to be hauled by road throughout or to rail-heads in Malawi and Mozambique. The Chinese builders of the Tan-Zam did an extremely good job in constructing the railway quickly and cheaply, establishing their own townships and rice farms along the route to make themselves entirely self-supporting during the construction period. However, they took security of the operation extremely seriously even to the extent of refusing to allow the General Manager of Zambia Railways and other Board Members to inspect work at the junction with their railway at Kapiri Mposhi. Having been seen off at gun-point from the end of the new railway, the Zambia Railways' officials may be forgiven for any subsequent difficulty found in achieving satisfactory co-ordination of traffic movements between the two lines.

ZIMBABWE
See Rhodesia/Zimbabwe

Extreme left, top: Zaire in colonial days circa 1918. A locomotive of the Chemin de Fer du Katanga takes water near Bukama.

Left, top: A train stands in Livingstone station, Zambia in the days of the federation with Rhodesia.

Left, centre and bottom: Two wayside stations, typical of the stops in Zambia on the Tan-Zam Railway.

(TCDD). However, modern Turkey under Kemal Attaturk, with Ankara as its capital, had first to be established and frontier disputes with Greece and Syria settled. The TCDD was not, in fact, formally established until 1927, the independent companies being absorbed over the next twenty years or so; the first railway in Turkey, the British Ottoman Railway, dating from 1860, was purchased in 1935. Since its formation, the TCDD has constructed over 2000 miles of new line to make up the present mileage of 6200, all (except for a short branch along the shore of the Black Sea) laid to standard gauge.

Turkish steam power favoured German practice, although locomotives from other sources have lingered on in service. Ten coupled motive power is particularly common, as befits a mountainous country. One fascinating oddity was a class of 2-6-0 by Hanomag which did not quite meet the axle-load limit and had to have a small pair of carrying wheels inserted between the second and third pair of drivers. Currently over 500 steam locomotives are reported as being in service although the main brunt of the work falls on 200 or so diesel locomotives. The Istanbul suburban services were electrified in 1955 and more recently a start has been made on the trunk line leading east from Haydarpasa towards Ankara.

There is much heavy construction in the mountainous regions which make up the greater part of the country, including the three-mile Amanus Tunnel southeast of Adana. Turkish railways presently carry some fourteen million tons of freight annually an average distance of 300 miles, using 19,000 freight cars. The annual passenger count is 128 million and there are 1100 carriages.

YEMEN

See map on pages 250-251.

In the days when Yemen was called Aden and ruled by the British, it had a 29-mile metre-gauge line running inland from the port. The line was built in 1916 for strategic reasons, since Arabia, as a rather loosely attached piece of the Turkish Empire, was then enemy territory. Indian equipment was used and an attempt to struggle on commercially after the war came to an end in 1929.

6
ASIA

Afghanistan **Bangladesh** Bangladesh Railway **Burma** Union of Burma Railways **China** Railways of the People's Republic of China **Hong Kong** Hong Kong Government Railways **India** Indian Government Railways **Japan** Japan National Railways	**Kampuchea (Cambodia)** Kampuchea (Cambodia) Railways **Korea** Korean National Railroad (South Korea) Korean Railways (North Korea) **Malaysia** Malayan Railway Sabah State Railways **Nepal** Nepal Government Railway Janakpur Railway **Pakistan** Pakistan Railways	**Philippines** Philippine National Railways **Sri Lanka** Sri Lanka Government Railway **Taiwan** Taiwan Railway Administration **Thailand** State Railway of Thailand **USSR** See Europe: USSR **Vietnam** Vietnam Railways System

AFGHANISTAN

See map on pages 250-251 or 278-279.

AFGHANISTAN RAILWAYS
Kabul.

History is full of examples of railways being built to strengthen tenuous political links; occasionally the opposite, railways *NOT* being built in order to weaken them, also occurs. A prime example is Afghanistan, which has the distinction of being the most populous country in the world to be without railways. However, the government has recently approved plans for a network of 1100 miles of standard-gauge railway connecting the capital Kabul not with nearby Landi Kotal, terminus of the Khyber Pass Railway in Pakistan but with Chaman (giving, with a break of gauge, a direct route to the sea at Karachi) and two points on the frontier with Iran, whose railways are also standard gauge. There is no link proposed with the Soviet system (on yet another gauge) at Kushka in the north. Diesel-electric traction is intended; an initial fleet of fifty locomotives has been proposed.

BANGLADESH

See map on pages 278-279.

BANGLADESH RAILWAY
Chittagong.

As an indication of her status as a pathetic victim of power politics, Bangladesh has for a railway system a collection of disconnected left-over bits of line, most of which were part of the Bengal–Assam Railway. They are separated both by gauge and by the River Brahmaputra which remains unbridged in Bangladesh.

Nevertheless, there are some remarkable structures; the 1915 Hardinge Bridge over the Ganges, on what was once the East Bengal Railway, the main line from Calcutta to Siligun (for Darjeeling), is 1.1 miles long and in the world class. There are fifteen spans and the pier foundations go down 160ft below low-water level.

Currently, on the metre gauge, 222 steam and 144 diesel-electric locomotives haul 926 passenger and 14,500 freight cars; on the broad gauge the figures are 115 steam locomotives, 34 diesel-electric, 276 passenger and 4300 freight cars. Seventy-two million passengers are carried; 2.7 million tons of freight are hauled an average distance of ninety miles. Expenses are 96 percent of receipts. In general Indian railway practice is followed.

BURMA

See map on pages 278-279.

UNION OF BURMA RAILWAYS
PO Box 118,
Rangoon.

Until 1937 Burma was part of India and the railways there had been constructed by the (British) Indian government, although initially leased for operation by a private company. The first line was opened in 1877, between Rangoon the capital and Prome on the Irrawaddy River. By 1934 it was possible to travel 723 miles up

country from Rangoon to Myitkyina near the Chinese Border, crossing the Irrawaddy near Mandalay by the 3950ft-long Ava Bridge, of sixteen spans. It still remains the only bridge across this river. The 1900-mile system that then existed remains substantially the same today; there are several separate sections connected by river ferries. There has never (quite) been a connection with the railway system of any of Burma's neighbours.

There was heavy destruction of the Burmese Railways during World War II; the Ava Bridge was out of commission for over ten years, until 1954. Another great bridge, the Gokteik Viaduct up in the hills on the Lashio branch, was also out of use for nearly as long. The Gokteik Viaduct is a steel trestle structure 320ft high and 2250ft long, of ten spans. Equally remarkable is the alignment of this line, which includes four reversals and a spiral in its climb to 3800ft altitude.

The system is metre gauge and Indian practice generally prevails. Current returns show 280 steam and 75 diesel locomotives, 1160 passenger cars and 11,000 wagons. Garratt articulated locomotives were supplied for the heavily graded (1 in 25) hill sections, but standard Indian types handled traffic elsewhere in steam days.

A symptom of the generally discouraging attitude of the Burmese government towards visitors is the fact that notices and station names are written only in Burmese script.

CAMBODIA
See Kampuchea

CEYLON
See Sri Lanka

CHINA

See map on pages 266–267.

RAILWAYS OF THE PEOPLE'S REPUBLIC OF CHINA
Peking.

Chinese Railway history started when a British company sought and won a concession for a nine-mile line from Shanghai to Woosung. The nobility, like the Eton College authorities forty years before, felt – quite correctly, as it turned out – that such a devilish device would undermine their time-honoured top position in society, but were not able to prevent construc-

Bottom left: A Burma Railways 2-8-2 + 2-8-2 Beyer-Garratt hauls a mixed train out of Sedaw. Note the British type semaphore signals. The second reversing station of this ascent can just be seen through the locomotive's smoke.

Bottom right: Tangshan station, China, in July 1976, only two weeks prior to the disastrous earthquake. This row of SY class 2-8-2 locomotives had just been completed at the works there.

Below: Peking station, 1976, with a class RM 4-6-2, which has just come off a train from Tientsin.

Page 262/263: Two diesels await their turn at Peking central station.

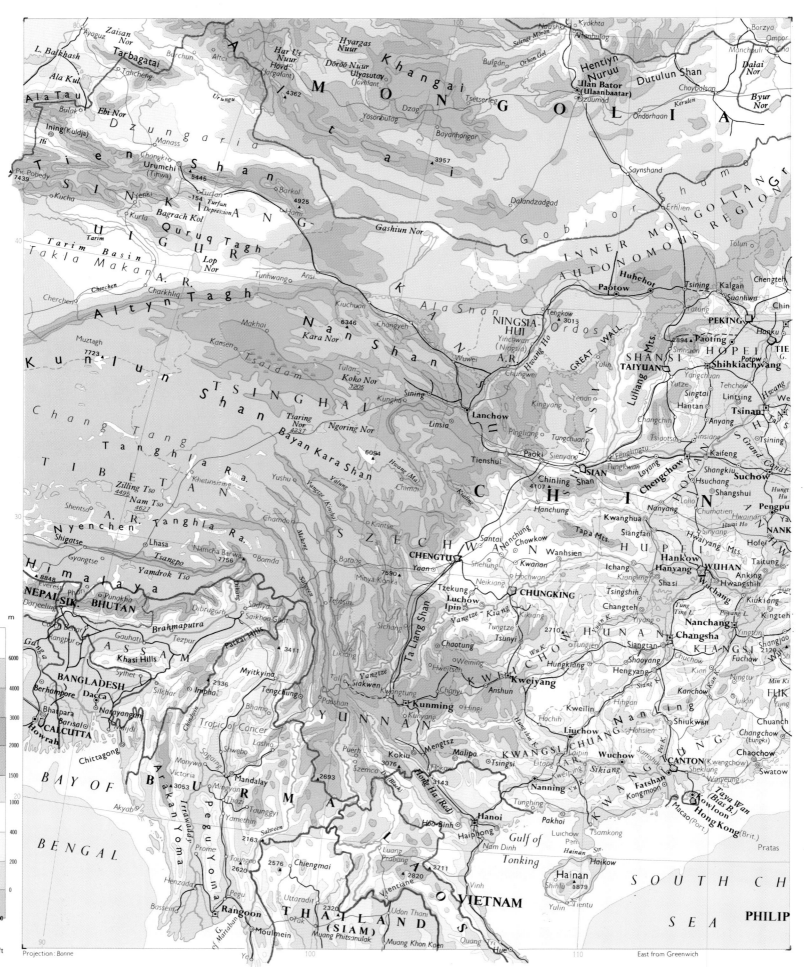

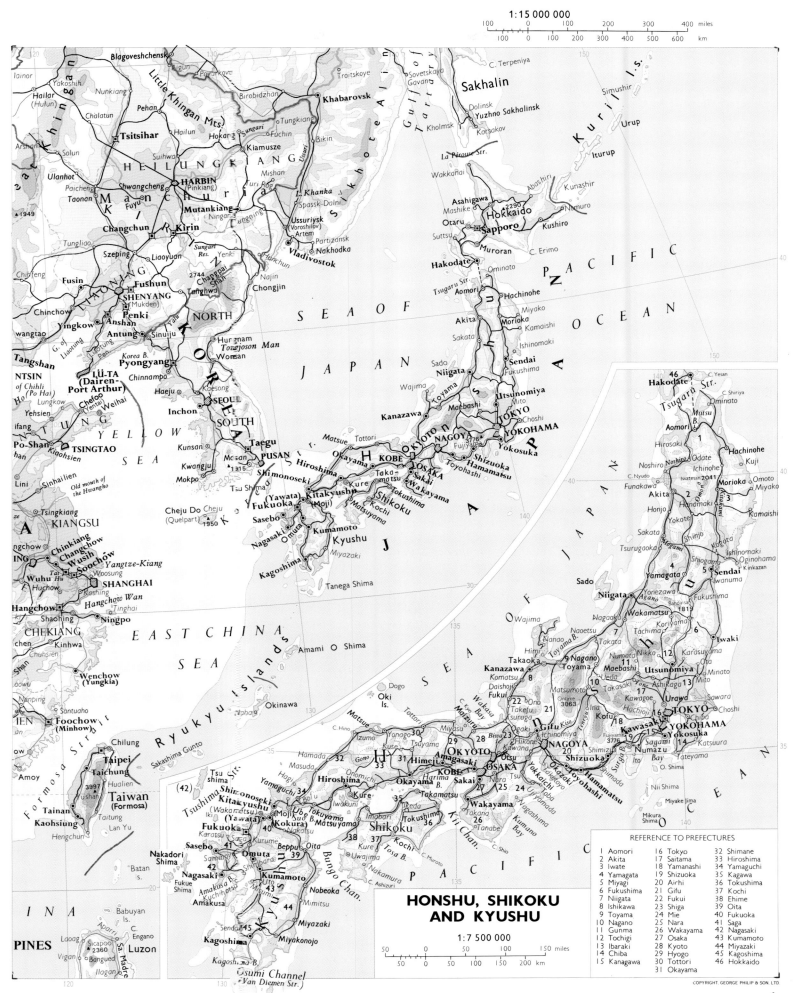

HONSHU, SHIKOKU AND KYUSHU

tion taking place. Accordingly, 2-4-0s *Celestial Kingdom* and *Flowery Land* began operations on 30 June 1876. The Mandarins, however, still had cards to play; in this case it is said that they caused bound coolies to be thrown in front of the train, thereby bringing home to the common people in a very realistic way the dangers inherent in the adoption of mechanical transport. A public outcry led to an apparently munificient gesture on the part of the Mandarins, who bought out the owners and had the railway destroyed, after only fifteen months of operation.

The first lasting line in China was the first section of a line which was intended to carry coal from the mining areas of Tangshan, on the northeast coast, to Tientsin. It eventually became part of the main line from Peking to Manchuria.

Again there were problems with the authorities and originally permission was only given to use mule traction. However, the European manager managed to build a locomotive from surplus material on hand at the collieries – it is said that on one occasion it was buried in the ground to conceal it from visiting officials – and in this way the Railway Age came to China. The 'Foreign Devils' concerned were in this case again British, but later concessions for railway building were also obtained by American, Belgian, French, German and Japanese interests. In spite of this variety of ownership, all the lines of national importance were built to standard gauge, apart from a line leading into what was then French Indo-China (now Vietnam). In due course all the lines were absorbed into the Chinese National Railways. No new foreign concessions were granted after 1908, and the formation of the Republic in 1912 led the way to a gradual take-over of the foreign systems. By 1930 (the date of the notorious 'Manchuria Incident'), there were 7200 miles of railway, all forming part of the National system.

A long period of war and revolution then ensued, during which the Chinese Railways System functioned spasmodically, according to the ebb and flow of the fighting. By the time that the Communists took power in 1949, only an estimated 4000 miles of line were operable.

This was an absurdly small system for a nation with a population five times and a land area twice that of the US, which had thirty times the railway mileage. Tremendous efforts were made by the new regime to provide the new China with an adequate rail system. Its extension during the postwar years by nearly 20,000 miles has not been paralleled elsewhere. For example, the Yangtze River formed a gap in the Peking-Shanghai Railway until 1969, when the great bridge at Nanking (fourteen spans, totalling 1830ft) was opened. The river was not crossed by rail even up-stream until 1957, well into Communist times. Much new construction was carried out in appallingly difficult country, leading to feats of railway engineering which also have no counterpart elsewhere during the last thirty years. Not forgotten also must be the amount of upgrading and doubling of existing main lines. Railways

now penetrate into the far corners of China; for example, there is a line to Urumchi in central Asia. Tibet, though, has still to be penetrated by rail. However, the Railway Technical Institute at Tientsin trains over 150 Railway Graduate Engineers each year and their work is gradually and literally leaving its mark in these tremendous but little known projects in the mountainous regions of western China. If present plans mature, there is little doubt that soon a 'Tibet Limited' will pull out of an enlarged Peking station on its journey to the still-forbidden city of Lhasa, crossing passes rivalling those of South America in the process.

In evaluating all this achievement, one must take account of the totalitarian nature of the regime, illustrated by the fact that Peking's magnificent central main station, completed twenty years ago, was planned, designed and built within twelve months. The democracies of the West could hardly do such a thing within twelve years! There are six platforms with twelve faces and, although it is a terminus, the main building is set at the side rather than the end, with the concourse at first floor level above the platform. Waiting rooms are provided for each main direction of travel, not only clean and comfortable, but almost luxurious. There are very fine dining rooms, nurseries and other amenities. The main signal box is just a room off one of the administrative corridors in the top floor of the block and above that there is a noble clock tower with a pagoda roof, which chimes 'The East is Red' at noon, three and six pm. There are 58 departures daily. Subtracting seven local ones, one finds that barely more than fifty main-line trains serve a capital city of some four million inhabitants, who have no private cars, no long-distance buses and only minimal air services.

Steam is very much in the fore in China, with around 5000 fiery dragons still in operation and 'March Forward' 2-10-2s still just (in 1978) rolling off the production lines at Tatung, northwest of Peking. It suits a country with much coal but little oil and a huge population to use this labour-intensive but simple machine for traction. 'People' 4-6-2s are used on passenger trains and a variety of 2-8-2s ('Liberation', 'Construction' and 'Aiming High') on shunting, trip and branch-line work. There are also some ex-Soviet 2-10-2s, secondhand after gauge conversion; their original name 'Friendship' is no longer appropriate. Most of the work is done with these very few types, the majority constructed since the rest of the world – except India – ceased to build steam.

During Mao Tse-Tung's 'Great Leap Forward' of 1958 to 1960, the Chinese Railways had some traumatic experience with do-it-yourself diesel locomotives and their premature large-scale production, so it is not surprising that they then set out to build the world's last steam locomotive factory as well as continuing steam production elsewhere. Although reliable diesel locomotives are now coming off Chinese production lines at the estimated rate of 200 per year, steam locomotives are also still

being built on a reduced scale. It is thought that the diesel fleet is currently between 1000 and 2000, of which more than half are Chinese-built. Electrification is at present on a small scale, far away amidst the mountains of central China, between Paoki and Chengtu. Some French-built locomotives form the basis of this operation.

The passenger trains of the Chinese Railways have a good deal to commend them. The soft-class sleeping cars are similar to the European first-class couchette, but kept spotlessly clean. At the modest speeds run, the riding is excellent and the catering in the dining car very much in the Chinese tradition, simple, fresh and good. Air conditioning has only been noted on the prestige run from the Hong Kong frontier to Canton. Hard class cars, of which there are both the couchette and the open-sitting variety are plain but also clean. The only feature towards which the Westerner might display a little caution are hole-in-the-floor toilets.

Freight operations are very much in traditional US style with great long trains of buckeye coupled bogie cars, hauled at high speed by big black 2-10-2s. In statistical terms it is estimated that 900 million tons of freight are hauled an average distance of 220 miles in a fleet of 210,000 wagons, the majority eight-wheeled.

In contrast to the American style of the trains, left-hand running on double track and raised platforms take after Britain. More cosmopolitan is the signalling which on the main line is mostly conventional multi-aspect colour light. Semaphore areas do exist and here at first glance signals do appear to be of old-fashioned British lower quadrant pattern; a closer look shows the arms to be of the American type but, because of the left-hand running, seen as if in a looking glass. Still deeper examination gives the impression that, when several arms are mounted on the same post, the aspects displayed and their meanings owe something to German inspiration. To complete the international picture, it may be added that in the old days the whistle boards on the Peking-Hankow Railway bore the French legend '*Sifflez!*', the whole of this reflecting the piecemeal way the Chinese Railway system was developed before World War I by different foreign powers.

EAST PAKISTAN
See Bangladesh

FORMOSA
See Taiwan

HONG KONG

See map on pages 266–267.

HONG KONG GOVERNMENT RAILWAY
Kowloon.

This 21.5-mile line is the stub end of the line from Kowloon – on the mainland just across from Victoria on Hong Kong island – to Canton in China. It was opened on 5 August 1911, was laid to standard gauge and was built with British capital. The new passenger station in Kowloon is very much after the style of and seemingly only a little smaller than Euston in London. One might expect something pretty grand in the way of trains to draw up at one of its six platforms. However, all there is is an hourly local train out to the frontier – as at Chicago, only pigs get a through ride. Passengers cross the border railway bridge on foot, noting (if they are so minded) the last Imperial four-bolt fishplate and the first Communist six-bolt one. A fleet of ten road-switcher diesels handles the traffic.

It should also be noted that Victoria is the last haunt of a once familiar rail-borne creature, the archetypical British double-decker street-car.

INDIA

See map on pages 278–279.

INDIAN GOVERNMENT RAILWAYS
Rail Bhawan,
Raisina Road,
New Delhi.

When they evacuated their Empire, the Romans left behind them in Britain and elsewhere – a system of law and a system of roads; the British in their turn left behind in India a corresponding system of administration and a system of railways, which, improved and modernized since independence, still form a great united network, ranking second in the world in size.

It was in November 1852 that the first passenger train conveyed officials and their guests from Bombay 25 miles to Thana on the first section of the Great Indian Peninsula Railway, now known as the Central Railway. Like most subsequent construction in British India, the GIPR was built by a privately financed company under a concession and guarantee from the government of India. Under the terms, a five percent dividend on its capital was guaranteed; in return, government traffic was carried free or at reduced rates, a measure of state control was imposed and any further profit was divided between the government

Above: The late Prime Minister of India, Pandit Nehru, drives the first electric engine to be built at Chittaranjan in 1963.

Top: Modernization has brought the diesel locomotive to steamy India but the country scene changes little.

Left: Hump-shunting at a marshalling yard near Shanghai, China.

and the shareholders. The government could exercise the right to take over the line after a certain passage of years.

Similar provisions applied to the East India Railway out of Calcutta, which opened its first section in 1854; the whole 1130 miles to Delhi began operating in 1864. A junction with the GIPR was formed at Allahabad in 1871, thereby opening rail communication right across the subcontinent. This was made easier by the foresight of the Governor-General, Lord Dalhousie (this was in the days before Viceroys), who imposed a uniform 5ft 6in gauge on the companies as a condition of granting the concessions.

The Indian Mutiny of 1857 came in the early stages of the period of railway construction. It has been argued that the coming of railways and the changes in the Indian way of life which their coming implied, was one major factor in sparking it off. Certainly one result of it was to ensure that the authorities did not drag their feet in providing India with a comprehensive railway system.

Alas, subsequent heads of government, Viceroys Lawrence and Mayo, did not maintain this insistence on a uniform gauge and introduced the metre-gauge for secondary lines. By the turn of the century there was even a through

Below: A Darjeeling-Himalayan narrow-gauge train on the ascent. Note the sand-men on front.

metre-gauge line between Delhi and Ahmadabad. Mayo is reputed to have said 'When we have an elephants load, we may use an elephant, but when we have only a donkey's load, we have to use a donkey', and the thinking behind this dubious analogy led not only to much metre-gauge construction but much narrow gauge as well, even in the plains where little advantage prevailed. In the mountains there were advantages; such lines as the Darjeeling-Himalayan with its 60ft radius curves would have been prohibitively costly as a broad- or even metre-gauge railway.

The military authorities stood no nonsense of this kind and strategic railways such as the Khyber Pass line (now in Pakistan) had to be broad-gauge to avoid the problems of transshipment from trains of one gauge to another.

The guarantee system (which later became considerably less advantageous to the investors) worked well and produced results; it by-passed government prevarication and took advantage of the Indian government's equally remarkable integrity and its ability to ensure that things were done properly. Even so, towards the end of the century there was some government-financed construction, particularly of so-called 'famine railways', which were built to bring in food quickly to areas where crops had failed. A few non-guarantee private companies also existed. In general there were few competitive or duplicated routes; one exception was between Bombay and Delhi, where both the GIPR and the Bombay, Baroda and Central India offered service.

In addition, the rulers of many of the larger princely states (that is one third of the total land area) constructed their own railway systems. On absorption in 1950 there were 7000 miles of such lines, of which the Nizam of Hyderabad's was the largest, extending 1375 miles.

From the 1920s onwards, the government exercised its option to take over the principal lines. First to go in 1925 were the GIPR and EIR companies. The Indianization of the lines was also begun. After 1925 the intake of young English engineers, for example, almost ceased. Subsequent recruitment was from India and, in fact, by 1947 there were a mere 200 British railway officers.

In 1947 came independence and partition, but, as stated earlier, well before this time the Indian government had acquired all the principal railways, although they still traded under the old names. Much mileage was lost to West Pakistan, East Pakistan (now Bangladesh) and Sri Lanka (Ceylon); in compensation, the lines in the princely states were acquired. The new boundaries were not convenient from a railway point of view and some otherwise pointless new construction was made necessary, particularly in order to maintain an all-Indian route to Assam. Alas, many refugees on trains crossing the new India–W Pakistan border were mas-

Extreme left, top: India's electrically hauled 'Sinhagad Express'. Note the bull-head track.

Extreme left, below: India's diesel-hauled 'Frontier Mail'.

Left: Chittaranjan (near Asansal, India) works in March 1965 where steam and electric locomotives are built side by side.

Below: A Western Railway of India train (shown here on the Northern Railway) from Delhi to Ahmadabad stops at Delhi Serai Rohilla station. The locomotive is YP class No 2750 – a 4-6-2 heading thirteen coaches.

sacred – as many as 3000 at a time – by opposing religious factions during this tragic period; rather strangely, British travellers were almost invariably spared.

Between 1950 and 1960 the old lines were reorganized into 'Railways' as generally shown below. Of course, the titles indicate administrative zones rather than separate systems:

Southern Railway[1]
Madras & Southern Mahratta, South Indian, Mysore*

South Central Railway
Indian peninsula, south-central area, south-west Maharashtra and Andhra Pradesh.

Central Railway[1]
Great Indian Peninsula, Nizam of Hyderabad's*, Scindia*, Dholpur*

Western Railway
Bombay, Baroda & Central India, Surashtra*, Jaipur*, Rajasthan*, Cutch*, Gaekwar of Baroda's*

Eastern Railway[2]
East India east of Moghal Sarai

South Eastern Railway[2]
Bengal–Nagpur

Northern Railway
Indian portion of the North Western Railway, Jodhpur*, Bikaner*

North East Frontier Railway[3]
Lines in Assam and approaches Darjeeling-Himalayan

Northern Eastern Railway[3]
Metre gauge lines north of the Ganges excluding lines in Assam and approaches.

Notes: * Princely State line.

1 In 1965 the South Central Railway was formed from parts of the Southern and Central Railways.
2 When originally formed the South Eastern Railway was included in the Eastern Railway.
3 In 1958 the Northern Frontier Railway was separated from the North Eastern Railway.

Aside from making good wartime neglect and going ahead with modernization, the greatest achievement since independence is self-sufficiency. In 1947 thirty percent of stores and equipment were obtained overseas; in 1977 the figure was five percent.

Civil Engineering

India is a country of great rivers and great rivers need great bridges. The story of the railway bridges of India is a book in itself. That strange story of Kipling's, *The Bridge Builders* ('The Day's Work') tells something of it. Among the problems are the unplumbed depths of alluvial soil, which means that foundations need to be sunk 150ft or more below water-level. The out-of-sight vertical height of a bridge's piers may total nearly a mile. Another difficulty is that rivers which are a trickle in the dry season and a mile or more wide in the wet, frequently decide to change their course.

Fortunately, from the earliest days, the Indians took effortlessly to the absorbing art of bridge building. One notes the retirement in 1945 of an Indian from the post of chief draughtsman in the Bridge Department of the North Western Railway and that he was the third generation of his family to be employed therein.

No problems are likely to arise which will overtax the skill and endurance of the bridge engineers and tradesmen. Indeed, the greatest river of Asia, the Brahmaputra, was not bridged at all until after Independence. The longest bridge in India – all but two miles in length – is over the little known Upper Sone River near Benares and dates from 1900. In all there are 111,000 bridges on Indian Railways, totalling over 680 miles in length.

Before independence, the principal seats of government moved into 'hill stations' during the hot summer. Most of these had railways, including Simla (the hot weather station for Delhi), Darjeeling (Calcutta), Ootacamund or 'Ooty' (Madras) and Matheran near Bombay. It is interesting to note the differing solutions adopted to solve the same problems on these world-famous lines.

Right: An Indian express train hauled by an Indian-built electric locomotive.

The Kalka-Simla line was a conventional, solidly built 2ft 6in gauge railway, sixty miles long. There are 103 tunnels including one three-quarters of a mile long. The ruling grade is one in 33 and the minimum curvature 120ft. Powerful 2-6-4 tank locomotives enabled train loads of the Viceroy's files and other traffic to be handled expeditiously. The line is now fully dieselized.

Between Siliguri and Darjeeling runs a line of similar length that conquers the mountains not by heavy engineering but by frequent spirals or Z-reverses and hideously sharp curvature, down in 60ft radius. The summit is at 8200ft altitude, the highest rails in India. The price paid is an average speed one-half of that of the Simla line.

The climb to 'Ooty' is achieved by the Abt rack and pinion arrangement. The gradient can be increased to one in ten; the forward speed is slow, but the speed with which height is gained is considerably higher. The original Swiss-built steam metre-gauge rack-and-adhesion 0-8-2 tank locomotives are still in service.

The 2ft-gauge Matheran line is remarkable in that problems on the mountain side are reduced to a minimum by using even sharper curves than on the Darjeeling line. Special locomotives were used, 0-6-Ts with a patent flexible wheel-base, and travellers are still startled to be met by notices saying (I quote) 'Oops, what a curve – 45ft radius!' Diesel traction is now used, with steam in reserve.

Indian railway stations both old and new are worthy of the great system they serve. Sonepur is noted for having the longest station platform in the world. The most magnificent is the Central Railway's terminus in Bombay. Incidentally, the actual Central Station, called Victoria Terminus, is a rather nondescript cinema-like 1930s structure, some distance from the centre of the city, serving another line.

Permanent way in early railways in India was of the British-chaired pattern with bull-head rails but soon the more usual spiked vignoles 'flat-bottom' became the norm. The signalling methods in use include the most modern colour light equipment, made in India under licence. The majority, however, is still mechanical and of great variety, but mostly British in origin. Staff, key and tablet working is usual on single lines and in addition, an Indian specialty – the use of ball-type tokens for this purpose.

Locomotive Landmarks

Indian Locomotive History can be divided into five overlapping periods; Primaeval (1852–1914); BESA (1903–1950); IRS (1926–1939); postwar steam (1947–1972); electric-diesel 1925 (to date).

Of the Primaeval period, *Fairy Queen*, an 1855 2-2-2 from the East India Railway is the most distinguished survivor, the grand old lady of the new railway museum at Delhi and still in working order. Otherwise 2-4-0s and 0-4-2s were the norm in the early days but outstanding was the 1880 'L' class 4-6-0 of the North Western and Bengal – Nagpur railways, built well before such behemoths were known in the home country. On the metre gauge, the 'F' type outside cylinder 0-6-0 was supplied to several systems. On the narrow gauge, one must salute the Darjeeling-Himalayan 0-4-0Ts of 1892 onwards, still in use on that most demanding line today.

The British Engineering Standards Association (BESA) designs were introduced in 1903, covering 4-6-0, 4-4-2 and 4-4-0 passenger designs and 2-8-0, 0-6-0 freight, etc. The 4-6-0s were still being built as late as 1950.

Corresponding 4-6-0s were constructed for the metre gauge. Many BESA locomotives – but not the 4-4-2s – are still to be found working, a tribute to their sound design.

Alas, the same comment cannot be applied to the IRS designs, mainly consisting of 4-6-2s of three different sizes (XA, XB, XC), and two 2-8-2s (XD, XE). The Pacifics had a reputation of being poor steamers, sluggish runners and – the XB particularly – bad riders to a point not only of discomfort but of danger. In the end, at Bihta, in 1937, one was derailed with the loss of 117 lives. An enquiry led to some modification, but the IRS broad-gauge designs never met the promises of their design committee, although some are still to be found in use. On the other hand the metre-gauge IRS YB 4-6-2 and YD 2-8-2 were satisfactory machines, while on the narrow gauge, generally the ZB 2-6-2 and ZE 2-8-2 remain the last word in steam power even today.

During World War II Lend-Lease brought quantities of American broad- and metre-gauge 2-8-2s to India. Their rugged characteristics showed up well in conditions there and led to an order being placed with Baldwins of the USA for the first batch of a new standard range of locomotives. So in 1946 there arrived in India the first WP 4-6-2. Later batches built in various countries brought the total to 755, to be eclipsed by the WG 2-8-2 which reached 2450. There was also a small WL 4-6-2 as well as three corresponding designs for the metre gauge, a YP 4-6-2, a YG 2-8-2 and a YL 2-6-2. A handful of ZP narrow-gauge 4-6-2s were also acquired, but insufficient for them to be regarded as a standard design. There are some 5000 of these excellent postwar locomotives in use, out of a total steam fleet of 8000. Many were built in India, in particular at the Chittaranjan Locomotive Works, set up in 1950

Passenger Trains and Statistics

Unusual nowadays among the world's railways are three classes of accommodation. It is true that the best night expresses 'Southern Cross' (Kuala Lumpur–Singapore) and 'North Star' (Kuala Lumpur–Butterworth) are only first and second class, while locals are second and third. Nevertheless the best day trains on the same routes ('Magic Arrow' and 'Golden Arrow' respectively) do cater for all three. An appropriately named 'Golden Blowpipe' serves the East Coast line. Through international trains run three times a week from Butterworth to Bangkok. Average speeds are in the 30–35 mph range, railcars being substantially quicker. Six million passengers are conveyed in a typical year using a fleet of 345 carriages. Brown and cream livery was the standard, but recently maroon with yellow lines has been used.

A recorded 8713 wagons (four-wheel and bogie) were used to convey 3.79 million tons of freight an average of seventy miles. Receipts are 97 percent of expenses.

The vacuum brake is used, together with chopper-type couplings. Wagons can be interchanged with the Thailand railways.

Above: One of the ubiquitous North British Locomotive Company Pacifics at work on the main west-coast line in days of steam.

Extreme left: A forest station on the metre-gauge Malayan Railway. Timber is a valuable export from the country.

The majesty of Kuala Lumpur Station, Malaysia.

Signalling and Operations

Present-day practice has evolved very much on British lines, with traditional semaphore signals and electric token working on most sections of the single line. Colour light installations also exist at Perai, Kuala Lumpur and Singapore.

Administration and Finance

The headquarters of the system are at Kuala Lumpur. It is administered as a public corporation under a general manager responsible to the Minister of Communications. Expenses in 1974 amounted to 87 percent of receipts. It is reported that studies are being made of the feasibility of constructing a transverse line running eastwards from Perai to the east coast.

SABAH STATE RAILWAYS
Kota Kinabalu,
Sabah.

The railway in Sabah, an outer province of Malaysia but then British North Borneo, was constructed between 1896 and 1905 and extends almost to 100 miles of metre-gauge line. It is situated on the west coast in the rice, rubber and timber producing areas. A quirk indicating its origin is that its trains provide first and third class accommodation only, as in pre-1950 Britain.

Five steam and fifteen diesel locomotives with ten railcar sets, 23 carriages and 150 wagons handle 175,000 passengers and 90,000 tons of freight annually. Expenses are 180 percent of receipts.

NEPAL

See map on pages 278–279.

NEPAL GOVERNMENT RAILWAY
Birganj,
Nepal.

JANAKPUR RAILWAY
Khajuri,
Nepal.

Nepal is a small mountainous kingdom on the northern frontier of India. Two short thirty-mile 2ft 6in gauge railways run from the border to rail-heads in the foothills. The older one, the 1927 Nepal Government Railway, which ran from Raxaul to Amlekhganj, is now reported chopped to a mere six miles. If true, even the naming of its seven steam locomotives (including two Garratts) after local gods has failed to avert this disaster. The other line, further to the west and known as the Janakpur Railway, appears still to be in operation from Jaynagar to Bizulpura.

Left: Passengers arrive to travel on this North Borneo Railway (now Sabah, a province of Malaysia) railcar by boat.

Bottom right: Landi Kotal, the terminus of the Khyber Railway.

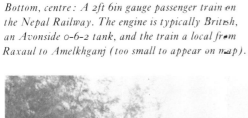

Bottom, centre: A 2ft 6in gauge passenger train on the Nepal Railway. The engine is typically British, an Avonside 0-6-2 tank, and the train a local from Raxaul to Amelkhganj (too small to appear on map).

Below: A modern Malaysian Railways diesel, the 8 a.m. 'Express Rakyat', leaves Singapore for Butterworth, 1978.

PAKISTAN

See map on pages 278-279.

As a nation, Pakistan is barely thirty years old; the British Raj may have succeeded in giving the old India a reasonable railway system but failed to give her unity. Hence, two wars and for many years, good undisturbed grazing on part of the old Lahore-Delhi main line. It is pleasant to record the recent re-opening of this once busy artery of commerce to traffic.

Ignoring the lines in what is now Bangladesh, the railways which Pakistan inherited consisted of the lion's share of the old North Western Railway (in 1946 the longest in British India), plus the Western portion of the metregauge Jodhpur lines. All are now amalgamated into a single state system.

PAKISTAN RAILWAYS – PR
Lahore.

The first section of the Pakistan Railways was a line to by-pass the un-navigable reaches of the River Indus near its mouth. It went inland from the seaport of Karachi 108 miles to Kotri and was known as the Scinde Railway. The ceremonial first barrow-load of earth was moved on 29 April 1858 and the line was opened on 13 May 1861. It was part of a plan for a rail and river route from Karachi (and hence, London) 1250 miles to Delhi. At first almost half the distance was by paddle steamer on the River Indus. In winter there is barely enough water

LANDI KOTAL

An American Locomotive Company diesel at the head of the Bolan Mail at Mach station, Pakistan.

to navigate; in summer the river can be up to fifteen miles wide without marked channels. Navigation was very much a hit and miss business and the consequence was that the Indus State Railway opened in 1878, giving a 2200-mile all-rail route – apart from the Indus ferry at Sukkur – from Karachi right across to Calcutta.

Because of the strategic importance of the legendary Northwest Frontier, then very much a live issue because of the aggressiveness of Imperial Russia (how history repeats itself), railways in this area were mainly financed and constructed by the government of India directly rather than by private enterprise.

The 1792-mile North Western Railway was formed in 1886 by the amalgamation of the state-owned lines and purchase of the private state-guaranteed ones. By 1947 it had grown to 6890 miles, including 53 miles across the Persian border. After partition, 1850 miles were lost to the new India, but 430 miles of metre gauge were to be added to make the new three-gauge Pakistan Western Railway. The old NWR had been solely broad and narrow (2ft 6in) gauge. In 1974, after East Pakistan had become the independent Bangladesh, the PWR became Pakistan Railways.

Large areas in the west of the country are devoid of railways (largely because they are virtually devoid of people also). One line which does thread this wilderness is the 455-mile Nushki Extension Railway out of Quetta, built for strategic reasons in World War I and (with the Germans approaching the Caucasus) re-

instated in World War II. Its terminus at Zahidan in Iran – the stretch across the border was recently handed over to the Iranians – may shortly be rail-connected, (except for three rail ferries) on standard gauge, to more familiar places such as Paris or London. The NER itself runs through country where stations are fifty miles apart and the whole annual rainfall of six to seven inches can fall in one day with dire results.

Civil Engineering
It is no accident that the civil engineering section dominates this account. Formidable and unpredictable adversaries which must be overcome are the River Indus and its tributaries, the Jhelum, the Ravi, the Sutlej and the Chenab. Furthermore, the unbending requirements of military strategy in demanding railways built to main-line standards in some of the most inhospitable country in the world, is another reason for civil engineers to come to the fore. The longest tunnel in British India, the 2.5-mile double-track broad-gauge Khojak tunnel, leads only to a dead end a few miles beyond the far portal, near the old fort of Chaman on the Afghan frontier.

Perhaps the very existence of this line, as well as that of its opposite number, the Khyber Pass Railway, meant that they never had to be used to transport troops in anger. On one occasion, the Amir of Afghanistan was invited to visit London and, in order to both honour and impress him, the great broad-gauge twelve-car Vice-regal special train was sent to Chaman

for his party to begin their journey. With four 2-8-0 engines, two at either end, the train set off up the 1 in 40 grade and entered the tunnel. Alas, in the smoke and darkness His Highness panicked and pulled the communication cord. It was some time before they got going again.

The Khyber Railway with its reversals, tunnels and spirals was an equally great achievement, partly because the engineering staff were, in a land where tribal custom rather than Imperial law prevailed, regarded by the tribesmen in the same light as a Victorian English gentleman might regard the pheasants and rabbits on his estate. In the end a 'close season' was negotiated for the daylight hours and the tribesmen made money as contractors for the building of the line.

It is possible that one or both of these strategic links (the former is the most likely) which now end at stop-blocks close to the frontier, might become commercial if Afghanistan goes ahead with her railway construction plan.

The overall length of the railway bridges on the PR exceeds 75 miles and their continued existence involves a constant battle against the forces of nature. Floods, earthquakes, winds, heat and cold are all on the grand scale. It should be noted that, at river crossings such as occur in Pakistan, not only has the bridge to be built but many miles of upstream containment works need to be constructed also. Even then a river may decide to seek new pastures, creating new gaps in the line, but leaving a great bridge high and dry.

The bridge with the greatest span is the

1962-built steel-arch Ayub Bridge across the Indus at Sukkur, replacing the Lansdowne Bridge, a cantilever structure, which when opened in 1889, held the record for the world's greatest span of 820ft. The longest bridge was the 1876-built Alexandra Bridge across the Chenab, on the line between Lahore and Rawalpindi, the length of which was originally 1.75 miles. There were 64 spans. As a result of river training works, the length was reduced by more than half in 1890, the girders being recovered and used elsewhere. The longest bridge then became the mile long Jhelum River bridge (on the same line) of fifty spans; it was completed in 1878.

Locomotive Landmarks

In common with the other railways in British India, the NWR took the standard BESA and IRS designs of steam locomotive. Some 600 (520 broad, forty metre and forty narrow gauge) are still in service, including the only BESA 4-4-os that remain. Before 1947, the NWR was burning 3500 tons of coal daily, all of which had to be railed from faraway Bengal. So, after independence, the steam fleet was rapidly con-

verted to oilburning and plans laid to dieselize as quickly as possible. The current diesel fleet numbers 500, the majority being General Motors standard units and, of course imported. Two main-line diesels supplied by Armstrong-Whitworth with Sulzer engines in 1935 had teething troubles which were never overcome, but this early enthusiasm for diesel power was the result of having so much mileage in waterless country.

Pakistan has virtually unlimited and, of course, inexhaustible resources in the way of water power for generating electricity. The busiest lines, those centred on Lahore, have accordingly been electrified – the 100 miles to Khanewal in 1974 and the 150 miles to Rawalpindi currently in progress.

In the past passengers on what is now the Pakistan Railway have suffered death from heat-stroke in the Sind Desert and frost-bite in the Zhob Valley, the narrow-gauge line on which the 7212ft summit of the system lies. On the Nushki extension one could be days away from rescue if breakdown occurred and the victualling of the box-van 'buffet cars' took this into account.

The famous 'Frontier Mail', Bombay to Peshawar, no longer runs beyond Amritsar and the 'Quetta Mail' no longer needs four steam engines driven all out to climb the twelve miles at 1 in 25 leading to the Bolan Pass, but the PR's slightly more prosaic services are both cleaner and quicker, the best trains having air-conditioned as well as dining facilities and first- and second-class accommodation. Romance, however, 'still brings up the 9.15', as Kipling (who was born and worked in Lahore) put it – or rather the 0900 Fridays only, Khyber Pass train from Peshawar, still steams with 0-6-0s front and rear.

Currently the Pakistan Railway carries 28 million tons of freight an average of 190 miles each year. The annual passenger count is 318 million. Expenses are 76 percent of receipts.

Top left: A diesel-electric locomotive on the Karachi-Lahore express.

Top right: A British-built inside-cylinder 0-6-0 works hard at the head of the weekly mixed train from Peshawar to Landi Kotal, Pakistan.

A train leaves Columbo, Sri Lanka.

PHILIPPINES

See map on page 302.

PHILIPPINE NATIONAL RAILWAYS – PNR
943 Claro M. Recto Avenue,
Manila.

The first railway in the Philippines was on the main island of Luzon. It was opened on 24 November 1892 and ran 123 miles northwards from the capital, Manila, to Dagupan. This was the 3ft 6in gauge Manila Railway Company, financed in Britain. Extensions followed, but bankruptcy and reorganization as the Manila Railroad took place in 1906. In 1917 the government was obliged to acquire the system. It was reorganized in 1967 under the present title.

Current returns show its extent as 'about 1052.679 km' (658 miles). Train services are unusual in that three classes of accommodation are provided plus first-class sleeping cars on overnight runs.

Seventy-six diesel locomotives, sixty diesel railcars, 140 carriages and 1700 freight cars handle 4.5 million passengers and 400,000 tons of freight, the latter hauled an average distance of 130 miles.

The small island of Panay has a seventy-mile public north-south line, dating from 1906; it was originally the Philippine Railway Company, but since 1975 it has been known as Phividec Incorporated; however, the scale of its operations may be judged from the fact that nine diesel locomotives do the work.

No public railways exist on the island of Negros, but there are numerous sugar plantation lines, believed still to exceed 1000 miles in total. Most are 3ft gauge, but the largest (the Victorias Milling Company at the northern tip of the island) was noted for having more than 200 miles of 2ft gauge line.

SRI LANKA

See map on page 278.

SRI LANKA GOVERNMENT RAILWAY
PO Box 355,
Colombo.

Until independence in 1947, Ceylon (as Sri Lanka was then known to the world) was part of India. It is an extremely beautiful island 400 miles long by 200 miles wide, just off the southern tip of the sub-continent. Its railways were part of the Indian system, linked to the mainland by a rail ferry as well as by that strange tongue of land known as Adam's Bridge. Apart from one short line near Colombo – known as the Kelani Valley Railway and familiar from film scenes taken there in 'Bridge over the River Kwai' – the system is (rather surprisingly) of 5ft 6in gauge. One would have thought that metre gauge would have been more suitable

vived into the diesel age. However, the short distances involved coupled with the policy of maintaining traditional services as far as possible meant that modernization did not avoid deficits proportionately heavier than any other state's, except Victoria, where revenue also currently covers only about 55 percent of expenses. Curiously enough, the narrower the gauge the lower the deficit, is the Australian rule at present.

Right: A C17 class locomotive pulls a freight train at Willowburn, South Australia.

Left: A Beyer-Garratt locomotive heads a ballast train en route to Yamba, New South Wales.

Below: The 5ft 3in gauge system in South Australia was one of the smallest on the continent, but had some of the most magnificent steam power, as exemplified by this streamlined 4-8-4.

Above: Australia's 'Overland Limited' hauled by trim English-Electric 1760 hp diesel locomotives.

Top: Crews change between Beyer-Garratt and diesel locomotives at Gladstone, South Australia.

Left: A South Australian streamlined steam locomotive.

TASMANIAN GOVERNMENT RAILWAYS
1 Collins Street,
Hobart 7000.

On a minute scale, the 520-mile 3ft 6in gauge system of the Tasmanian Government Railways (now a division of the Australian National Railways), exemplifies the Australian railway situation. Scenic, short-haul, not very busy, little abridged, and uneconomic, with its last quite good prestige passenger train recently axed, the system faces a rather questionable future, like a number of lines on the mainland.

Extreme left, top: Emu Bay Railway's 'The West Coaster' train at Rosebery station, Tasmania in steam days.

Left: The 'Tasman Limited' leaves the country station Ross in Tasmania.

Bottom left: The 'Tasman Limited' winds through typical Tasmanian countryside, 25 miles north of Hobart.

Below: The inaugural through-train from Sydney arrives at Dynon in the Melbourne suburbs on 3 January 1962.

VICTORIAN GOVERNMENT RAILWAYS – Vicrail

67 Spencer Street,
Melbourne 3000.

This is the smallest state, its greatest dimensions east to west some 500 miles and north to south some 250. Except for the mountainous region north-east of Melbourne, most of the area is well-served by the 4400-mile 5ft 3in-gauge network of the Victorian Railways; however many lines in the wheat-growing north-western plains carry little traffic and some limited cuts in mileage have taken place. Passenger services are still maintained over a high proportion of the network, although Vicrail's passenger rolling stock contains many elderly wooden-bodied vehicles, not all built since 1900. Even the suburban electric services in the Melbourne area, which are on a very large scale indeed, are still heavily dependent on coaches which before motorization fifty or so years ago had served many years behind steam power. There is some modern stock in suburban and inter-

city service, but not a great deal of it. Speeds are however somewhat higher than in other states, and the line maximum is 80 mph.

The steam locomotive fleet was a modern and up-to-date one, with handsome machines of individual character and unified style not much like those anywhere else in the world, although perhaps reminiscent of Indian practice. The broad gauge was, of course, one similarity. Dieselization, as always, has brought uniformity, although each state does possess a different colour scheme. Apart from the Melbourne area, where an underground line is now being built (Sydney's lead in this department having become intolerable), electrification is confined to one line running to the eastern coalfields area.

A brief account of this system's present situation would not differ *materially* from that of New South Wales (mentioned beforehand), although this compression misleads if it implies much uniformity in many other respects between very different operations. Revenue received is only 55 percent of expenses.

Top left: Victoria's only narrow-gauge Puffing Billy *passenger train has been restored to regular running from Belgrave to Menzies Creek in the Dandenong Ranges near Melbourne. It is the first time in the century-long history of the Victorian Railways that a narrow-gauge railway line has been re-opened. Restoration of the service was made possible by a volunteer organization – the Puffing Billy Preservation Society. This popular train runs to regular schedules at week-ends and public holidays, and is available also for special trips. It connects at Belgrave with electric trains. On the first trip into the hills, following restoration of the line on 28 July 1962,* Puffing Billy *is here seen, with steam and smoke belching from the funnel, crossing the Monbulk Creek trestle bridge in the Dandenong Ranges.*

Bottom left: A diesel-hauled train leaving Spencer Street Station, Melbourne, Australia.

Below: Melbourne's Jolimont passenger yard with the railway workshops to the right. Nearby is Flinders Street station which handles more traffic than any other Australian station.

WESTERN AUSTRALIAN GOVERNMENT RAILWAYS

Westrail Centre,
Box 5 1422, GPO,
Perth 6001.

This system, with a total of some 3800 route miles, eighty percent of which is 3ft 6in gauge and the rest 4ft 8½in (with about ninety miles of mixed gauge), is the exception to most Australian rules. Thirty years ago it was almost more typical than any other: then all-3ft 6in gauge, with a very large mileage of infinitesimally used branch lines, mostly loops circuitously joining points already connected, and a tiny centre of gravity around Perth. In 1957, at a stroke, over 800 miles were summarily closed, which had the effect of removing from the working timetable only those lines with less than one scheduled train *per week*. Then came the standard gauge, and conversion of the 400-mile Perth to Kalgoorlie section, including a brand-new

double-track mixed-gauge line up the mountain barrier outside Perth, followed by closure or conversion of other branches in the east of the state. Then came the mineral boom, and a great increase in business. And so, contrary to all reasonable expectation, the WAGR still earns its expenses

As in Queensland, steam locomotives tended to be small, though not so excessively so; the V class heavy freight 2-8-2s of 1955, the last new steamers (ordered after sad experience with the first batch of diesels) would have passed muster on a minor branch line in South Africa. Modern power is adequate but unremarkable. Passenger services, surprisingly perhaps in view of the scanty population of the state, have always been a bit better. The old narrow-gauge transcontinental express on the Perth-Kalgoorlie leg offered its passengers hot showers in 1938; the same run now offers the fastest run in Australia (averaging just over 50 mph overall). Some very respectable trains

run on other routes (though understandably not very often).

Separate and distinct from the Western Australian Government Railways, and indeed a thousand miles distant in the northern part of the state, are four very new railways, all opened since the mid-1960s, and built to carry iron ore in large quantities from mines to ports, and nothing else. Extremely heavy trains, weighing up to 18,000 tons, on heavy track controlled by CTC (and busy enough in one case to need double line on heavy grades), all in desert or semi-desert with no town of any size within a thousand miles, clearly involve the managements of these concerns (for their railways operate only as a part of the mining undertaking) in a set of very different problems. One piquant illustration of this was the import of a 'Castle' class 4-6-0 from England to the Hamersley Iron Company's line in 1978, to work recreational trains and provide mechanically minded staff with harmless amusement.

Left: The 'Trans-Australian' express at Perth station soon after its arrival from Port Pirie.

Bottom left: The special ministerial train at the opening of the railway from Perth to Kalgoorlie on 1 January 1897.

Below: The combined 'Trans-Australian' and 'Indian-Pacific' trains en route to Perth. Note the 3ft 6in and 4ft 8½in gauge tracks alongside.

Above: Twin diesel units haul a 3800-ton train of grain hopper wagons somewhere in Western Australia.

Extreme left: One of Western Australia's northern and very modern iron-ore hauling railroads. Built to last using modern techniques, these tracks can carry 18,000 tons at a time.

Left: The giant Mt Tom Price iron-ore train is made up of either 175 ore cars with two locomotives hauling, or 200 cars with three locomotives hauling. In the latter form it is 1.25 miles long and transports 20,000 tons of ore. It reaches speeds of 80 mph. This Hamersley Iron Ore train runs between Mt Tom Price in the north of Western Australia and the port of Dampier. The locomotives were made in Canada and the 100-ton capacity ore cars were made in Japan.

Right: Iron ore in the West Australian outback on the Mount Newman Railroad.

Extreme right, top: A mixed train on the rack section between Solok and Bukittinggi on the island of Sumatra in Indonesia. The locomotive is a Japanese-built 0-10-0 of 1962.

Bottom: Villagers wait for the morning mixed train to Bukittinggi.

INDONESIA

See map on page 302.

INDONESIAN STATE RAILWAYS
Perusahaan Jawatan Kereta Api,
Jalan Gereja No 1,
Bandung, Java.

The Indonesian Republic includes a great many islands large and small, but most of them backward and undeveloped. Railways have always been confined to the three islands of Java, Sumatra and Madura. Java, some 750 miles long east and west and an average of 75 miles north and south, is a fertile, densely populated land with an ancient history of civilization; of volcanic origin, it is still studded with semi-active volcanoes and with many mountain ranges. There are some 3500 route-miles of railway in Java forming a single fairly dense system. Sumatra is much larger, but less fertile and less developed while every bit as mountainous; approximately 1000 route-miles of line survive in three widely separated systems. Madura, a small island off the Java coast, once had over 100 miles of railway but only one line now survives.

The first railway in Java was a standard-gauge line from Semarang to the central Java capital of Jogjakarta, and dates from 1864.

Development of the network in all islands was relatively unplanned, with most lines built by private capital to serve agricultural purposes; a state railway organization, however, came to control the main lines and some sixty percent of the mileage by 1939. The 3ft 6in gauge was soon chosen as standard, although the standard gauge survived at Jogjakarta until converted rather hurriedly during the Japanese occupation 1942–45; various relics of it remain.

By the 1930s the Javanese state railway system was extremely modern and well-equipped, with some electrification, automatic signalling, modern hump yards and well-maintained tracks on which ran absolutely the best and fastest 3ft 6in gauge express trains in the world. Twenty years later, after wars, revolutions, and a decade of highly quarrelsome and disorganized independence, not many of these high standards remained; in fact the system was by then perhaps the world's most ramshackle. Travellers' tales told of jungle creepers festooning catenary wires; photographs showed marshalling yards taken over as shanty towns, with families squatting in two-storied comfort in abandoned wagons (that is, inside the body and between the wheels); wheezing and antiquated woodburners dragged short trains of rotting coaches packed inside and outside with smiling customers. Since those years, a more stable administration has brought much recovery, and probably most of

the remaining dilapidations are due to competition from unrestricted road transport.

In Sumatra the course of events was much the same. However, although narrow-gauge lines in Java are strictly local affairs, the Atjeh Tramway of 2ft 5½in gauge, running some 300 miles in the northwest of Sumatra from north of Medan to Bandar Atjeh once had a much greater importance. This was closed in 1970 pending gauge conversion, and although some fifty miles have since reopened to 3ft 6in traffic it is uncertain what has become of the rest.

Locomotive Development
Early conditions favoured the use of small and lightweight, usually four-coupled, machines; an enormous variety once existed and many still survive and are occasionally active. Worth special note is a considerable number of van-bodied tram engines. Underlying this plethora, however, developed a fleet of powerful and advanced main-line steam locomotives, reaching a peak between about 1910 and 1930 with some compound Pacifics, some express passenger 4-6-4Ts, some impressive 2-12-2Ts for heavy freight haulage on mountain lines, and several varieties of Mallet culminating in some American 2-8-8-0s. After 1945 100 very workmanlike heavy 2-8-2s were acquired from Germany. The majority of locomotives, naturally, were Dutch, although there were also many British, German and Swiss products.

Many types were also to be found in Sumatra, though the Deli Railway at Medan had its own characteristic types and the system based at Padang, which had sections of rack line to reach coal mines, has some German-, Japanese- and Swiss-built ten-coupled rack-and-adhesion tanks, some built as late as the 1960s.

Political conditions ensured the survival, in a manner of speaking, of the steam fleet much longer than otherwise expected; even when cessation of 'confrontation' with the Western powers led to the commencement of loans and grants-in-aid from Western sources for the purchase of diesels, difficulties in keeping these more complex machines mobile has meant that steam has made some surprising comebacks. But very often the condition of the machines leads to deplorably bad performance and the results can give little pleasure. Diesels are in general European, and although a large number of diesel-hydraulics were acquired from Germany, more recent purchases have been diesel-electric. Much of the electrification in the Djakarta area was kept going rather in the manner of steam, but it is currently being refurbished although not extended.

Train Services and Rolling Stock
Main-line passenger services have never been quite as bad as they might have been, and some indication of pre-1939 standards survives. Sufficient new modern (though often spartan)